MONEY IN CLASSICAL ANTIQUITY

This is the first book to undertake a comprehensive analysis of the impact of money on the economy, society and culture of the Greek and Roman worlds. It uses new approaches in economic history to explore how money affected the economy in antiquity and demonstrates that the crucial factors in its increasing influence were state-formation, expanding political networks, metal supply and above all an increasing sophistication of credit and contractual law. Covering a wide range of monetary contexts within the Mediterranean over almost 1,000 years (*c.* 600 BC–AD 300), it demonstrates that money played different roles in different social and political circumstances. The book will prove an invaluable introduction for upper-level students of ancient history, while also offering perspectives for future research to the specialist.

SITTA VON REDEN is Professor of Ancient History at the University of Freiburg/Germany. She is the author of *Exchange in Ancient Greece* (1995) and *Money in Ptolemaic Egypt* (2007) and co-editor, with Paul Cartledge and Paul Millett, of *Kosmos: Essays in Order, Conflict and Community in Classical Athens* (1998).

KEY THEMES IN ANCIENT HISTORY

EDITORS

P. A. Cartledge
Clare College, Cambridge
P. D. A. Garnsey
Jesus College, Cambridge

Key Themes in Ancient History aims to provide readable, informed and original studies of various basic topics, designed in the first instance for students and teachers of classics and ancient history, but also for those engaged in related disciplines. Each volume is devoted to a general theme in Greek, Roman or, where appropriate, Graeco-Roman history, or to some salient aspect or aspects of it. Besides indicating the state of current research in the relevant area, authors seek to show how the theme is significant for our own as well as ancient culture and society. By providing books for courses that are oriented around themes it is hoped to encourage and stimulate promising new developments in teaching and research in ancient history.

Other books in the series

Death-ritual and social structure in classical antiquity, by Ian Morris
978 0 521 37465 1 (hardback), 978 0 521 37611 2 (paperback)

Literacy and orality in ancient Greece, by Rosalind Thomas
978 0 521 37346 3 (hardback), 978 0 521 37742 3 (paperback)

Slavery and Society at Rome, by Keith Bradley
978 0 521 37287 9 (hardback), 978 0 521 37887 1 (paperback)

Law, violence, and community in classical Athens, by David Cohen
978 0 521 38167 3 (hardback), 978 0 521 38837 5 (paperback)

Public order in ancient Rome, by Wilfried Nippel
978 0 521 38327 1 (hardback), 978 0 521 38749 1 (paperback)

Friendship in the classical world, by David Konstan
978 0 521 45402 5 (hardback), 978 0 521 45998 3 (paperback)

Sport and society in ancient Greece, by Mark Golden
978 0 521 49698 8 (hardback), 978 0 521 49790 9 (paperback)

Food and society in classical antiquity, by Peter Garnsey
978 0 521 64182 1 (hardback), 978 0 521 64588 1 (paperback)

Banking and business in the Roman world, by Jean Andreau
978 0 521 38031 7 (hardback), 978 0 521 38932 7 (paperback)

Roman law in context, by David Johnston
978 0 521 63046 7 (hardback), 978 0 521 63961 3 (paperback)

Religions of the ancient Greeks, by Simon Price
978 0 521 38201 4 (hardback), 978 0 521 38867 2 (paperback)

Christianity and Roman society, by Gillian Clark
978 0 521 63310 9 (hardback), 978 0 521 63386 4 (paperback)

Trade in classical antiquity, by Neville Morley
978 0 521 63279 9 (hardback), 978 0 521 63416 8 (paperback)

Technology and culture in Greek and Roman antiquity, by Serafina Cuomo
978 0 521 81073 9 (hardback), 978 0 521 00903 4 (paperback)

Law and crime in the Roman world, by Jill Harries
978 0 521 82820 8 (hardback), 978 0 521 53532 8 (paperback)

The social history of Roman art, by Peter Stewart
978 0 521 81632 8 (hardback), 978 0 521 01659 9 (paperback)

Asceticism in the Graeco-Roman world, by Richard Finn OP
978 0 521 86281 3 (hardback), 978 0 521 68154 4 (paperback)

Ancient Greek political thought in practice, by Paul Cartledge
978 0 521 45455 1 (hardback), 978 0 521 45595 4 (paperback)

Money in Classical Antiquity, by Sitta von Reden
978 0 521 45337 0 (hardback), 978 0 521 45952 5 (paperback)

MONEY IN CLASSICAL ANTIQUITY

SITTA VON REDEN

CAMBRIDGE
UNIVERSITY PRESS

CAMBRIDGE UNIVERSITY PRESS
Cambridge, New York, Melbourne, Madrid, Cape Town, Singapore,
São Paulo, Delhi, Dubai, Tokyo, Mexico City

Cambridge University Press
The Edinburgh Building, Cambridge CB2 8RU, UK

Published in the United States of America by Cambridge University Press, New York

www.cambridge.org
Information on this title: www.cambridge.org/9780521459525

First published 2010

Printed in the United Kingdom at the University Press, Cambridge

A catalogue record for this publication is available from the British Library

Library of Congress Cataloguing in Publication data
Reden, Sitta von.
Money in classical antiquity / Sitta von Reden.
p.   cm. – (Key themes in ancient history)
Includes bibliographical references and index.
ISBN 978-0-521-45337-0 (hardback)
1. Money – Greece – History.   2. Money – Rome – History.   I. Title.   II. Series.
HG237.R43   2010
332.4′938 – dc22   2010022869

ISBN 978-0-521-45337-0 Hardback
ISBN 978-0-521-45952-5 Paperback

To Florentin

Contents

List of figures and tables

FIGURES

TABLES

List of maps

Preface and acknowledgements

When in the 1990s I mentioned to Michael Crawford that I was planning a book on ancient money, he advised me to investigate one coinage, and look at one local monetary economy, before embarking on the larger project of money in classical antiquity. I took his advice, studied Ptolemaic coinage and money, and more than ten years later returned to the original plan. I learnt that any presumed 'nature' of ancient money is very different if you use different kinds of evidence, and that any single type of evidence provides a limited perspective. From the correspondence of Cicero, and the volumes of coinage calculated to have moved around the Roman empire, the ancient monetary economy strikes us as very advanced and widespread. In contrast, personal letters, tax receipts, bills and bank accounts surviving from Greco-Roman Egypt suggest that there was a huge discrepancy in economic behaviour between those who had a great deal and those who had very little money at their disposal. Greek and Roman authors, moreover, lead us to believe that outside the great cities and their imperial outreach people did not know money, living primitive lives in huts and woods, and bartering their goods in a natural economy. But archaeology tells a different story: coinage was present in remote places and most 'barbarians', too, had some form of money.

Thus presenting a small volume on money in classical antiquity (*c.* 600 BC–*c.* AD 300) does not do full justice to the most important aspect of its subject: forms and impact of money varied tremendously from place to place. Its functions and meaning were perceived very differently by different people and social groups. And, scholars have offered highly controversial interpretations of the place of money in antiquity, without these interpretations being always mutually exclusive. The aim of this book is therefore to nurture an understanding of the complexities of money and monetization in classical antiquity, and the possibilities of exploring them by means of the various kinds of evidence available.

Many colleagues and friends have helped me to find my way through the forest of complex issues. Henry Kim and Christopher Howgego opened my eyes to the large amount of social and economic information to be gained from coinage. Andrew Meadows drew my attention to the issue of circulation and the role of weight systems and standards in the formation of ancient monetary networks. Many discussions with Jean Andreau, Dominic Rathbone, Gary Reger, Walter Scheidel and Bert van der Spek made it possible to write the chapters on credit and price formation. Vincent Gabrielsen, Joe Manning, Paul Millett and Neville Morley strengthened my belief that money works within particular cultural and social contexts. Greg Woolf pointed me to the fascinating subject of coinage and money in Britain and Gaul. David Schaps showed me that there is a clear answer to every question if only you pose the question properly. The editors of the *Thesaurus Cultus et Rituum Antiquorum*, in particular Betrand Jaeger and Richard Buxton, made me look at money in cult and ritual. Chapter 7 is based on the research for that project. Richard Seaford and Leslie Kurke were stimulating conversation partners when I focussed on the symbolism of money. Many others commented helpfully at conferences and seminars, in particular Peter Bang, John Davies, Richard Duncan-Jones, Johannes Hahn, Marietta Horster, Wim Jongman, Katharina Katsari, Elio Lo Cascio, Josh Ober, Robin Osborne, Ute Wartenberg, Gregor Weber and Jonathan Williams. Special thanks go to Paul Cartledge, Peter Garnsey, Elizabeth Hanlon, Jodie Barnes and Mary Morton from Cambridge University Press, who edited the manuscript and saved me from some foolish errors. Patrick Todt at the University of Freiburg very professionally prepared the index for this volume. Yet the book would never have been completed without the generosity, encouragement and patience of Paul Cartledge who commissioned it and oversaw its slow progress over many years.

I dedicate the book to my son Florentin with love and thanks for all the small sacrifices he made without complaint. He has the burning desire one day to make more money than his parents. May he succeed in that, but yet not lose his endearing curiosity in other things the world holds in store.

Greek and Roman monetary system and coin denominations

1 talent = 6,000 drachmas (not coined)
1 mina = 100 drachmas (not coined)
1 (silver) stater = four or two drachma pieces ('tetradrachm' or 'didrachm')
1 drachma = 6 obols
1 obol = 8 chalkoi

Obols, half-obols and chalkoi were usually coined in bronze from the fourth century BC onwards. A gold coin, called chrusous = 20 silver drachmas, was coined by some mints from the second half of the fourth century BC onwards.

ROMAN (LATE REPUBLICAN AND IMPERIAL)

1 (gold) aureus = 25 denarii
1 (silver) denarius = 4 sestertii
1 sestertius = 4 asses
1 dupondius (bronze) = 2 asses (bronze)
1 as = 2 semises (bronze)
1 semis = 2 quadrantes (bronze)

The sestertius was minted intermittently, first in silver, but from c. 23 BC in a copper-zinc alloy. The aureus was not minted regularly before the time of Julius Caesar. Until c. 130 BC there were 10 rather than 16 asses to the denarius. Other denominations, such as the antoninianus (from the time of Caracalla, c. AD 215) = two denarii, were minted for limited periods of time.

List of abbreviations

Abbreviations of ancient sources, journals and modern works used in this book can be found in S. Hornblower and A. Spawforth *Oxford Classical Dictionary*, 3rd edn, Oxford 1996, pp. xxix–liv. References to editions of papyri follow the conventions in J. F. Oates *et al. Checklist of Editions of Greek, Latin and Coptic Papyri, Ostraca and Tablets*, 5th edn, Bulletin of the American Society of Papyrologists Suppl. 9. Atlanta 2001 (also http://scriptorium.lib.duke.edu/papyrus/texts/clist_papyri.html)

In addition I have used the following:

CH	*Coin Hoards*, vols. 1–9. London, Royal Numismatic Society, 1975–2002.
GHI	R. Meiggs and D. Lewis *A Selection of Greek Historical Inscriptions*. Oxford [rev. repr.] 1988
IGCH	M. Thompson (ed.) *An Inventory of Greek Coin Hoards*. American Numismatic Society. 1976–9.
OGIS	W. Dittenberger *Orientis Graeci Inscriptiones Selectae*. Leipzig 1903–5.
RO	P. J. Rhodes and R. Osborne *Greek Historical Inscriptions 404–323 BC*. Oxford 2003.

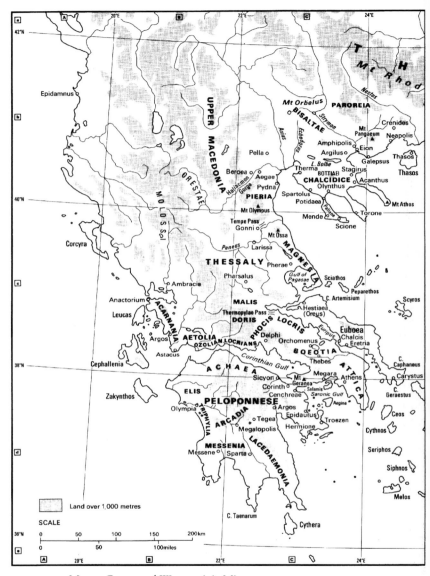

Map 1: Greece and Western Asia Minor

xviii

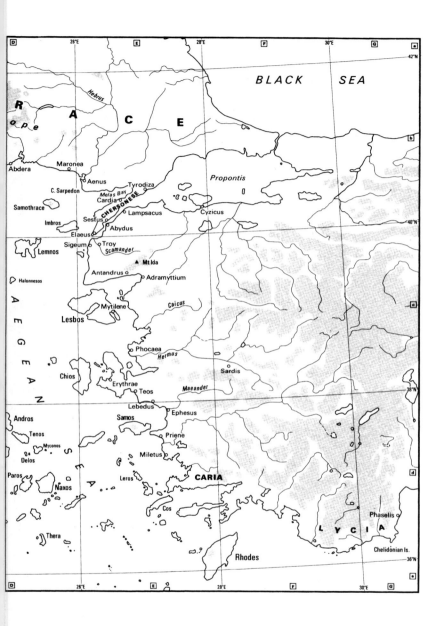

BLACK SEA

T **R** A **C** **E** ope

42°N

Abdera

Maronea

Aenus Tyrodiza

Propontis

C. Sarpedon *Melas Bay* Cardia CHERSONESE

Samothrace Sestus Lampsacus Cyzicus 40°N

Imbros Elaeus Abydus

Sigeum Troy

Scamander

Lemnos ▲ Mt Ida

Halonnesos Antandrus Adramyttium

A Mytilene *Caicus*

E Lesbos

G Phocaea

E *Hermus*

A Chios Sardis

N Erythrae

Teos *Maeander* 38°N

Lebedus

Andros Samos Ephesus

Tenos Priene

Myconos Miletus

Delos

Paros Leros CARIA

Naxos

Cos

Thera LYCIA Phaselis

Chelidonian Is.

Rhodes 36°N

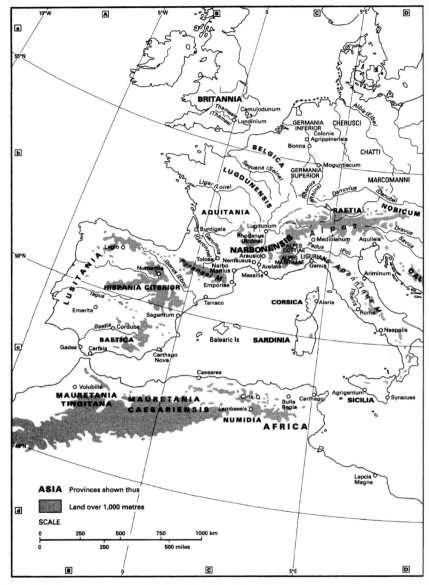

Map 2: The Roman empire at the time of the Julio-Claudian emperors

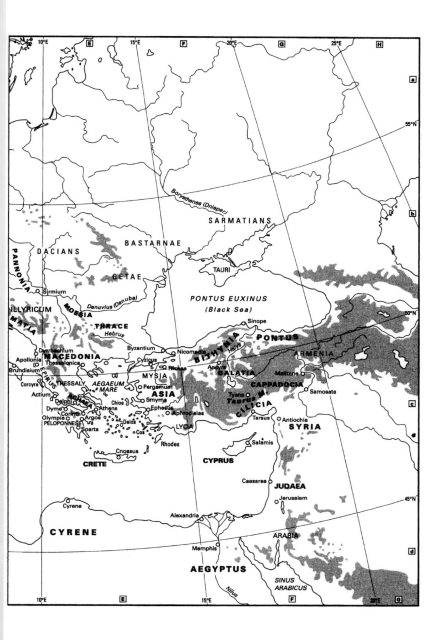

Introduction

One of the surprising phenomena in world history is the success of money. Money is more easily lost than gained; it requires a host of laws, regulations and controls to work and have value; in the form of coinage it costs something to be produced; and – above all! – it makes people dependent on anonymous authorities such as governments, federal institutions and central banks. Money destabilizes wealth and social relationships, and transforms tangible, useful property into mere options for the future. While it has created immense riches for some, and reasonable well-being for many, it has also created more extreme forms of poverty and the most spectacular economic crises the world has ever seen. Rather less surprisingly, there has been much resistance to monetization, and many political thinkers whose views were influential in other respects had serious objections to the use of money.[1]

There is the other side of the coin. As Aristotle in his imagined history of the origins of coinage writes:

When mutual help grew stronger and people imported what they needed and exported what they had too much of, coinage came necessarily into use. For the things that people need by nature are not easily carried about, and hence men agreed to employ in their dealings with each other something which was intrinsically useful and easily applicable to the purposes of life, for example, iron, silver and the like. Of this the value was at first measured simply by size and weight, but in the process of time they put a stamp upon it to save the trouble of weighing to mark the value (*Pol.* 1257a 31–8).

The thoughts of Aristotle still resound in a famous passage by John Stuart Mill (1806–73) defining the advantages of gold and silver coinage:

By a tacit concurrence, almost all nations, at a very early period, fixed upon certain metals, and especially gold and silver, to serve this purpose [of purchase]. No

---

[1] We shall return to the critics of money in the epilogue of this book.

other substances unite the necessary qualities in so great a degree, with so many subordinate advantages... They were the most imperishable of all substances. They were also portable, and containing great value in small bulk, were easily hid; a consideration of much importance in an age of insecurity. Jewels are inferior to gold and silver in the quality of divisibility; and are of very various qualities, not to be accurately discriminated without great trouble. Gold and silver are eminently divisible, and when pure, always of the same quality; and their purity may be tested by a public authority... To the qualities which originally recommended them, another came to be added, the importance of which only unfolded itself by degrees. Of all commodities, they are the least influenced by any of the causes which produce fluctuations in value.[2]

Money in the form of gold and silver coinage was so successful, according to Mill, because it is portable, imperishable, divisible, stable in value and easily hidden. It made value measurable and comparable and thereby allowed more complex transactions to take place over time and distance. It facilitated exchange and reduced the costs of transactions.[3] Socially, it created greater trust in the justice of transactions as it provided a means of recompense for the supply of goods and services as well as compensation for injuries and injustice.[4] It transformed simple markets into powerful distribution mechanisms. In its early history in Greece it liberalized labour relationships, warfare and politics as well as having made possible the first Western democracy.[5] Its anonymity and exchangeability at the same time increased the freedom of individuals, and choice.

And yet, the counter-intuitive assumption that the success of money was not quite as predictable as the story of its success suggests helps us to focus on the conditions of its becoming one of the most powerful instruments of human intercourse. If we assume that people sacrifice many valuable objectives in order to integrate money into their everyday lives, and that governments have to invent many regulations in order to keep the value of their currencies stable and functioning, we can begin to think about the stories behind the history of money. In whose interest was it to

---

[2] J. S. Mill *Principles of Political Economy* [1848]. London 1909, bk. 3, ch. 7.2.

[3] The more technical term 'transaction costs', frequently recurring in the following chapters, is borrowed from Neo-Institutional Economic Theory, where it refers to three forms of costs. According to Ronald Coase, who introduced the theorem into the debate, there are three categories: (1) search costs that occur when parties find out about relative prices, (2) costs that occur in the process of negotiation, such as the costs of reaching an agreement or drafting contracts, and (3) costs of uncertainty and complexity that occur in long-term contracts (Coase (1937); see also Williamson (1975); and Frier and Kehoe (2007): 117–19 for brief discussion).

[4] Thus especially Aristotle in a much-discussed passage of the *Nicomachean Ethics* (*EN* 1133a) with Meikle (1995): 129–46; and below, chapter 1.

[5] Schaps (2004) for each of these aspects.

use and improve the use of money? What kind of transactions benefited from money, and why? What kind of incentives, or incentive structures, supported the use of money? What rules of behaviour made monetary payment, monetary exchange and monetary wealth accepted forms of social interaction and status signification? Most of all, what political, social and cultural systems made certain forms of money acceptable and other monetary systems collapse? It soon turns out that in contrast to common perception money does not 'do' anything by itself. Through money the complexity of relationships, exchange and wealth increases as it links an ever increasing amount of transactions that without money are separate and distinct. But money is not a phenomenon unchanging over time. It develops as individuals, social groups and governments allow it to perform certain functions. Put more technically, money is ruled by human institutions, norms and social as well as political forms of organization. In order to understand the history of it, one has to understand the dependence of money on these institutions, norms and socio-political contexts.

MONEY AND COINAGE

Some important distinctions need to be introduced before we explore the development of money. Money, in contrast to coinage, has never been deliberately invented (either by traders, citizens or states), but comes into being as regular transactions are made by means of the same medium. When rents are regularly paid in grain, or bride prices customarily rendered in gold and silver, these media become forms of money. When different kinds of payments are regularly made with the same medium, and this medium itself becomes a desirable object for the purpose of exchange, the medium takes over additional monetary functions. If an obligation is not discharged, but remains pending as a debt expressed in terms of one particular medium, this medium also takes on a monetary function. When a payment or exchange is made, a common standard by which different items are compared in value helps to assess the equivalence of the payment or exchange. When any of these forms of payment become institutionalized, that is, many people make them in the same way, money comes into being. For convenience, therefore, money can be defined by four basic, but interdependent, functions.[6] It is a *means of exchange* if people make payments for goods and services; it is a *means of payment*, if people

---

[6] Polanyi (1977): 99, 104 f., 107–9; further functions are suggested by Einzig (1966): 444 f., 458–63; Schaps (2004): 12–15, and Seaford (2004): 16–20 for discussion.

pay taxes, rents and penalties; it is a *store of value*, if people keep it in a treasure box, display it at home, or put it in a bank account; and it is a *unit of account*, if people compare the value of different goods on the basis of that medium, or account for debts, future payments, and so on. Yet still today new functions of money arise. For example, when investment companies began to provide loans based on the virtual money of investors speculating on the profits of tax relief or changing interest rates, they introduced a new function of money (let's call it money as a *means of virtual payment*).[7] As institutionalized transactions change over time (bride price is no longer paid, transactions with virtual money become more popular), concepts of money fluctuate alongside changing forms of collective behaviour.

In the past, people often used different media for different monetary purposes. Gold and silver, for example, were used as stores of value, together with salt as a medium of small exchanges and animal hides for larger transactions. Grain was used for the payment of rents and taxes, while at the same time other objects were used as accounting units or for the comparison of value.[8] Such forms of money are sometimes called *limited-purpose money* as they lack the complexity of functions all-purpose money fulfils. Such moneys also lack the capacity to be transformed into other monetary functions (so-called *fungibility*) which some monetary theorists regard as the essence of money.[9] Yet once again, the fungibility of money is never total, nor has there ever been any evolution from limited to all-purpose money. For example, in antiquity human beings (such as slaves) could be bought with money, but education, political service and warfare only gradually became paid jobs – much to the regret of conservatives like Plato and Isocrates. For a time within the medieval period, sins could be absolved with money, whereas sacred relics were regarded as impossible to be traded commercially. In more recent years, it has been debated whether the conditions of human life, such as health, blood or fresh air should have monetary value and thereby become subject to some supply-and-demand mechanism. Human labour can be purchased like sex and pleasure, but we resent the idea that human emotions can be obtained commercially.[10] Therefore, money is never used for 'all purposes' nor is it fully 'fungible'.

---

[7] Arguably, this can be regarded as a form of using money as a unit of account. But as the loans are not stable sums, but dependent on speculative amounts, it ought to be regarded as a new function of money – which, incidentally, our legal systems do not yet fully control.

[8] Appadurai (1986); and Parry and Bloch (1989), introduction, for some examples in an anthropological perspective.

[9] Polanyi (1957): 264; see, however, Melitz (1970); cf. Seaford (2004): 18 f.

[10] For these examples and, more generally, the politics of 'commodification', see the introduction in Appadurai (1986).

It is more helpful to consider money within social and normative contexts that bestow upon it, and prohibit, particular usages.

Moving on from the shifting sands of money, we find that there are special forms of money which are more readily defined. An exceptionally important one in Western history has been gold and silver minted into coinage. The first coins in ancient Greece were made of precious metal and carried an authoritative stamp which, as Aristotle accurately described, certified its weight and value. In principle, coinage can be issued by any authority, such as temples, individuals, states or firms, but in antiquity there was not much debate over who should have the right to coin. In ancient China, by contrast, it was an important issue whether governments or private entrepreneurs should have the right to issue coins.[11] Another issue not known from classical antiquity, but seriously considered in ancient China, was whether coins should be replaced by some other object or commodity. The fact that certain questions arose in one rather than another monetary culture shows that precious metal coinage, too, is not a natural consequence of monetary evolution, but a specific historical development.[12]

There were also other forms of money than coinage in antiquity. In archaic Greece, for example, coinage was a departure from the use of silver and gold units of weight used as means of payment and exchange in many public and private transactions.[13] In the fifth century BC, bronze and copper coins were a departure from the exclusive use of precious metal as money. The shift from precious to (some) base-metal coins was a conceptual challenge as the latter destabilized the value of money that so far had been linked to what was assumed to have universal value. In late-fifth-century Athens the emergency issue of (silver-plated) copper coins provoked an outcry like a moral disaster.[14] It was the practical solution to a pressing scarcity of silver, yet at that time raised the question of the value of money. How far should the state (or citizens) have the power to issue valid coins the value of which depended on political decision rather than intrinsic value? Given that the debased coinage did circulate, there must have been a new consensus, not acceptable to all, but generally promoted by the collective citizen body, that monetary value could be based on political decision rather than universal, or super-natural, qualities such as those residing in

[11] Williams (1997): 155; a comparison of Mediterranean with Chinese traditions of coinage proves very instructive; Scheidel (2008); Schaps (2007).

[12] Persuasively argued by Kurke (1995) and (1999).

[13] E.g. Kroll (1998); (2001); (2008); and Kim (2001a and b).

[14] Kroll (1976) and (1979) on these coins; von Reden (1995): 114–15 with Aristoph. *Frogs* 734–49 for the social implications.

gold and silver. The introduction of bank notes later in Western history represents a similar transformation promoted by the combined power of state authority and central banks. By this time, however, users had long become accustomed to promissory notes on paper as forms of money beyond coins. Cash-less forms of money such as transferable credit notes, cheques, or bonds, which make possible storage and transfer of money by means of written or electronic notification, have once again transformed notions of money, and shifted trust in the stability of precious-metal value (e.g. Mill, above) to a rather precarious trust in the stability of law and monetary regulation.[15]

MONEY: TERMINOLOGY AND CULTURE

Given the historical embeddedness of money, it is unsurprising that neither the Greeks nor the Romans had a term that precisely matches our word 'money'. Both languages had words for coins (*nomisma/nummus*), or cash (*argurion/argentum*: 'silver'), but the general terms *chremata* (resources) in Greek and *pecunia* ('cattle money') in Latin differed from our word 'money' (deriving rather arbitrarily from *moneta*, a cognomen of the goddess Juno in whose temple coins were sometimes minted). The Roman jurist Iulius Paulus (early third century AD), who for legal purposes attempted to define money, suggests that *pecunia* included not just coins but *omnes res*, all things. Thus he writes:

> The designation *pecunia* does not only include coinage but absolutely every kind of *pecunia*, that is, every substance (*omnia corpora*); for there is no one who doubts that substances are also included in the designation of *pecunia* (*Dig.* 50.16.178).

The fact that a lawyer felt the need to define *pecunia* beyond coinage shows that commonly *pecunia* was associated with coinage as much as money is associated with physical currency today. Similarly, when Aristotle discusses the art of money-making (*chrematistike*) he distinguishes it from another kind of *chrematistike*, the art of increasing the wealth of a household (*Pol.* 1257b40 ff). For clarification he calls the latter *ktetike* (the art of managing property) but the two were very close. This was so because *chremata* did not refer just to coins, but to all movable objects a household contained. In the *Nicomachean Ethics* Aristotle describes *chremata* as 'everything the value of which can be measured in terms of coinage' (*EN* 1119b26). Beyond the superficial identification of money with coins, both *chremata* and *pecunia*

---

[15] Hart (1986) for the gradual transformation of perceptions negotiating this shift.

were broader categories, just as nowadays money comprises more than coins, notes and plastic cards.

In antiquity, however, the concept of money was closely linked to valuable objects (*chremata/res*). And so monetary value, too, was considered to be the price (*time/pretium*) of objects that were purchasable. Since both Aristotle and the Roman jurists were well acquainted with price variation, monetary value was clearly perceived as a social rather than intrinsic factor of objects.[16] Moreover, as in both Greece (by the fourth century) and Rome base-metal coins were minted, it was the stamp of the coin rather than the intrinsic value of precious metal that was regarded as constituting the value of money. Paulus, once again, argued that monetary value was created by the public stamp (*forma publica*) rather than the fact that coins had a substance (*substantia*).[17] Rather more provocatively, Pliny the Elder called money *rerum pretia*, the price of things (Plin *NH* 33.1).[18] *Rerum pretium* was the value bestowed upon gold and silver in the first instance, but even in the case of precious metal was not beyond social influence. Debates over monetary value took place within the contested opposition between value by convention and represented by the power of governments on the one hand, and universal, sometimes supernaturally defined, value represented by the substance of metals and useful objects on the other. As stamped coins were money only within the boundaries of one political system, but monetary exchange took place across such boundaries, other valuable objects – *chremata, res, merces* (commodities) – had to be conceptually included into the category of money.

The value of modern money is based on central banks, international civil and banking law as well as technical conditions such as widespread literacy, the print industry, and electronic data transmission. This has created greater reliability of monetary transactions beyond national and political boundaries and thus brought about a notion of money that is less dependent on the intrinsic value of objects as opposed to state authority. Instead, concepts of money depend on the market, an (almost) global monetary network of transactions, an equally global economic culture, and central banks that fix exchange rates of national or local currencies. In antiquity international capital markets and international laws did not exist, while banks were run by private entrepreneurs whose international relationships depended on their own business contacts. State and social power over the value and supply of money were felt more strongly, while

---

[16] Meikle (1995) for Aristotle's distinction between use value and exchange value.
[17] *Dig.* 18.1.1 with Wolters (1999): 341–62; cf. Lo Cascio (1996).
[18] Further discussed below in the epilogue.

highly exchangeable objects were readily included into the category of
money. This does not mean that Greek and Roman money had not fully
matured. Rather, different forms of economic and political organization,
conditions of transaction, monetary institutions and forms of law suggested
a narrower and at the same time broader notion of money than is current
today.

MONEY IN THE ANCIENT ECONOMY

While functions and meanings of money are dependent on a wide range of
social and cultural conditions, it is most strongly associated with markets
and the economy. An economy may be defined as the production, distribution and consumption of things, each involving exchange, payment and
storage of valuable objects as well as relationships and institutions which
organize these activities. Indeed, as money has become the major means
of interaction and communication in the economy, it has also become its
major signifier: any relationship in which money is used is part of the
economy, while monetary relationships are regarded above all as economic
ones.

Ancient authors, too, associated money with economic exchange. But
'the economy' was not the same in antiquity as it is today.[19] *Oikonomia* in
Greece referred to the task of managing a household, be it private, royal
or public. It included strictly economic aspects, such as managing material resources, minting coinage and administrating finances, but also social
aspects such as choosing and training a suitable wife and household staff.
There was, moreover, no attempt to treat production, distribution and
consumption as related activities that constituted an autonomous system
linked through money and markets. Each had their separate social and
political aspects which could not be dissociated from their material side.
This was a matter both of perception and social reality. Labour relationships, for example, were frequently not regulated by money but in the
form of personal dependence (slavery and long-term tenancies) or within
the household where free labour was unpaid. Exchange and credit, moreover, were not always just monetary relationships but were embedded in
relationships of patronage and friendship with social consequences in the
interaction with neighbours and friends.[20] Although people identified a
sphere of commerce which was identified above all with markets, harbours

---

[19] See for discussion the section 'Economic context' in the bibliographical essay at the end of this
book.
[20] Millett (1991); Verboven (2002).

and money, and marked by special rules of behaviour, laws and sites, any connection of that sphere with production and consumption did not make immediate sense.[21] Despite the fact that there was something comparable to what we regard as economic activities, they were lumped into different categories. This created important differences between ancient and modern economic behaviour as well as perceptions of money.

Unfortunately, the problem has been discussed in highly ideological if not polemical fashion over the past decades. There are above all two major issues. Firstly, scholars have asked (in rather un-historical fashion) whether or not the ancient economy was similar to the modern, despite its obvious difference in size and complexity. This discussion has entered textbooks as the primitivist vs. modernist debate. And secondly, and more sensibly, it has been debated whether or not the ancient economy can be analyzed within the terminology and ideas of modern economic theories which were developed for modern market economies. This is the so-called substantivism vs. formalism debate.[22] Moses Finley, the most famous proponent of the 'substantivist' position, argued that the ancient economy was radically different from a modern (post-nineteenth-century) market economy and thus could not be understood within modern theoretical terms. Finley drew attention to the largely self-sufficient agrarian household as the major (social) site of production and consumption. As exchange was significant in cities only, and these cities, rather than being centres of production were places where wealth produced in the rural hinterlands was consumed, Finley attributed a very limited role to money.[23] Money for him was above all coinage serving as a means of exchange and payment in the non-productive cities of relatively small political entities. Neither was it a medium regulating demand (consumption) and supply (production), nor did it link local markets to larger exchange networks beyond. In *The Ancient Economy* he argued firstly that all monetary exchange was cash exchange and there were no such things as fiduciary money, that is, money not backed up by precious metal coinage or bullion. This made the volume of money very small, and in turn demonstrated its limited use. Secondly, credit did not increase the volume of money in circulation, but was used for instant needs when cash in hand was scarce. This frequently happened due to slow circulation and the fact that surplus cash was kept in hoards rather than being spent or invested. Thirdly, money did not convey market information and was not used as an accounting unit to make rational

[21] Von Reden (1995): 105–26.
[22] The debates are well summarized by Schaps (2004): 18–26; Cartledge (2002); and Davies (1998).
[23] For the following Finley (1985): 115 f.; 132–5; 166–9; 141–3; and *passim*.

economic choice possible. The famous example of Columella, the owner of several large estates in Italy and author of an agricultural manual in the first century AD, suggested that even large players in the economy were not able to calculate the profitability of alternative investments. Therefore, cash-cropping and surplus-production for markets and export were never pursued systematically, so that trade and market exchange could not have significant effects on monetization. Fourthly, ancient governments had no monetary policies. Minting was guided by state expenditure rather than market considerations and concerns for a stable currency. Metals, weight systems and designs were adopted according to the immediate interests of civic communities, emperors or kings, with disastrous consequences for the monetary system. Moreover, since each local community took pride in its own coin designs and weight system, monetary transactions across political boundaries remained cumbersome and inefficient. Given the limitations of ancient coinage and money, the Mediterranean region remained economically fragmented, even at the height of the Roman empire. Local price formation was independent of inter-regional markets, which barely existed anyway, and the imperial monetary tax economy was a political economy superimposed upon otherwise local and particularized systems of production and consumption.

Most, if not all these positions have been contested in recent years, but also the issues have changed.[24] Finley wrote within an intellectual climate in which the liberal market economy and its theoretical basis in the form of classical and Neo-Classical Economic theory had to be protected against the challenges of communitarian economic models, especially the socialist system of the Soviet Union. Defenders of the market model, including ancient historians, aligned their perceptions of the past with their present ideas of progress and described the ancient economy as an earlier version of the Western system.[25] Critics of the system or those who, like Finley, did not believe quite so firmly in the market model as the only rational form of economic organization, drew out the possibilities of communitarian distribution systems, grounding their arguments, too, in pre-capitalist examples of the past. Ancient economies, with their ideological if not real focus on communitarian institutions such as households and small political communities, and economic cultures in which reciprocal social exchange or political redistribution, rather than markets, functioned as major distributive mechanisms, served both

---

[24] Von Reden (2002) for a summary of responses to Finley; Harris (2008), introduction, for a sketch of recent issues.
[25] Nafissi (2005): 17–54.

as historical examples and trans-historical paradigms for alternatives to the Western market economy. Finley's account of ancient money was not a disinterested description of money in antiquity, but an argument against the historical use of liberal and neo-classical conceptualizations of money.

Since the collapse of the socialist systems which represented the last significant alternative to the liberal market model, academic interest in the ancient economy has changed. Instead of contrasting communitarian and liberal economic models, historians and economic theorists have turned to consider economic growth and development in both global and historical perspectives. Once again the relationship between economics and culture, in the past and in the present, is at stake, but discussions depend no longer on the glorification of Western markets (though possibly on the glorification of growth). As economists have begun to theorize markets as culture-dependent and therefore variable distribution mechanisms, new perspectives on pre-modern economies have emerged.[26] This may turn out to be particularly fruitful for research on the ancient economy which does not seem to be characterized either by long-term economic stagnation, or by capitalist market development.

The question of growth, difficult to measure as it is in the absence of sufficient amounts of relevant quantitative data, has become central to recent debates on the ancient economy. It is uncontroversial that there was some, even considerable, economic development in the Mediterranean between the archaic period and the Roman empire. Population increase, urbanization, the development of imperial cities like Alexandria, Antioch or Rome, and the growth of monetization itself can be taken as reasonable indications of long-term economic growth.[27] At the same time, environmental factors, technological limits, comparative data, and the host of aspects that distinguish pre-modern from modern economies suggest that sustained economic growth in terms of an effective increase in per-capita production was no more than 'modest' throughout antiquity.[28] Given this frame of long-term economic development, on the one hand, and limited short-term productive growth, on the other, the impact of money on ancient society was neither 'limited' nor 'considerable'. Quite beyond these polar opposites, it is better to ask under what circumstances money could have effects on the economy and what these effects may have been.

---

[26] Introduction in Morris, Scheidel, and Saller (2007) with North (1990); Bang (2008).
[27] Ibid.; see also Reger (2006).   [28] Saller (2005): 265.

MONETARY DYNAMICS, MARKETS AND STATE EXPENDITURE

I shall argue throughout this book that money was a dynamic that under changing political and social circumstances increased the complexity of transactions and reduced costs. A reduction of the costs of transactions is a vital condition for an increase of the efficiency of economic activity and thus economic performance.[29] This monetary dynamic was neither continuous nor just dependent on the growth of markets, state expenditure or volumes of coinage in circulation. Rather, factors such as the increasing 'connectivity' of the Aegean in the late archaic period, the Athenian empire in the fifth century BC, the conquest of the Persian empire under Alexander the Great, or the growth of the Roman empire during the republic and principate, mostly rapidly rather than continuously improved the conditions for monetary circulation and the expansion of what I shall call 'monetary networks'.[30] At the same time, institutional (normative) factors such as the imperative in granting and returning credit, the financial aspects of friendship, the ideological emphasis on social and communal munificence, and many other more localized rules of behaviour supported a monetary credit economy which in turn increased the efficiency of money.[31] The consolidation of currencies as a result of imperial taxation, and increasing legal security of Greek and Roman citizens, provided a third factor for positive monetary development.[32] Against the long-held scholarly consensus that moral reservations of the Greco-Roman elite against monetary, interest-bearing loans prohibited the growth of a monetary economy, I shall suggest that the culture of credit was a vital condition for the dynamic development of money in classical antiquity.

I shall take political structures, institutions, and normative behaviour, rather than a simple explanatory dichotomy between either the increase of state expenditure or the growth of markets, as the prime conditions for the growth of monetary economies in classical antiquity. Social networks of exchange, large estates, armies, and tributary systems provided equally, if not more, important contexts for the circulation of goods and money than markets. The impression may be an accident of our evidence which privileges the activities of elites, soldiers and governments to the cost of

---

[29] Frier and Kehoe (2007): 117–19.
[30] B. Cohen (1998); (2004) for monetary networks, Horden and Purcell for the 'connectivity' of the Aegean from the archaic period onwards.
[31] Millett (1991); Verboven (2002); Cohen (2003) and (2008) with a different emphasis.
[32] Frier and Kehoe (2007); and, less theoretically, von Reden (2007a).

the ordinary civil population. But arguably it is just these groups, collaborating with and using imperial structures, that created a major stimulus for the movement of goods across the Mediterranean – because of their consumption habits and control over large portions of surplus production.

In several chapters of this book I shall draw attention to the extent to which the 'private' and 'public' (state) economies were linked in practice. This does not only refer to private by-loads on ships carrying taxes in kind, or the combined function of communication lines used for military purposes and trade, but also to the use by individuals, traders and entrepreneurs of administrative and legal infrastructures (not least coinage itself) which were created for public or taxation purposes, and the virtual identity of private and imperial interests in the exploitation of land and manpower. Arguably, this created a much more dynamic monetary economy than the apparently subordinate role of ancient markets suggests.

The polar opposition of the relative impact of either state expenditure or market development, which has so dominated twentieth-century debates on monetary development, is based on a questionable distinction between public (state) and private (market) economic sectors. Although it is possible to distinguish between private enterprise and public (state) finance, the distinction is often not very helpful for coming to terms with the conditions of the Greco-Roman economy. The collective property of the *polis* in classical Greece, for example, was a category economically and legally distinct from that of the private property of individual citizens and their *oikoi*. In Rome, the emperor Augustus made a point of distinguishing his own property (*patrimonium*) from the imperial treasury, the *fiscus*, and the (republican) public treasury, the *aerarium*. Both Greek and Roman law, furthermore, knew the idea of managing property on behalf of somebody else (e.g. an estate owner, an administration, emperor, or king). Thus in principle, private and public financial resources were separated, and there were legal categories for keeping private and public (imperial) exploitation of these resources distinct. But in practice the cross-over was great, and the question of whether monetary policy, monetary development, minting, legal development and monetization were driven by state or private interests (the market) is ill-posed.

First of all, the legal distinction of private and public property that is known from both classical Athens and republican and imperial Rome was not universal. Property rights were not homogeneous throughout the Greco-Roman world.[33] The diversity of land-tenure regimes in the ancient

---

[33] Frier and Kehoe (2007): 134–42.

Mediterranean brought with it an equally great diversity of property rights over land and yields which could efface the distinction between, for example, ('public') taxes and ('private') rents.[34] Not only were such systems part of the Greco-Roman economy, but in the course of imperial expansion new socio-economic and fiscal systems were incorporated without being totally transformed. In the Hellenistic concept of monarchy, for example, the kings were the ultimate owners of all land, and the 'public' royal economy was identical with the 'private' economy of the kings. This seems to have left some vestiges in the Roman imperial financial system in which an emperor's *patrimonium* was both his private possession and an asset of the government.[35] On the one hand, the emperor was not just a wealthy citizen who occupied a public position and funded public projects out of his own pocket: the emperor's property, the *patrimonium*, was passed from one emperor to his successor not by private will, but as part of the transfer of the office once it had been formalized as such. At the same time, the *patrimonium* gradually established claims to a number of public sources of income and, although it was in theory managed separately from the state finances, its administrative personnel became an integral part of the state bureaucracy. Given the great interface between public and private interests and investments, the participation of emperors and kings in markets and trade, and the diversity of property rights within the Greco-Roman economy, the attempt to distinguish between state economy and market economy becomes difficult. In fact, the particular interdependence between the economic interests of states and the 'private economy' of their leaders and elites created a particularly powerful background for the development of money and its circulation.

In between 'public' and 'private' individuals and their households there were other social groups and organisations which influenced the development of money. Temples and (public) cults were important participants of ancient economies, but tend to escape the notice of economic historians.[36] Temples were landlords and proprietors of substantial amounts of movable treasury, while cult observance could involve large expenditure. On the one hand temple finances were supervised by secular officials, which suggests that the property of a god or goddess was regarded as an asset of the collective body of citizens. On the other, temples also advanced loans to the governments and cities to which they belonged, so in this respect they were private creditors. Moreover, the sacrifice industry in ancient cities,

---

[34] For examples from Ptolemaic Egypt, Vandorpe (2000).   [35] Rathbone (1996 a): 315 f.
[36] Temple finance tends to be a subject in its own right and is poorly integrated into economic history; a notable exception is Reger (1994).

and the ruler cult of eastern cities and kingdoms under Greco-Roman rule, involved economic activities taking place at the interface between private and state economy. It is noteworthy that the economic activities of large urban temples and cults were fully monetized, and even highly innovative in their monetary strategies. Instead of representing a traditional, backward-looking element in ancient economies, both temples, and kings and emperors acting as religious figures, integrated money into their economies and bestowed upon it a symbolism that was favourable for its circulation.

AIMS OF THIS BOOK

In line with the idea of the Key Themes series, this book is intended to offer guidance for the study of a central aspect of Greco-Roman antiquity. This means that it should be an introduction to students who are new to the field. However, a stimulating textbook should also offer some perspectives for further research. Achieving this double goal turned out to be a rather difficult task. Research on ancient money is rapidly advancing, leaving little room for standard knowledge and much for further exploration. My tentative path through this jungle is to present a book in non-technical language with clear signposts to the evidence. I wish to offer new perspectives on this evidence rather than just taking stock.

The time frame of the book is 'classical antiquity', which I have taken to comprise roughly the millennium from the seventh century BC to the third century AD. Developments before and after this period would have increased the perspective, but also expanded the size of this volume. For that reason I also had to be selective in the choice of topics and geographical as well as social contexts. As it is now agreed that there was no one cohesive ancient economy to be encompassed in a single model, there is also no simple way of describing money within the multiplicity of more or less connected regional economies.[37] Given the increasing awareness of the great diversity of socio-economic structures within the Mediterranean, and the questionable boundary between the Greco-Roman and Near Eastern systems of production and exchange, the task of writing a monetary history of the Mediterranean over a period of 1,000 years must be surrendered to collaborative projects. My own expertise lies in the Eastern Mediterranean from the classical to the Hellenistic periods. For the Western Mediterranean and the Roman world, I had to draw more heavily on the work of others.

[37] Cartledge (2002); Davies (1998).

This might be regarded as a shortcoming, but it was worth taking the risk in order to encourage comparison and contrasting.

I start with the subject of monetization, that is, the development of money and coinage. But I do not wish to establish 'origins' of money (chapters 1 and 2). As will become clear in subsequent chapters, monetization was a continuous and geographically fragmented process which in many respects extended well into the third century AD, and beyond. By considering different cases of monetization, I wish to draw attention to a range of institutional conditions which promoted the growth of monetary economies in Greco-Roman antiquity. In the third chapter I shall explore the expansion of monetary networks. Money becomes a more effective medium of transaction the more people use it in the same form and for the same purposes. The expansion of networks in which compatible forms of money or coinage circulated was a vital condition for money to increase its effects. At the same time, the way in which monetary networks developed in antiquity suggests that there was no continuous expansion towards a single monetary zone. Monetary networks appear to have expanded and contracted in response to changing political conditions. In the fourth chapter, I shall look at ways in which money (coinage) was used efficiently by being combined with other forms than cash. Credit and cash-less forms of payment based on monetary units made the amount of coinage in circulation work harder and thus increased its power and impact. The question of who used credit and cash-less payments under what conditions and for what purposes is important for the issue of the impact of money on different ancient economies.

Prices and their regional and inter-regional fluctuation are indicators of the efficiency of monetized markets, and of market integration. But, as I shall argue in chapter 5, whether or not ancient markets were integrated temporarily or in the long term,[38] the material we have does not normally allow proper analyses of price formation beyond a very narrow chronological and geographical frame. There is some evidence to suggest that people believed in some equilibrium of grain prices throughout the Mediterranean. But even under comparatively good conditions of evidence we are unable to prove this belief, nor answer the question of how 'normal prices' were established and re-established over a period of time (chapter 6). In chapter 7 I shall look at the role of temple and cult finance in the process of monetization and monetary economics. The question of how temples

---

[38] The most recent and innovative approach to this much discussed question is Bang (2008), esp. 93–110.

and cults contributed and responded to the economies surrounding them has been addressed so far only in the case of the Apollo temple of Hellenistic Delos (Reger (1994)). Broadening the perspective towards a wider range of urban and rural temples in the Eastern Mediterranean, I shall suggest that many Greek temples pursued breathtaking financial strategies so far unattested in any other public or private context. Rather than being resistant to the use of money, temples contributed importantly and possibly innovatively to the development of money. Moreover, the way in which sacred finances were increased and enhanced through interest-bearing loans and endowments allows a glimpse into the relationship between money and agricultural land within the management of productive resources.

In the epilogue I shall turn to the perception of money and coinage. As it happens, in pre-modern societies such perceptions tended to be critical and disconcerting rather than favourable and constructive. But instead of wishing to confirm perennial anxieties about the nature of money in pre-modern societies, I shall draw attention to the highly specific direction of such worries. Rather than being a timeless influence on the social and moral fabric of any society, money seems to provide a suitable platform for the expression of concerns over collective values.

CHAPTER I

Monetization: issues

INTRODUCTION

If you consult an ordinary dictionary, you will find monetization defined as establishing something (e.g. gold or silver) as legal tender in a country. If legal tender had been a pervasive concept in antiquity, and if coins had been the only tender, monetization would then refer to the introduction of coinage.[1] But when we consider that valuable objects and metal bullion, too, were tendered by custom or public approval, we find that monetization was not a process involving solely the establishment of coinage by governmental act. In this chapter we will explore monetization more broadly as the development of monetary institutions, intertwined as they were with the development of coinage. In the second chapter I shall compare a number of different cases and forms of monetization in the Greek and Roman world.

It is open to question whether it was economic or political institutions that brought into being money and coinage. The problem is linked to the major controversies in the debate over the ancient economy. Those who see a significant development of markets from an early period of classical antiquity onwards tend to link monetization to the transformation of a barter economy into a market economy.[2] Those who believe that markets were relatively late developments in ancient history emphasize that monetization was a result of community building and state development.[3] According to the latter view, the need for a common standard of value and

---

[1] Legal tender refers to the legal prerequisite that this form of payment must be accepted in settlement of an obligation. There is no clear evidence before the Athenian Standards Decree of the second half of the fifth century BC (below, chapter 3) that states decreed by law that their coinage, or any other tender, had to be accepted in their domestic or other markets they controlled. We do know, however, that states regulated which tender was approved in settlement of payments to their treasuries (e.g. *IG* XII.9 1273 + 1274, 2–3 (Eretria c. 525 BC), referring to *chremata dokima*). Such regulations come close to the legal enforcement of a tender, though not being quite the same. For further discussion and literature, Figueira (1998): 52–8; 398 f.; Körner (1993): 273–5.

[2] Most recently Schaps (2004) and (2008).

[3] For theoretical discussion, Giacomin and Marcuzzo (2007).

unit of account in which obligations between citizen collectives and individual citizens could be settled was prior to the need for a common means of exchange. Any kind of public payments, be they made in a military, political or economic context, provided the context for the development of monetary media, and remained the major force in their spread. It follows, for them, that ancient governments did not make monetary decisions with a view to fostering markets, but according to their own monetary needs.[4]

As was suggested in the introduction, the relative impact of states and of markets on the development of money and coinage cannot be fully separated. The development of money presupposes a range of institutions to be in place, and in turn reinforces their importance. Monetization as defined above cannot take place without a recognized central authority and some kind of administrative as well as legal apparatus enforcing standard weights, measures and regulations governing monetary transactions. If, however, there are no markets or individuals who accept money for further payments and exchange, it does not circulate.

The money that is likely to have preceded coinage in Greco-Roman antiquity is bullion, that is, unstamped pieces of precious metal exchanged according to their weight.[5] For such money to function there needs to be a recognized unit of metal weight and an official certification of standard weights in the area in which they are deemed valid. The earliest monetary unit of weight known in Greece was the mina subdivided into variable numbers of drachmas further subdivided into six oboloi. In Rome, the standard unit was the libra (pound) subdivided into twelve unciae. Extant weights show that standard weights were issued by local authorities and certified by a stamp.[6]

While the development of money was on its way, there was in Greece an accelerated dynamic towards the formation of *poleis* with distinct identities, territorial boundaries, political, legal and administrative institutions, as well as some idea of collective political and military action. Demographic growth, changing forms of warfare, the emergence of written law, the struggle for power among members of old and new elites, as well as intensified inter-state relationships, were all part of this complex development.[7] Among the many concerns that ancient authors associate with lawgivers and tyrants of the archaic period was control over metals and the specification of the units of weight by which they were measured.

---

[4] For the debate, see von Reden (2002); for the demand-oriented approach to minting, now Hollander (2007); (2008).
[5] Crawford (1985); Kroll (1998); (2008); Kim (2001b).   [6] Crosby and Lang (1964).
[7] Osborne (1996): 161–242.

Perhaps not accidentally, regulations were remembered above all in those areas known to have minted coinage first. The literary tradition has Pheidon, tyrant of Argos but also controlling Aegina some time in the seventh century BC, reform measures and weights as well as invent coinage (Strab. 8.3.33; Hdt. 6.127; cf. Arist. *Ath. Pol.* 10). As coinage is attested neither in Argos nor in Aegina during the somewhat shadowy lifetime of Pheidon (*c.* seventh/early sixth century BC), this must have been a reform of those weights and measures which in the second half of the sixth century, when the first coins appear in Aegina, underpinned the monetary system. Solon of Athens (*c.* 600 BC) is said to have reformed the weights of Athens, counting a different number of drachmas to the mina (Arist. *Ath. Pol.* 10.2). This system was adopted from the cities of Euboia, which also began to mint coinage early.[8]

The relatively small size of Greek *poleis* and their advanced internal organization were beneficial to the successful standardization of weights and measures within a bounded political territory, and thus to the development of money. In other ancient social formations, such as the tribal (*ethnos*) states of central Greece, or the kingdoms of northern Greece and temperate Europe, there was no similar degree of communal action and therefore no similar concern for establishing unified weights and monetary units. Macedonia, for example, had a bewildering array of local weight standards as well as local coinages well into the fourth century.[9] Only by the time of Philip II had one ruling family concentrated enough power to issue a 'national' coinage; and this coinage was introduced for external purposes only, not to replace the large number of internal currencies. The independent states and tribes of Italy and central Europe had no need to establish common political structures before they were conquered by the Mediterranean powers. Celtic coins in each area were produced of consistent weight and metallic composition, thus likely representing local weight systems and currency values; but there was no attempt to make them compatible with each other.[10] In Pharaonic Egypt, too, there was no official weight and currency system that was valid throughout Egypt. Local temples were in charge of producing their own weights and measures as well as certifying the purity of the silver they issued. Some coins were produced because of their acceptability among mercenaries and other foreign recipients, and hence in the late fifth century imitations of Athenian tetradrachms were produced in some quantity for foreign but not internal use.[11]

---

[8] Kroll (1998).   [9] Kraay (1976): 131–41.   [10] Allen (1980).   [11] Van Alfen (2002).

MONEY INTO COINAGE

In Solonian Athens, as in some other Greek cities at around the same time, payments to and from the public treasury were calculated in monetary units without coins being struck. Several laws attributed to Solon stipulate monetary penalties for injuries, expressed in drachmas of silver, although it is certain that coinage had not yet reached the Greek mainland. It was above all the leading magistrates and jurors who were liable to be fined for neglecting their duties. Thus in the earliest extant law surviving from Dreros in Crete we read (*GHI* 2 (*c.* 650–600 BC)):

May God be kind! The city has thus decided: when a man has been a *kosmos*, the same man shall not be *kosmos* again for ten years. If he does act as *kosmos*, whatever judgement he gives, he shall owe double, and he shall lose his right to office as long as he lives, and whatever he does as *kosmos* shall be nothing. The swearers shall be the *kosmos* and the *damioi* and the Twenty of the city.

We do not hear what kind of payment the *kosmos* owed in case of giving judgement without the right to office. Yet the shield description in book 18 of the *Iliad*, fixed in writing around 700 BC, gives an emblematic picture of public litigation:

And the heralds kept the people in hand, as meanwhile the elders were in session on benches of polished stone in the sacred circle and held in their hands the staves of the heralds who lift their voices. The two men rushed before these, and took turns speaking their cases, and between them lay on the ground two talents of gold to be given to that judge who in this case spoke the straightest opinion.[12]

In the fictional Homeric scene, the judge receives a fixed sum of gold as a reward for his sentence, while in the Cretan law the sum to be paid back is calculated on the fine the *kosmos* had imposed. Yet both texts suggest that communal life in the pre- and early archaic period, especially in its role of settling conflict, required a medium with which obligations were paid in the public sphere.

In sixth-century Athens the administrative office of the *naukraroi* (some sort of financial board dealing with temple or naval finance) dealt with payments in silver, and some payments made to victors in local games were calculated in drachmas.[13] Epigraphic evidence points to penalties reckoned in drachmas or staters in several *poleis* from the seventh century BC onwards.[14] It is also important to note that the earliest coin hoards of

---

[12] Hom. *Il.* 18.503–8 (trans. Lattimore).   [13] Kroll (1998).
[14] Körner (1993): nos. 46 A; 61 B; 72; 77; von Reden (1997).

the second half of the sixth century BC include a mixture of coins, rings, ingots, and pieces of precious metal, suggesting that in the early period of minting bullion and coins were used together. In Greek sanctuaries of Southern Italy and Sicily, too, large, round ingots and chopped chunks of ingots have been found as dedications to the god or goddess. Some have local coins attached or melted on to them.[15] In early Rome, bullion almost certainly served as a medium with which armies and tribute were paid before the first coins were minted for that purpose in the early third century BC.[16] But silver bullion was not used just for large payments to and from state and temple treasuries. The fact that the first Greek and Ionian coinages already comprised tiny specimens has been taken to suggest that coins were inserted into a pre-existing system where also small transactions were made on the basis of silver.[17]

Yet it has been questioned whether bullion served as money to the same extent as coinage from the mid-sixth century onwards.[18] In comparison to the Near East, where transactions in bullion went back at least two millennia by the time the first coins were struck, the tradition of bullion money in Greece was weak and short-lived. In the fictional epics of Homer, once again, personalized precious metal containers were exchanged among heroes and their guest friends, but they were neither used according to units of weight nor associated with more than one sphere of exchange. The four monetary functions, which we identified in the Introduction, seem to have been spread over several media serving as what we called limited-purpose money.[19] Gifts and recompense (*apoina* or *Wergeld*) were paid in the form of precious metal containers, textiles and slaves. The standard of value used to measure the value of brides and prestige objects was the ox rather than precious metal. Trade was conducted not with bullion, but on a barter basis as an exchange of goods for goods: wine was exchanged for metals, hides or slaves. From the eighth and seventh centuries BC onwards there is evidence of precious metal vessels (cauldrons and tripods) being used as means of payment. Iron spits widely used for cooking sacrificial meat may also have served monetary functions.[20] But from all that we know such items were counted out by number rather than weighed on the scale as bullion.

The use of bullion as a means of payment and exchange is much more articulated in the evidence from Babylonia and Mesopotamia.[21] What is

---

[15] Kroll (2008): 24–6.   [16] Crawford (1985).   [17] Kim (2001b).
[18] Thus Schaps (2004); (2008).   [19] Donlan (1981); (1981–2); (1989).
[20] Schönert-Geiss (1987); Wells (1978); Kroll (2001); and e.g. *BCH* 1938, 149–66; *ICret* IV 1; IV 8ₐ₋d.
[21] Le Rider (2001).

more, silver there served several inter-related functions in a broad range of relationships. Payments to and from the state were made in silver, rents and taxes were paid in this form, trade was conducted and loans made in silver.[22] In the famous law codes of Hammurabi and Eshnunna (early second millennium BC) amounts of silver were fixed as penalties for criminal offences and unfulfilled rental obligations; prices for goods and amounts of tax were payable in that form; and there were loans of silver the interest rates of which were regulated in terms of units of silver.

The social and political context within which both the Mesopotamian law codes and the use of silver as a means of payment emerged may serve to explain why here silver became a form of all-purpose money. Palaces of the smaller and larger kingdoms were redistributive centres regularly dealing with the income from tribute and the disbursements of gifts and food rations. Agrarian production was based on communal rather than private property, creating occasions for regular small-scale lending, borrowing and exchange. In the law code of Eshnunna, the king establishes himself as the authority over weights and measures. Extant weights from Assyria in the form of lions carry inscriptions which certify their validity as a standard.[23] Silver as a medium of exchange and payment, unit of account and store of wealth circulated in a dense and complex network of institutionalized relationships which, in combination with weights and measures fixed by royal authority, transformed silver into a form of money. In Greece during the early archaic period, neither the amount of silver in circulation nor the density and frequency of homogeneous (institutionalized) obligations seem to have reached the scale of those known from the Near Eastern kingdoms.

The situation rapidly changed in the seventh century. There was a dramatic increase of exchange relationships visible in the material culture, an equally dramatic development of settlement, and a notable orientation towards the Near East from which both cultural habits and silver were imported.[24] At around the same time tyrants and lawgivers began to reform weights and measures in the area of their influence. A concept of *chremata* emerged that represented some concept of money.[25] Only a couple of generations later, and almost overlapping with the developments just outlined, the first coins were struck. Whether bullion filled an identical range of functions as coinage did subsequently is a question that cannot be answered until we have a better understanding of the use and circulation of

[22] Van de Mierop (1992).   [23] Zaccagnini (2000); Mitchell (1990); Fales (1995).
[24] Kroll (2001).   [25] Morris (1994); Kurke (1995).

metals and bullion money. It is certain, however, that bullion and coinage merged, and for some time were interdependent forms of money.

It is, however, noteworthy that coinage made a much greater impact on Greece than it did on the Near East. As Schaps notes:

The invention of coinage came at the end of a long process of the monetization of Near Eastern society. The technology of making coins was trivial and had been available for a long time . . . For Lydians and Phoenicians, perhaps, the difference between coins and the other forms of silver that they were accustomed to was no more than a quibble.[26]

In Greece, although important steps towards the development of all-purpose money were made before coinage, it gathered pace with the introduction of coinage. Once coinage was adopted, the use of bullion as a means of payment and exchange declined rapidly.[27] It continued to function as a store of wealth, and occasionally served to transport large amounts of money over distance. But hoards combining coins and bullion disappear after the sixth century BC. Very little is certain about the practices in those communities – most notably Sparta – that neither minted their own nor employed foreign coinages for domestic purposes. But there is little evidence that, by the classical period, they used bullion instead. A wide range of goods, especially grain, other produce and textiles, are more likely to have been used rather than metals.

The spectacular spread of coinage in the Aegean during the late archaic period is at least partly explained by the role of coinage in the process of establishing identity in Greek political communities. The production and reproduction of local imagery on a daily means of exchange created social cohesion and a focus on a collective political centre through meaningful symbols. At the same time coins facilitated both internal and external transactions by making them independent of scales and weights. It has been argued that Aegean coinage is notably different from other coin traditions where coinage was neither made of precious metal nor carried a figurative stamp.[28] While the use of precious metal represents the function of coinage in inter-regional transactions where this material was equally valued, the stamp reflects the local political significance of institutionalized transactions. The ideological function of coinage promoted and stimulated the use of coinage both within and among competing cities, despite the fact that monetization could have progressed, if not at the same pace, without coinage.

---

[26] Schaps (2004): 16.   [27] Harris (2006).   [28] Scheidel (2008).

The nature of the spread of coinage demonstrates how much the success of coinage was linked to Greek institutions and culture. After the adoption of coinage by major Greek *poleis*, minting spread along the main axes of Greek overseas migration into the Black Sea region, Sicily and Southern Italy, Cyrene, Spain and Southern France. From the late sixth century BC onwards it spread to Thrace and Macedonia in the Northern Aegean, followed by Lycia in south-western Asia Minor. Persian silver coins, by contrast, were minted in the period of conflict with the Greeks in the first half of the fifth century BC, and hoard finds are concentrated in Asia Minor where contact with the Greeks was most intense. Achaemenid coinage was above all an extension of, and response to, Greek coinage.[29] The same holds true for the satrapal coinages of Western Asia Minor, and for the city of Carthage which began to issue gold and silver coins at the end of the fifth century BC, most likely to pay for the war against the Greeks in Sicily. In Egypt imitations of Athenian coins were struck in the middle of the fifth century, most likely to pay for Greek mercenaries. The earliest silver coins of Rome in the third century BC were minted for some unknown purpose in Greek Campania without much impact on the city of Rome itself. The coinages of the Persian empire, Carthage, early Rome and Egypt had little influence on domestic taxation and exchange as long as coins were treated internally as bullion. In Egypt, where we have the best knowledge of monetization under Greek influence, coined money took root in all economic sectors which the Ptolemies controlled, but the vast sector of cereal production that remained dominated by native and local power relationships remained largely unaffected by Greek coinage.[30]

MONETIZATION WITHOUT COINAGE

Monetization in Greece, then, was intertwined with the spread of coinage. It became increasingly dependent on the circulation of coins, but was not co-extensive with their use. As we suggested in the introduction, any valuable object could be regarded as a form of money as long as its value was measurable in terms of monetary units ('had a price'). Consequently, many strategies were adopted to compensate for a lack of cash. Among these were the conversion of cash obligations into kind, the use of monetary assets other than coins in settlement of obligations, the use of monetary units as a reference point in the exchange of goods for goods and credit (see further chapter 4). In order to distinguish monetization from the spread

[29] Scheidel (2008).   [30] Manning (2007) (2008); Migeotte (2002): 41–9.

of coinage, we need to distinguish between institutions that promoted the use of coinage, and those that promoted monetization more generally.

Payments to and from political governments, in particular army pay, penalty charges, payments for service to the city or *polis*, public festivals and games, as well as to office holders and magistrates were dominated by coinage.[31] Ancient governments seem to have both claimed and made these payments regularly in certified coinage and thereby demonstrated some commitment to coined money. The need to pay monetary taxes and tributes also promoted the use of coinage, although tax farmers, who bought the right to collect a certain tax from the taxpayers, could accept taxes in other forms than those in which they were levied.[32] Private rental payments, wages, market exchange and foreign trade, by contrast, were not directly controlled by governments and thus in principle were open to the use of any form of payment. Local markets were controlled by market officials, but only in exceptional circumstances do we hear that they enforced the use of any particular tender (see above, note 1). Different forms of money and coinages arrived here by means of circulation, and their acceptability ruled the game. However, the need to pay monetary tolls and indirect taxes, as well as custom and expectation, in practice will have restricted the choice of payment media among contracting partners.

Massive fluctuation in the coin supply was typical of ancient monetary economies.[33] Some places, such as the cities of Crete and many Cycladic islands until late in the fifth century BC, did not mint their own coins but used an approved foreign coinage instead. Even in places which had their own mints, temporary cash flow problems were a recurrent problem. Coinage was like other commodities subject to supply and demand, which both affected interest rates and commodity prices. In the third century AD, the Roman lawyer Gaius stated the problem in general terms. Observing that prices of goods varied widely from one place to another in the Roman empire, he related this phenomenon rather than to the supply-and-demand mechanism of goods to the variable rates of interest payable on monetary loans:

Granted that currency has a uniform value everywhere, in some places it can be raised easily and at low interest, while in others only with more difficulty and at a high rate of interest (Digest, 13.4.3 *Preamble*).

---

[31] Howgego (1990).
[32] Turner (1984) for tax-collection practice in Ptolemaic Egypt; Woolf (1998): 44 for Gaul; Howgego (1994): 16–20 for the interfaces of collecting taxes in cash or in kind.
[33] Bresson (2005) for discussion.

The Diocletian Price Edict of AD 305, moreover, was the most comprehensive attempt to fix maximum prices for commodities and services in the face of a highly variable coin supply throughout the territory of the Roman empire.[34] Commodities, especially grain, were used when coinage was scarce. A Greek business agent in the Ptolemaic Fayum once complained to his manager that he had expected to be able to buy fodder with grain, but found that nobody accepted grain as payment (*PSI* IV 356 (mid-third century BC)). The letter demonstrates both the potential and the limits of grain as money in ancient markets.

Temporary or localized shortages of coinage were no real impediment to monetary transactions. The absence of monetary institutions, however, was such an impediment. If key obligations – taxes, rents, wages and debts – are not settled in either coinage or monetary units of account, an area can be regarded as not monetized. Unfortunately, such places are by nature poorly documented. There is much speculation about the way in which goods were exchanged in places beyond the reach of written and numismatic evidence. Barter is often assumed to have been the dominant mode of exchange in non-monetized societies. But anthropologists emphasize that barter is a non-social form of exchange typical of hostile and non-co-operative environments rather than harmonious social collectives (see figure 1).[35] Moses Finley argued that, typically, ancient peasant households which were remote from urban centres and not subject to rental obligations and taxation were largely self-sufficient, and thus did not have to exchange much at all.[36] According to a more optimistic assessment of exchange among rural peasants, lending, borrowing and sharing were typical strategies for ancient peasant households.[37] It is important once again to think in institutional terms rather than to adopt crude polarities between city and countryside, self-sufficiency and market exchange, or practices typical of peasant and of tenant economies.[38] Coin finds in remote places and rural areas help to correct an all too simple distinction between urban monetization and rural barter or cash-less gift-exchange.[39] Taxation, public wage labour and military service, as well as cash-cropping were important ways of driving coinage into the countryside and integrating remote places into monetary circulation despite their distance from an urban centre.[40] Conversely, once a whole payment structure of wages, rents and taxes was

[34] Meissner (2000) for the interpretation of the much-discussed Price Edict in these terms.
[35] Humphrey and Hugh-Jones (1992).   [36] Finley (1985) *passim.*
[37] Millett (1984) for the peasant economy in early archaic Greece.   [38] Bloch (1967).
[39] Howgego (1992): 20–2; de Ligt (1990): 33–43; against Crawford (1970): 45.
[40] De Neeve (1990), and below.

Figure 1: Interethnic barter

effected by obligations expressed in coinage, they could easily dispense with ready cash. We shall explore such situations in later sections of this chapter.

MONETIZATION AND THE CIRCULATION OF METALS

Since bullion and coinage were the main forms of money in antiquity, the availability of metal was an important condition for monetization.[41] Some scholars have argued that a relative scarcity of monetary material is a necessary cultural pre-condition for such materials to be endowed with value.[42] But for a monetary economy to take off, sufficient amounts of monetary material must be in circulation in order that regular obligations can be expected to be discharged in monetary form. It is therefore not entirely coincidental that the first coins of Asia Minor were struck in electrum, which is in rich supply in the area where the first coins were produced. Gold and silver, too, are naturally supplied in Lydia and help to explain the switch from electrum to gold and silver coins at the time of the Persian take-over of Lydia in the mid-sixth century BC. Attica, one

---

[41] Carradice and Price (1988): 48–50.   [42] Einzig (1966); Polanyi (1977).

of the first areas to produce coinage, has productive silver mines in Laureion and Thorikos where some exploitation started in the early Bronze Age. The discovery of the rich ores at Maroneia some time before 483 BC, moreover, gave a major boost to coin production in Athens and in the Aegean more generally.[43] Siphnos in the Cyclades was famous for its gold and silver mines in the archaic period which gave this island an outstanding position in the trade network of the Aegean.[44] In Northern Greece, there were gold and silver mines in Macedonia, Thrace and on the island of Thasos, which may explain their early adoption of coinage. The gold and silver ores of Thasos and Thrace helped to finance Macedonian imperial ambitions in the fourth century BC and raised coin circulation in the Aegean to a new level. The spread of Roman precious-metal coinage was intimately linked to Rome's imperial expansion. Beginning with the acquisition of the mines in Carthage and Southern Spain after the Hannibalic wars in the late third century BC, north-western Spain, Gaul, Britain, the Danube provinces and Asia Minor became vital resources for the Roman metal supply.[45] The immediate effects on coin production of incidental gains in precious metal, such as the discovery of the Maroneia ore just mentioned, the capture of the Persian treasury by Alexander the Great, the Carthaginian payments to Rome after the first Punic War, or the Roman conquest of Spain, Bosnia and Dacia during the reign of Augustus, show the high sensitivity of the coin supply to the availability of metal.[46]

However, many minting states, most notably Aegina, did not have their own silver resources nor imperial access to foreign mines. Still more puzzling is the fact that chemical analyses of most coinages reveal that their metal came from a great variety of foreign sources, even when local mining was possible. The exploitation of metal resources – iron, bronze, copper, gold and silver – is regarded as a central motivation for exchange in the Bronze Age as well as Greek overseas settlement during the archaic period.[47] The circulation of metals for coinage, too, may be understood in this context. The extraordinary achievement of archaic Aegina, and later the Ptolemies, of sustaining a monetary economy without domestic silver resources was possible only against the background of circulating metal.

---

[43] Rutter (1981); Osborne (1985): 116 for the relationship between the exploitation of these mines and state finance.

[44] Horden and Purcell (2000): 346.

[45] Wilson (2002) for a dramatic picture of the scale of mining in the Iberian provinces.

[46] Howgego (1992) for further discussion of these examples.

[47] Osborne (1996): 113–15; Horden and Purcell (2000): 346–9.

Although still poorly explored in detail, the circulation of metal and the development of precious-metal money in the Eastern Mediterranean were interdependent phenomena. Just as the circulation of metals was a condition for bullion and coinage to become money, so the demand for metal became a reason for trade and violent looting of both treasuries and mining resources.[48]

In the first 200 years of monetary history, silver was the dominant monetary metal in Greece. Gold, electrum and either copper or bronze (both called *chalkos*) were metals of regular coinages outside the mainstream monetary networks of Greece only. Gold was struck in quantity in the Persian empire, where the gold daric was part of a regular bi-metallic coinage. Greek Lampsakos, too, struck a gold coinage for about forty years in the fifth century BC, although it was minted on the weight standard of the daric and thus created specifically for this exchange network. Carthage struck gold coins early in the fourth century BC, probably because of the relative abundance of gold in comparison to silver in Africa, but again its economy was peripheral to that of the Greco-Roman world, and the coinage served above all external military purposes. Electrum was the preferred metal among mints in northern Asia Minor and created a regional coinage among the cities in the Black Sea area.[49] Base metal had some monetary tradition in iron-rich northern Etruria where the so-called *ramo secco* (dry branch) bars produced from a metal with high iron content had some monetary function at least from the sixth century BC onwards.[50] In Greece, however, gold and bronze for a long time were not regarded as suitable for coinage.[51]

The reluctance of the Greeks to strike gold coins is not quite as readily comprehensible as their reluctance to strike base metal. Gold used as a store of value and means of payment is known from the epics of Homer, but it does not seem to have circulated much in the real world of archaic Greece. It rested in the treasuries of palaces and temples, developing into a reserve that was minted in times of emergency.[52] In Athens an emergency gold coinage was struck in 407/6 BC from the gold melted down from seven victory statues dedicated to Athena on the Acropolis, when other cities also minted gold coins temporarily.[53] In Rome the first gold coinage

---

[48] Howgego (1992).   [49] Figueira (1998): 92–109 for numismatic detail.   [50] Burnett (1989).

[51] Aristoph. *Frogs* 743–9; Athen. 669 D; Thuc. 2.13.5; Kurke (1999): 307 f. for further examples.

[52] Howgego (1995): 9; Seaford (2004): 30–2 for a comparison of gold and silver in Homer.

[53] Aristoph. *Frogs* 720–33 with scholia. See also Thompson (1970); Kraay (1976): 69 f.; Howgego (1995): 111 f.; and Kurke (1999): 306 f., for the discomfort this is supposed to have caused among the Athenians.

(*c.* 220–215 BC) is likely to have been related to the emergency situation of the Second Punic War.[54]

Despite their origin in emergency situations, gold coinages had massive effects on the amount of money in circulation. When Philip II seized the Thracian gold mines of Krenides (later Philippi) in the mid-fourth century BC, this is likely to have had both economic and ideological motivations and effects. The coinage he struck from the alleged 1,000 talents of gold derived from the mines annually carried a head of Apollo, marking Philip's positive relationship with Delphi and aspiration of becoming leader of all Greece.[55] But apart from its symbolic impact, the Macedonian gold coinage increased the stock of money and made available a means for paying and transporting large sums. Alexander the Great further increased Macedonian gold coinage, minting it as far east as Babylon and Susa. This was the money with which officers were paid and with which donations were lavished on subjects, a practice which continued well into the Roman period.[56] A passage of Josephus shows that the stipends to the soldiers besieging Jerusalem in the first century AD were paid in aurei and denarii (Jos. *BJ* 5.9.1–2). Suetonius mentions an increase in army pay in the form of three aurei under the emperor Domitian (Suet. *Dom.* 7.3).[57] The aggregate value of gold in comparison to that of silver coinage must have been highly variable over time and place, but could form a considerable proportion of the combined total. In first-century AD Pompeii, the proportion of gold within the total number of coins in circulation was enormous. Analyses of eighty-four coin groups buried at Pompeii in AD 79 revealed that two thirds of the total value of coins found was struck in gold.[58] Duncan-Jones has estimated that, from an estimated total supply of coinage of *c.* 21,000 million sesterces in the mid-second century AD, almost 60 per cent were minted in gold, some 30 per cent in silver and less than 10 per cent in bronze.[59] In the Hellenistic period, however, gold was struck only intermittently. By the end of the fourth century BC the successors of Alexander the Great ceased minting gold. It continued to play a role in Egypt where the gold mines of Nubia supplied the Ptolemies with the raw

---

[54] Howgego (1995): 112; also for the context of this coinage. [55] Diod. 16.8.6.
[56] The Raphia Decree (Thissen, *Studien zum Raphia Dekret*, Greek Text A, 1–20) mentions a donation of 300,000 chrusoi as a donation to the army after the battle of Raphia in 217 BC; but the reference to gold coinage in this context is likely to have been just conventional; von Reden (2007): 76; cf. note 59 below.
[57] Lo Cascio (2008): 170.
[58] Howgego (1995): 10 f.; Duncan-Jones (2003); but see Andreau (2008) for a possible bias of this evidence.
[59] Duncan-Jones (1994): 168–72; Jongman (2003) for a discussion of these figures.

material for additional as well as prestigious money. Royal munificence in Egypt was expected to be paid in chrusoi (gold coins).[60]

At the time when gold coinages brought additional coined money into the Mediterranean cities and empires, the production of bronze coinage also became popular. Whether the two developments were both related to an increase in the demand for coinage is debatable. Both copper and bronze (an alloy of copper and tin) had been widely available in the Greco-Roman world, where they were used for utilitarian and artistic purposes from the third millennium BC onwards.[61] The principal places of copper production were Chalkis and Cyprus, which both derived their names from these resources, Anatolia in Asia Minor, Etruria, Bruttium and Elba in Italy, as well as Spain. Tin was imported from Eastern Iran and Anatolia, and later Britain and Spain. In face of the abundance of copper, it is surprising that silver rather than bronze became the preferred monetary medium in Greece. In earlier research the preference for silver was regarded as an indication of the priority of high-value payments over small-scale exchanges in the early monetary economies of ancient Greece.[62] But the fact that tiny specimens of silver coins have now been detected renders this explanation implausible.[63] When bronze coinage began to become acceptable money, first in some Sicilian cities in the mid-fifth century BC and a little later on the Greek mainland, it did so as a token coinage, representing a face value above its metal content. In the Cretan city of Gortyn it is assumed that bronze coinage in the fourth century BC was literally forced upon its citizens by law (*IC* IV 162). Yet while the contribution of bronze coinage to the general stock of money was low, its contribution to the development of local cash economies was considerable.

It is worth asking why states began to mint base-metal coinages when they had been reluctant to do so previously. Answers may be sought in a greater demand for coinage in the market and for a more convenient means of payment in small-scale exchanges. Fractional silver coins were tiny pieces, the value of which was difficult to tell apart. A greater need of states to make small payments can also be assumed, as the development of new infrastructures and urban building increased the amount of public wage labour from at least the mid-fourth century BC onwards.[64] There was also a greater number of mints and greater mint activity as a result of Macedonian military expansion, which not only produced more coins but increased the degree of monetization in the Hellenized parts of the Eastern

---

[60] Cuvigny (2003).   [61] Osborne (1996): 113 f; Horden and Purcell (2000): 345 f.
[62] Kraay (1964).   [63] Kim (2001b); but see still Scheidel (2008).   [64] Von Reden (2007b).

Mediterranean. All this combines to form the assumption that there was a greater demand for coins both in the cities and countryside, and in the army.[65] But it is too simple to construe the adoption of bronze coinages just in terms of a greater demand for coined money. Token coinages required considerably more political regulation and trust in the issuing authority than any precious-metal currencies. Governments had to put considerable effort into making such coinages acceptable so that they would circulate. This is encapsulated in the story of the Athenian general Timotheos enforcing a bronze coinage on his soldiers stationed at Olynthos in 364 BC. The soldiers accepted the coinage only after Timotheos had made large concessions to the merchants from whom the soldiers bought their supplies. He promised the merchants that he would exchange for this money all the crop that was available in the region as well as the booty that reached them; and that he would compensate them with silver for any bronze coinage that was still left in their hands thereafter (Arist. *Oik.* II.2.23).

The history of monetization in Hellenistic Egypt, moreover, provides a case for both the role of bronze coinage and the large amount of regulation and control such a coinage required. At the beginning of the third century, Ptolemy II introduced a large regular bronze coinage comprising not only small fractional denominations such as obols and half-obols, but coins up to one drachma. Egypt had no silver resources, and the amount of silver available does not seem to have satisfied the demand for money which was required by the degree of monetization which Ptolemy II envisioned (see below). As with any other token currency, the nominal equivalence of bronze to silver coins was regulated by law, and an agio (fee) of about 10 per cent was charged on the exchange of bronze for silver. The coinage circulated because it was accepted for local taxes and state purchases. Local administrations, moreover, paid for produce and public wages in bronze.[66] In combination with the Ptolemaic royal banks, which had the exclusive right to exchange currency and control the value relationship of silver and bronze, the system worked well for about eighty years. By the time of Ptolemy III (243–224 BC) silver became so scarce within Egypt that bronze seems to have become the only coinage used in the Nile valley by the late 230s. Towards the end of the century, the monetary system of the third century collapsed. For a number of reasons, such as internal political trouble, dynastic discord, a decline of economic and military power within the Mediterranean, and the loss of major provinces, the nature of Ptolemaic power within Egypt changed. It seems, although we cannot be certain, that

---

[65] Hollander (2008).   [66] For details, von Reden (2007a): 58–70.

the central Ptolemaic government lost the degree of authority which had been necessary to maintain the monetary system of the third century. A monetary crisis ensued which resulted in the revaluation of the bronze coins at their proper metallic value. This was no more than about one sixtieth of their former fiduciary value in the silver standard.[67] Henceforth the bronze coinage became an independent currency in which most goods, services and taxes were paid. Although nominally wages and prices increased to exorbitant levels, there was no real price increase (see below, chapter 7). However, when bronze coins were reckoned against silver staters, they had much lesser value and seem to have been tendered at the market value of their metal content.[68]

Base-metal coinages, when having a fiduciary value only, required a degree of state regulation not comparable to that of the precious-metal coinages typical of the classical and archaic Greek cities. By the time the Romans adopted coinage, the process seems to have been reversed. Using at first heavy bronze bars, the value of which was equal to the value of their metal, the Romans raised the face value of bronze coins when the demand for coinage increased. In the following chapter we shall look in more detail at individual cases of monetization, the conditions of its spread, and the relationship between monetization and coinage which this process involved.

---

[67] The nature of the monetary changes is difficult to understand, but price levels seem to have jumped up quite consistently by a factor of sixty at the end of the reign of Ptolemy IV. In the second century BC they climbed further by factors of two and four; Reekmans (1948) and Maresch (1996) for discussions of the evidence. Cadell and Le Rider (1997) for grain prices only.

[68] Von Reden (2007a): 70–8; Maresch (1996); and below, chapter 6.

CHAPTER 2

Monetization: cases

ATHENS AND OTHER GREEK *POLEIS*

Writing in fourth-century Athens, Aristotle had two explanations for the origins of coined money (*nomisma*). In the *Politics* he points to the intrinsic value of metals, and their use as coins in trade among people with no social or political connection (*Pol.* 1257a 31–8, quoted on p. 1). In the *Ethics*, by contrast, he suggests that coinage had its origin and principal function within communities. By convention (*nomos*), citizens had given value to legal tokens (*nomismata*) in order to achieve justice in exchange. These tokens compensated those who provided services to another citizen at precisely the value of the benefit produced for the exchanging partner. They thus provided the possibility of compensating each citizen for the different use value of their products:[1]

> The number of shoes exchanged for a house (or for a given amount of food) must correspond to the ratio of builder to shoemaker. For if this does not happen, there is no exchange and no community . . . All goods must therefore be measured by some one measure, as we said before. Now this unit is in truth 'need' *(chreia)* which holds all things together . . . But coinage has become by convention some kind of representative of utility; and this is why it has the name *nomisma* – because it exists not by nature but by law and convention (*nomos*) (*EN* 1132b 20–34).

Aristotle's assumptions are unlikely to represent faithfully the reasons why coinage was adopted in archaic Greece, but they capture the combination of functions that it performed in the fourth century BC. Coins served both internal and external purposes, they were a convention and a convenience, and they had token as well as intrinsic value. The real reasons that made civic governments mint their first coins in the sixth century BC are not known and may in fact have varied; but it is more important to ask why they were so successful in the particular context of the Greek *polis*.

---

[1] Will (1954) (1955); Meikle (1995); and Amemiya (2007): 150–3 for both these much discussed passages.

Coins and money are acceptable because of their exchangeability which in turn depends on some collective desirability. The best evidence for the prestige of precious-metal money (though not necessarily coinage) happens to come from places other than Athens. Money as a measure of value is strikingly attached to a payment in kind represented in a famous inscription in honour of a Cretan scribe called Spensithios at around 500 BC.[2] Spensithios had received extensive honours and a 'wage' (*misthos*) for his expert skills of writing down and remembering the affairs of the city. The reward was in kind – public maintenance (*trophe*), exemption from taxes (*ateleia*), fifty jars of wine, and some other goods. He found it important, however, to total the value of the receipt in monetary terms: the wine and the goods together were worth twenty drachmas. This seems to have been an important aspect of the reward despite the fact that the text had no accountancy purpose. It has survived on a metal belt (*mitra*) worn underneath a garment close to the body. It was a personal gratification rather than a public document.

The totalling of *chremata* in monetary terms also occurs in another context of symbolic significance. An early sixth-century BC inscription from the Samian Heraion records the votive offering of two Perinthian citizens probably of Samian origin (Perinthos was a Samian foundation), dedicating a tithe to the goddess of their mother city:

Meniskos, son of Xenodokos, Demis, son of Pythokles, and the Perinthians dedicate to Hera as a tithe a golden Gorgon, a silver Siren, a silver cup, a bronze lamp stand – together amounting to 212 Samian staters – and this stone. (*SEG* XII 391)

Samos was one of the earliest minters of electrum coinage, but had no or little coinage at the time when this dedication was made. The island was famed for its extraordinary power and wealth which are presumed to have derived from the great number of contacts it entertained with the Greek and non-Greek world and which were displayed by means of prestigious dedications in the temple of Hera from the eighth century BC onwards.[3] The Heraion itself was magnificent, and after its reconstruction in the sixth century BC was regarded as the largest temple ever seen in Greece (Hdt. 3.60). The dedication of the Perinthians that was of considerable value by any standards of the ancient world was part of a conspicuous display in a competitive world of 'peer interaction'. Just as in the case of the Spensithios reward, monetary units served as a standard of absolute value and at the

---

[2] Jeffery and Marpurgo Davies in *Kadmos* (1970), fig. 1, side A. Thomas (1992): 69–71.
[3] Osborne (1996): 93 and 272 ff.

same time related the intrinsic value of objects to the accounting structure of particular communities.

The earliest evidence for reckoning in monetary units at Athens as enmeshed within the Solonic tradition. Alongside the use of bullion in money in several of the laws ascribed to Solon (see above), it appears in the accounting structure of sacrificial offerings, where one *medimnos* of grain was deemed equivalent to one sheep, or one drachma (Plut. *Sol.* 23.3). Isthmian victors were rewarded with 100 Athenian drachmas and Olympic ones with 500. Someone who delivered a wolf for killing was rewarded with 5 drachmas, a young wolf was worth one drachma (*ibid.* 23.4). It is by no means certain whether these sums were paid out in the form of silver or in any other form, as was the case with Spensithios, but both passages show the preferred use of monetary units in constituting relationships of value as well as measuring prestigious payments in bullion or kind.

On a grander scale, monetary wealth was demonstrated at Delphi in a competitive display of piety and power. Most impressively, this was achieved during the rebuilding of the Apollo temple which had burnt down by accident in the sixth century BC. Herodotus tells the story in connection with the exotic generosity of the Egyptian king Amasis, who contributed 1,000 talents of bronze in contrast to the meagre 200 minai (of silver?) contributed by the Greeks of Naukratis (Hdt. 2.180). The largest share, however, was shouldered by the Athenian family of the Alcmeonidai, then in exile, who took over the contract of rebuilding, overspent massively, and thereby facilitated their return to Athens. That monetary display was involved in the execution of the project is clear from the fact that the Alcmeonidai were later accused of having bribed the Delphic oracle while overseeing the construction work, a suspicion that was ready to hand when money had been involved (Hdt. 5.62.3). Spending large monetary sums for the benefit of communities and temples was a powerful means of gaining and enhancing influence and power. An astonishing explicitness about the monetary sums expended, where modern sentiment requires reticence, shows the high status attached to money.

The prestige associated with monetary payments provides the normative background for the great acceptance of certified lumps of silver in a wide range of relationships. The ideological meaning and promotion of coinage in the representation and self-representation of *poleis* remained an important aspect of monetary culture throughout antiquity. The memory of Themistocles who had persuaded the Athenians to apply a windfall supply of Laureion silver to the construction of a fleet against Aegina, the transfer of the treasury of the Delian League to Athens, and the monetary power that derived from this resource, were important aspects of Athenian monetary identity in the classical period.[4] They were symbolically reinforced by the publication of the tribute quota lists on the Acropolis of Athens (see below), the display of tribute coinage at the City Dionysia, one of the major religious festivals at Athens, and the publication of the temple inventories that summarized and totalled their possessions in monetary units of metal weight.[5] By the middle of the fifth century BC, money symbolized the strength of Athens in contrast to Spartan weakness, and was a hallmark of democracy and sea power.

Turning from the prestige of money to its functions, we need to focus on the transactional structure of ancient *poleis*, and Athens in particular. Several aspects of the process to which the emergence of money must be related have been mentioned in the previous chapter: a greater degree of internal cohesion and civic interaction (including reward for political service), a greater focus on the collective citizen body with one religious and political centre (including ritual and games), increased inter-state relationships and overseas settlement (colonization). Under the surface of the development of ideological meanings of money there lay particular social and economic structures that promoted the use of bullion money and coinage in Greece.

Alongside the many political and religious occasions for monetary payments emerging in the archaic *polis*, and the growth of trade, there was an increase in the amount of regular (institutionalized) rental payments resulting from a new land-tenure regime in Athens. One change that has rarely been considered in the context of the Solonian reforms is the legal abolition of share-cropping arrangements in favour of independent peasant holdings and fixed-rent tenancies.[6] The precise status of the so-called *hektemoroi* (sixth-part tenants) who surface in the literary tradition of Solon's reforms is not fully understood, but it must be fairly certain that they were comparable to the semi-free share-croppers who continued to be attested in Thessaly, Crete, Magna Graecia, Sparta, Egypt, some parts of Herakleia Pontika, Asia Minor and the Near East well into the Hellenistic period.[7] In share-cropping contracts, rental claims are formulated as proportions of the actual harvest rather than as fixed sums specified before the rental period. Share-croppers, often representing collective ethnic groups, tended

---

[4] Kallet-Marx (1993) (2001); for the literary negotiation of this identity, see Kurke (1999).
[5] Harris (1995).
[6] For the significance of fixed-rent tenancies vis-à-vis share-cropping contracts, see Kehoe (1988); Morris (2001) and Osborne (1996): 221–5 for alternative interpretations.
[7] Rathbone (1989).

to be more closely tied to land and landlords than contractual tenants; because of their semi-free status, they may also have enjoyed a degree of patronage and social care. In practice, however, their economic situation was at risk because of their potential full enslavement, since unfulfilled rental obligations were compensated for by a loss of personal liberties rather than by payment of a penalty. In fixed-rent contracts, by contrast, the rent was negotiated at the beginning of the contractual period, and had to be paid (in cash or kind) regardless of the size of the actual yield. If the rent remained unpaid by the stipulated time, the landlord had no right of redress, but to a penalty equivalent to, or a multiple of, the rent.

If, as is commonly assumed, the abolition of debt-bondage was a major step towards the formation of a free citizen body at Athens, and if the liberated *hektemoroi* became the landless *thetes* in the Solonian citizen census, the reforms had important effects on contractual relationships in Athens as well as on the development of institutionalized monetary payments.[8] They initiated a shift from share-cropping to fixed-rent tenancy agreements and a new regime of rental obligations fixed in terms of specified sums of 'cash' or kind. The specification of such monetary sums also may have been linked to the establishment of the equivalences associated with Solon's legislation (see above). In turn, the reforms provided a stimulus for surplus production necessary to meet agrarian rental obligations (in the classical period regularly paid in cash rather than kind) and to pay for seasonal labour. Changes in the agrarian labour and land regime were not exclusive to Athens, which is deemed to have been a late rather than an exceptional case of the social and economic transformation that took place in the Aegean world during the archaic period.[9] Just as the transformation taking place in the first half of the sixth century BC provided a context for monetary exchange to expand within and between *poleis*, monetization (rather than coinage) was a condition for the development of a system of free independent small holdings that characterized Athenian society for several centuries. The first, rather small, issues of coinage appear in Athens during the reign of Peisistratos around 550 BC.

Athenian coinage increased massively at the end of the Persian wars (479 BC),[10] and once again at the height of the Athenian empire from the middle of the fifth century BC onwards.[11] Both these boosts of coin production affected the degree of monetization in Athens and beyond.

---

[8] Thus Plut. *Sol.* 13, 2; but Morris (2001) for an alternative view on the social background of the *thetes*.
[9] Morris (1987). [10] Rutter (1981). [11] Meadows (unpublished).

Athenian democracy, which was predicated not least on the monetary payments made by and to the citizens, was financed at first by the income of
imperial revenues and subsequently by the success of the Athenian monetary economy itself.[12] The money that was paid to the city by its allies and
wealthy citizens mobilized coinage and stimulated circulation throughout
the Aegean (see next chapter). By the time of the Peloponnesian War, not
only military stipends, public and private wages, rents and commodity
prices, but also social payments such as dowries and *eranos* loans (see glos-
sary) regularly appear as sums of cash. The lease and exploitation of the
Athenian quarries and mines were fully monetized, including the payment
of wages and transport. Magistrates, councillors, jurors, citizen soldiers,
rowers and labourers employed in the massive building projects of the fifth
century BC were all paid in coin. Athens did not tax its citizens directly, but
its substitute institutions, *eisphora* and liturgies, mobilized coinage within
the *polis* and prevented it from being hoarded or lost in export. Liturgies
were obligatory financial services of the 1,000 or so wealthiest citizens and
resident aliens who were required to undertake work for the state at their
own expense, such as equipping a warship for one year, training a chorus
for the festivals, or coaching a team for the athletic games. The financial
outlay for the relatively small liturgy of training a chorus was roughly 300
drachmas, equivalent to the annual income of a skilled worker. Equipping a
warship reached a scale of one talent (6,000 drachmas), probably a quarter
or third of the entire property of the one who was required to perform that
service. It has been argued that the need to generate cash for public service stimulated cash-cropping and surplus production on large estates and
might have served as a reason for wealthy land owners to generate a monetary profit on their estates.[13] It has also been argued that the attempt to
avoid these burdensome obligations made many potential liturgists invest
their money in credit so as to obfuscate the level of their real wealth.[14]
This, in turn, produced profit for the investors and had positive effects on
economic performance in Athens as a whole. It is debatable whether the
number of people who adopted such strategies was significant enough to
stimulate economic growth in real terms, or whether the texts from which
examples are known over-represent such cases, but it must be unquestioned

---

[12] Schaps (2004): 124–37 discusses the major aspects of the link between democracy and monetization
from the sixth century BC onwards; this included the monetary generosity of ambitious politicians
(e.g. the Alcmeonids and Cimon); public building initiatives (e.g. that of Pericles); and the many
instances of the 'recirculation of wealth . . . through the state by means of money' (137).

[13] Osborne (1991).   [14] Cohen (2003).

that the liturgical system not only swallowed large sums of cash, but also created incentives to direct money into other channels.[15]

Both literary and epigraphical sources create a picture of almost full monetization of the Athenian *polis* by the time of the mid-fifth century BC. Romantic pictures of rural money-less tranquillity, such as that intimated by Aristophanes in the *Acharnians* (33–9), need not concern us much. Payment to members of the council (on which most citizens living in the countryside served at least once in their lives), cash stipends to citizen armies and the fleet, the expectation of cash dowries (often financed by mortgage), as well as deme festivals which were also financed by liturgical service (Whitehead (1986a): 164) directed cash into the entire Athenian countryside, if only at times and in small amounts. But cash-cropping for urban and foreign markets, and the exploitation of quarries and mining districts, brought considerable amounts of money to the immediate hinterland of the city and deme centres.

Greater impediments to the free circulation of money were, as Finley argued, the only limited markets available for land and labour.[16] The widespread availability of slave labour limited the market for labour and held wages at the same level for over two centuries (see chapter 4). The importance of landed property for civic status, moreover, put some ideological limits on the commodification of land so that the largest store of wealth was not easily converted into cash. A thriving mortgage industry turned land into temporary cash; but in the absence of competitive interest rates and long-term tenancies generating a regular cash income for absentee landlords, cash circulation is likely to have been much slower, and monetary fortunes much smaller than in the Roman republic and empire.

MONETIZATION UNDER GREEK INFLUENCE: EGYPT

Until the Greco-Macedonian conquest in 332 BC Egypt had no regular coinage. Occasional coinages had been produced in Memphis in the late fifth century BC, arguably serving to pay Greek mercenaries; an Aramaic-speaking garrison at Elephantine in southern Egypt had used shekels and imitations of Athenian tetradrachms within its military district during the fifth century.[17] There was also a small issue of Athenian imitations under Artaxerxes III Ochus during the second period of Persian domination (359/8–338 BC). Interestingly, the issue bears the legend '[coin of] Artaxerxes Pharaoh' in demotic Egyptian script and therefore is unlikely to have been

---

[15] Thus Morris (1994).   [16] Finley (1981b); (1986).   [17] Van Alfen (2002).

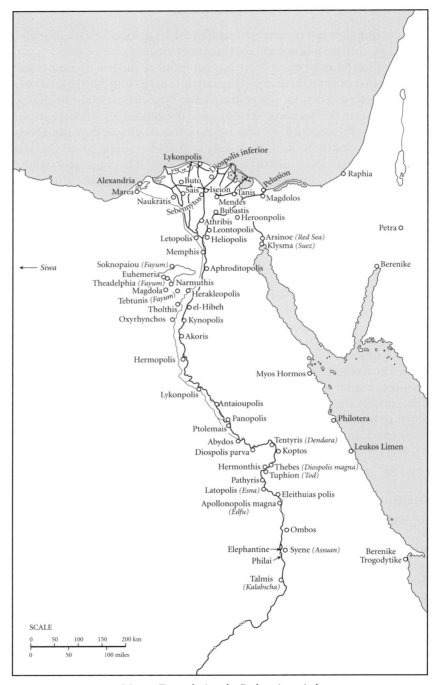

SCALE

0   50   100   150   200 km

0   50   100 miles

Map 3: Egypt during the Ptolemaic period

used for transactions with Greeks in the first instance. Finally, foreign coins had reached the country in some quantity from the late sixth century onwards. They are attested in Pharaonic matrimonial contacts as payment of staters, and in hoards as *Hacksilber* (cut pieces of precious metal), probably circulating at its bullion weight.[18] Pharaonic Egypt, however, is a particularly good example of a society that had money without using coinage. Baskets of grain, vessels of oil, weighed bronze and foreign silver in total fulfilled most monetary functions. Over the long period of ancient Egyptian history some were used as measures of value, others as stores of wealth, and all of them were in particular contexts accepted as a means of payment. But none of these was used as all-purpose money throughout Egypt. Crucial conditions for the circulation of a general currency, such as universally recognized weights and measures or a central administrative apparatus of regulation and control, were absent. The Pharaonic 'state' was a conglomeration of communities and regions loosely held together by bureaucracy and ritual. Large temples, such as the temple of Ptah in Memphis or that of Amun in Thebes, had certified the value of bullion, but these certifications had been valid only as far as the influence of the temples reached.[19]

Coinage was introduced into Egypt by Alexander in 332 BC, but a regular mint was not opened before 326/5 BC. In the meantime, the satrapy had been dependent on the Macedonian and other imperial mints which remained the major centres for the supply of coinage when production of coinage in Egyptian mints began. By 318 BC coin use in Egypt was still dominated by the posthumous Alexander coinage produced in Macedonian mints in Amphipolis and elsewhere. Of the total number of silver tetradrachms known from a large hoard of Demanhur in the Nile Delta, less than 5 per cent were minted in Egypt between 326/5 and 318 BC.[20]

The circulation of Macedonian coins in Egypt was at first very limited. Reliable details of the famously ruthless administration of Egypt under the governor Kleomenes of Naucratis between 331 and 323 BC are unknown, but one of his major financial projects must have been the construction of Alexandria masterminded by the Rhodian architect Deinocrates and supervised by some military engineers. In addition, temple inscriptions refer to building and restoration projects in the name of Alexander the Great during this period.[21] An anecdote in the pseudo-Aristotelian *Oikonomika*

[18] Lüddeckens (1960); Pestman (1961) esp. 103–5, for examples.
[19] Van Alfen (2002); von Reden (2007a): 31–3; Reinach in *P. Ryl.* III, S. 76; Sethe-Partsch *P. Bürgsch.*, S. 236; Pestman (1961): 105 for the certification of silver by temples.
[20] Duyrat (2005).   [21] Huss (1994).

suggests that under Kleomenes local administrators of the *nomoi* (districts) were required to pay taxes in money which was procured from the sale of grain for export (II. 2.33). The same text also mentions several ruses by which Kleomenes extracted money from priests, wealthy residents and local administrators engaged in commerce. If the stories are true, money was used at the top of the local administration and in markets by people employing economies of scale. There is no indication that any taxes were collected in cash from the ordinary population, or that large parts of the population were involved in the commercial transactions generating this cash. During the first ten years of Greco-Macedonian rule, coinage circulated among the overlapping groups of temple elites, Alexandrian wealthy estate holders and governors of districts. Its circulation was stimulated by the monetary taxation of these groups and the commercial affairs they undertook to raise that money.[22]

The introduction of coinage into Egypt served political and fiscal purposes. From a political point of view it created a focus on Alexandria, the new capital from the late 320s onwards. It was a strong mark of foreign domination. From the time of the take-over of the Egyptian satrapy by Ptolemy, son of Lagos, one of Alexander's generals, in 323 BC, the imperial Alexander coinage that had circulated in all conquered areas was gradually transformed into an Egyptian currency minted in Alexandria. First, the legend on the coins changed to that of '[coin] of Ptolemy', and in 306/5 BC, when Ptolemy proclaimed himself king of Egypt, he put his own portrait on the coinage. Because of the limited silver resources in Egypt and Ptolemy's increasing demand for coined money, the weight of the stater was reduced from the Athenian standard of 17.2 g, used for the posthumous Alexander coinages in the other successor empires, to a mere 14.3 g, close to the Rhodian standard. In order not to lose the heavy coins in private hoards, all incoming full-weight coins had to be exchanged against light-weight Egyptian ones at an exchange of one to one. This gained the mint 3 g of silver per silver stater, 1.5 g of gold per gold stater, and the fee that was charged for re-minting. The so-called Ptolemaic 'closed currency system' was the first of its kind in antiquity. It could be implemented internally because Egypt was a comparatively centralized state and it was accepted externally because Egypt was the main supplier of grain which neither traders nor cities could boycott.

The internal economy of the vast temple estates to which most Egyptian agrarian property was attached remained largely unchanged during

---

[22] Manning (2007); von Reden (2007a).

Ptolemaic occupation.[23] Major transformation occurred alongside the Ptolemaic system of taxation which was introduced under Ptolemy I in the first forty years of Ptolemaic rule (323–279 BC). Taxes and rents on crown and temple land planted with cereals continued to be levied in terms of grain. Fodder crops, however, fruit gardening, fishing, animal husbandry, trades and manufactures, any sale transaction (esp. of land), and land and river transport, were taxed in cash. The tax on wine and oil, the production of which was monopolized by the state, occupied some middle ground. It was collected in kind but then sold by licensed retailers so as to reach the treasury in the form of cash. The Greek tax-farming system, moreover, in which contractors and their sureties guaranteed the annual income of one monetary tax to the state, allowed some flexibility in the collection process. The system guaranteed a fixed tax-income to the state, but also ensured that it was in monetary form. It is likely that not all tax-payers were able to pay their taxes in cash, and some payments were converted only by the tax-farmers, possibly at their own profit.[24]

Thorough monetization of the Egyptian countryside began under Ptolemy II (279–243 BC) when a general monetary poll tax was introduced in combination with a new bronze coinage. Under the first Ptolemy, only small fractions had been minted in bronze, as was typical in other parts of the Greek world. From 265 BC onwards, not only were large denominations up to one drachma minted, but the pieces themselves had an unprecedented size (up to 9 cm in diameter). It is most likely that the innovation was directly related to the introduction of the salt tax, which was in fact a poll-tax levied on each household according to its number of men, women, slaves and animals. It was only a small sum, but was thoroughly collected on the basis of census declarations which required a massive administrative effort.[25] Most local commercial taxes henceforth were paid in bronze coinage. Many were claimed in silver currency, but in practice paid in bronze with an agio charged on top. The Ptolemaic bronze coinage became the main currency in the countryside, while Greek settlers, members of the army and administration, and the citizens of Alexandria handled both coinages side by side.

For reasons that are not entirely clear, silver coinage became increasingly scarce in Egypt in the second half of the third century.[26] From about

---

[23] Manning (2003); (2007).   [24] Turner (1984); Bingen (1978a).

[25] Clarysse and Thompson (1995); (2006), for the vast papyrological documentation concerned with that process.

[26] Changing conditions of Egyptian trade, on which the influx of silver depended, are regarded as the major cause of the decline of silver resources in the middle of the third century BC and its

230 BC onwards hardly any silver is attested in the Egyptian countryside, and even payments to foreign countries – most notably the subsidies to Rhodes after its devastating earthquake in the early 220s – were paid in bronze coinage.[27]

It seems that before the decline of silver currency in Egypt, the income of bronze money was applied above all to local expenditure, especially the rural irrigation system which required regular maintenance.[28] Large 'gangs' of labourers were recruited in a system of corvée which in Pharaonic times had been rewarded with food rations (grain and beer), but under the Ptolemies paid in cash and kind. The introduction of the salt tax, the monetization of corvée labour, the creation of a large bronze currency, and the transformation of the Pharaonic economy into something more familiar to the Greeks were probably related processes. Beer, for example, which used to be a major component of food rations in pre-Ptolemaic Egypt, was no longer requisitioned by the administration directly as a tax in kind, but sold in the market and taxed in cash. A similar monetary cycle was created in the case of oil, linen and some foods, the production and retail of which used to be under the control of temples, but was now monopolized by the government selling licences to the retailers of these goods by auction.

How far was Egypt monetized in the first generations of Ptolemaic rule? As far as monetization in terms of coinage is concerned, it remained limited compared to the vast economy of cereal agriculture that dominated Egypt. But the economy in coin came to interact with the economy in grain. Most payments could be made in grain, while grain stores were run by accounting structures similar to those of banks.[29] There was a fixed conversion rate between units of coin and grain independent of the fluctuating market price of the latter. Grain accounts were kept in similar form to coin accounts, and there was a certain liberty about the form in which payments were accepted and made. There is the general impression, although it cannot be proved, that liquidity in terms of coinage was low even among the wealthiest in Ptolemaic society. Individuals and the administration used cash efficiently, setting off one kind of obligation against others, converting cash obligations into kind and using the cash of third parties to make payments.

---

reappearance under Ptolemy VIII (183–116) and Ptolemy IX (116–107 BC); Maresch (1996): 7–11. Wallace (1938) emphasized the profligacy of Ptolemy III Euergetes as a major reason for the decline of silver resources in Egypt.

[27] Noeske (2000).   [28] Von Reden (2007a): 60–70.

[29] The classic analysis is Preisigke (1910); but see also Bogaert (1988); and von Reden (2007a): 79 ff.

The Greek monetary economy based on coinage was gradually introduced into Egypt. It was successful because of the complex monetary policy of the first three Ptolemies which extended from their own ideological and practical propagation of coin use, a careful combination of traditional and new systems of payment and taxation, to the creation of small cycles of monetary taxation and payment in the countryside. It was part of a more fundamental transformation of economic, administrative and legal structures that were introduced at first in areas of Greek settlement in the Fayum and adjacent areas, as well as in the Greek cities of Alexandria and Ptolemais in Upper Egypt which both, unfortunately, are poorly represented in the papyri. Combined with the deliberate transformation of the economy was a cultural policy that promoted the Greek language, encouraged the participation of native personnel in the Greek administration, and sought some co-operation with the native temple elites whose own power was predicated on the acceptance of the Pharaoh. The success of the monetary system was closely linked to the success of the political regime and declined as soon as the authority of that regime declined.

ROME

Early Roman monetary history is not documented well, which creates an unfortunate bias of extant sources towards the adoption of physical objects such as coins and metal bars.[30] Yet both the adoption of coinage almost 200 years after communal political action is firmly attested, and the fact that the first coin issues were small by comparison to Rome's financial needs, suggest that the use of coinage and monetization were distinct processes in Rome. Our extant literary sources, however, elide the distinction. As Michael Crawford observes:

Relentlessly modernising, they persistently discuss the early Republic in terms of the monetary conventions of their own times, including, of course, the use of coinage, and in terms of the economic thought, if that is not too grand a term, of the late Republic and early Empire, heavily influenced by Greek experience.[31]

In contrast to the Greek cities, where the development of coinage went hand in hand with the development of civic institutions, in Rome of the

---

[30] Our knowledge of early Roman monetary development depends almost entirely on the work by Crawford (1985) and Burnett (1982) (1987) (1989). Other accounts, including my own, are based on their research; succinct summaries can also be found in Cornell (1995): 394–7; and Hollander (2007): ch. 4.

[31] Crawford (1985): 17.

early republic coinage was introduced at first to regulate relationships with other states. There is no archaeological evidence of Roman coinage before *c*. 320 BC when the first small series of bronze coins were minted for use in Campania, notably with a legend in Greek. Because of their production in Neapolis (modern Naples) and their local circulation pattern, the first Roman coins have rightly been regarded as belonging to the history of Neapolis rather than Rome itself. Silver coins had been used in the Greek cities of Sicily and Southern Italy from the sixth century BC onwards, while 200 years later non-Greek towns in Campania, Apulia and Lucania began to mint their own coins on the Greek model. In Rome itself, regular issues of coins, cast rather than struck, do not appear before the 270s BC or even later. Despite their production in Rome, even those do not seem to have been used predominantly in the city itself, but for payments in the surrounding areas. The most interesting aspect of Rome's early numismatic history is that it reflects the multiplicity of Roman relationships with other places. Each relationship was conducted on the basis of a different monetary medium which only eventually merged into one system by the mid-third century BC.

Shifting our focus from coinage to money, we find that the use of monetary units of bullion weight appears first in the laws of the Twelve Tables (mid-fifth century BC). Minor injuries, in contrast to major offences, were punished with payment of monetary sums reckoned in asses of bronze (table 8.3–4). One literary tradition attributes the first money – mistakenly the first coins – to the mythical king Servius Tullius (Timaeus *FGrHist.* 566.61 = Pliny *NH* 33.43). This has been taken to mean that it was this king who introduced monetary units in order to facilitate the population census which is also attributed to his reign.[32] It is, however, unnecessary to link monetary history to a shadowy mythical inventor. As in the case of archaic Greece, the transformation of a census rating based on agrarian produce, and the emerging system of public litigation involving the payment of penalties, provide sufficient explanation for the establishment of a standard of value and means of payment in terms of bullion weight in fifth-century Rome.

An ancient hypothesis has it that the word *pecunia* was derived from the word *pecus* (cattle). According to this theory, fines in early times were specified in quantities of cattle and sheep (Plin. *HN* 33.42). Later laws laid down equivalences between numbers of animals and quantities of bronze (DH 10.50.2; Gellius 11.1.2; Festus 268–70). This approach has

---

[32] Cornell (1995): 288.

been rejected as unhistorical, not least because the etymological argument is unfounded.[33] It should be noted, however, that scholars dealing with the Solonic legislation give more credence to the assumption that rates of conversion were established in early monetary history to make agrarian and metallic wealth equivalent (see above). In Rome, this may have been linked, if not to the conversion of cattle value, to the conversion of agrarian produce derived from public land into monetary census qualifications on which army recruitment was based from the late fifth century BC onwards.[34] The so-called Servian census is recorded only on the basis of a calculation in terms of asses of bronze (Liv. 1.43; DH 4.16). One might speculate that, as peasants were recruited into the legions, the property qualification for the lowest class was fixed at the level of the value of the two-*iugera* (0.5 ha) allotment which settlers in the Latin colonies received.

It is almost certain that the gradual incorporation of Italian land into Roman territory led to an increase in tribute payments to the Roman government. Livy connects the first imposition of tribute on public land with the introduction of army pay during the siege of Veii at the end of the fifth century BC (Liv. 4.59.11–60; cf. Diod. 14.16.3). It is possible that tribute from the Latin and Etruscan peoples was paid in the form of un-coined bronze, which in turn provided the means for weighing out the legionaries' pay. But once again no contemporary evidence is available, and it is possible that a more complex interdependence of tribute, army pay and other transactions based on convertible rates of metal weight and goods promoted monetization in Rome before the first pre-weighed pieces of metal were issued under state authority.

Scanty vestiges of early monetization within the city of Rome are complemented by abundant evidence for monetary developments outside Rome. Etruscan bronze ingots bearing simple designs in the form of a twig (therefore called *ramo secco* (dry branch) bars by modern scholars) occur in hoards throughout northern and central Italy as well as in Latium.[35] The earliest specimens from a hoard in southern Sicily can be dated to the sixth century BC, but *ramo secco* bars still occur in hoards deposited in the third century BC. They were produced in Etruria but seem to have been a form of movable wealth throughout the Etruscan sphere of influence. They may have been used for payment in a variety of transactions within and between communities, but it is not certain that they had any connection with the Roman monetary system. Above all, they do not seem to have

---

[33] Cornell (1995): 288; and Crawford (1985): 19 f. [34] Crawford (1985): 24.
[35] Crawford (1985): 5.

been produced to any consistent weight standard.[36] The Romans, however, adapted to this tradition by producing a signed bronze bar (*aes signatum*) and fixed it at a weight of five asses each. The first extant pieces date to the late fourth or early third centuries BC and are roughly contemporary with the first bronze coins produced in Neapolis. Most interestingly, they were produced not from the Etruscan type of unrefined copper, but from the leaded tin bronze that was used for Greek bronze coins of that time. Round bronze discs produced from the same metal as *aes signatum* and also based on the as standard seem to have been fractions for use in smaller trans-actions from the first quarter of the third century BC onwards. They are extant in six denominations, from the as down to its twelfth (one uncia). These so-called *aes grave* (heavy bronze) disks were cast rather than struck and seem to have been an amalgamation of the Etruscan tradition of heavy bronze bars and the Greek tradition of round coins.

Rome produced struck silver and bronze coins based on the Greek drachma system from the mid third-century BC onwards. While silver coins were struck centrally in Rome, bronze coins were minted in several places to different weight standards. Mints of bronze coinage extended from as far north as the Latin colony of Cosa near Rome to Palermo in Sicily.[37] Moreover, the two types of coinage did not circulate in the same areas. Bronze coins are found mainly in the areas where *aes grave* and *aes signatum* continued to circulate, while silver use was concentrated in Campania. There is no question that all coins were struck by Roman authorities, yet they seem to have been designed for different payments. Only a generation or so later were the various elements of the disconnected monetary system integrated. The production of *aes signatum* ceased, while the silver coins took over the function of large denominations by being equivalent to three *aes grave* asses. This incidentally, represented a real rather than fiduciary relationship of value between silver and bronze coins of 1:120.

The Roman production of several monetary media in third-century BC Italy shows in singular fashion that the introduction of coinage in Rome was not based on a single initiative. It differs significantly from the cases of archaic Greece and Hellenistic Egypt where more central planning seems to have driven the introduction of coinage. Greek *poleis* produced coinages from the start in a range of related denominations, while the Ptolemies introduced the Greek monetary system in the form of a tri-metallic coinage.

---

[36] Burnett (1987): 4 ff., also for the chronology of the following.   [37] Burnett (1987): 5.

We do not have to look very far for explanations of the different development in Rome. Both Roman *aes signatum* and coins were contemporary with Roman expansion into Italy. They reflect an increasing engagement in several regions with established monetary traditions. The construction of the Via Valeria towards the central Apennines and the extension of the Via Appia into Campania happened during the same period and represent both contacts and construction costs at a considerable scale. The minting of the first Campanian coinage with the Greek legend *Romaion* ('[coin] of the Romans') may be linked with the Roman treaties with Neapolis in 326 BC or, if a later chronology is adopted, with the Roman conquest of Campania in 304 BC.[38] The first production of *aes signatum* may be connected with Rome's campaigns in Etruria, Umbria and Central Italy. But precisely what were the purposes of the first Roman *aes* bars and Greek-style coinages remains a matter of speculation. No direct connection between coin finds and army movements can be established archaeologically, and thus there is no reason to follow later Roman historians who, observing contemporary practice, believed that coinage was invented to pay Roman soldiers.[39] The most important conclusion to be drawn from the numismatic evidence is that coinage was a subordinate phenomenon of monetization; for by any reasonable calculation the amount of money earned and spent by the Roman state in the first half of the third century BC was much greater than the small amount of coinage and *aes* bars reckoned to have been produced could have covered.[40]

An incontrovertible link between coin production and army payment emerged by the end of the Second Punic War (218–214 BC) when Rome rapidly increased its coin production. Already during the time of the First Punic War the nominal value of bronze coins had been increased so as to become a token money like in Greek coin systems. Arguably the Romans learnt to use their metal reserves more efficiently and monetary usage allowed the transition from commodity to token money. The periodical minting of gold coins in between the first two Punic wars also points to an increasing need for coined money.[41] In 214 BC a monetary reform created a totally new monetary system in which the dominant coin was the silver denarius, replacing the silver didrachm which in smaller quantities had been minted parallel to the South Italian coin systems. The fractions of the denarius continued to be minted in bronze, with 10 asses to the denarius.

---

[38] For the former, Cornell (1995): 394; for a later chronology, Burnett (1987).
[39] Burnett (1987), against Crawford (1985): 22 f.   [40] Burnett (1987): 12 f.   [41] Harl (1996): 30.

Further fractions went down to one uncia, valued at one twelfth of an as, or 120th of the denarius. Incidentally, Roman fractional coinage suggests that price levels in republican Rome were much lower than in the contemporary Greek world where the smallest denomination (one chalkous, if minted at all) represented one 48th of a silver drachm, or 2.5 times the value of an uncia.

Despite thorough monetization of army and tribute payments, it would be wrong to conclude that most payments in Italy were made in the form of coined money by the end of the third century BC. Rome's political and economic success took off at the beginning of the second century, clearly noticeable in the combined political, economic and monetary crises (or, at least, transformations) taking place within the kingdoms of the Eastern Mediterranean. From the mid-second to the mid-first century BC there was yet another significant increase in the production of Roman coinage, and the value of the as was once again decreased (now being equivalent to one sixteenth of a denarius).[42] The capacity of the Roman economy to absorb larger volumes of coinage was apparently far from being exhausted. Yet it is problematic to infer from greater volumes of coinage produced a greater degree of monetization, even if we equate monetization with coin use.[43] Already by the second century Roman coins had virtually replaced and extinguished local coins in Italy and Sicily, and similar developments took place in Spain and southern Gaul at the end of the first century BC (see next chapter). Imperial expansion also led to new urban foundations, development of arable land, a growing number of Roman citizens and people with Latin rights, access to new mines and metal resources, the growth of the city of Rome itself, and probably a population increase in absolute terms.[44] Thus quite simply Roman people used more money. Despite it being likely that there was a real increase in the degree of monetization during the late republic, we need to look once again for institutional change rather than just noting that more money was around.[45]

The army was a major stimulus for monetization.[46] According to an argument advanced by David Hollander, soldiers not only were paid in coin but, returning home, introduced monetary practices. Soldiers mostly came from, and returned to, rural areas where home production and local social exchange ruled the economy. On campaign, however, they not only

---

[42] Crawford (1969); Hopkins (1980) extrapolated from these figures volumes of coinage in circulation which has turned out to be highly controversial: Howgego (1992) for a summary of the debate; Hitchner (2005) for a cautious resuscitation of Hopkins' argument.
[43] See Howgego (1992) for the number of factors to be considered.   [44] Scheidel (2007): 45–9.
[45] Howgego (1992) and Hollander (2007).   [46] Hollander (2005).

had been paid in coin but had become accustomed to money and markets for consumption as well as the exchange of booty which tended to be sold quickly at a profit (Liv. 10.17.4; cf. Polyb. 10.17). Army service was a 'bridging' occupation, that is, an occupation that affected subsequent social and economic accomplishment. Hollander assumes that in rural society traditional farmers lived side by side with more commercially minded peers. Increased urbanization created new demands on the hinterland of cities and enforced a transformation of the rural economy that, Hollander suggests, was driven by the innovative dynamic of soldiers and veterans. Above all veterans, who were settled in *coloniae* (military settlements) within hostile environments, provided a vital stimulus for monetization: they introduced cash-cropping, monetary exchange and monetary investment into areas yet unfamiliar with coinage.

Another stimulus to monetization in Italy was the growth of villas (large agrarian estates) typical of the Roman elite from the late republican period onwards. From the time of Cato the Elder (mid-second century BC), but best attested during the first centuries BC and AD, villa economies in Italy (and later North Africa and Gaul) specialized in cash-crop production, especially of oil and wine.[47] Elite investment in stock-raising for commercial purposes is evident in the late republican period and increased still further in the subsequent two centuries.[48] A system of landholding in which absentee landlords rented out their land in short-term tenancies subject to monetary rents forced small tenants into cash-cropping for local or Roman markets.[49] Yet the situation was not uniform throughout Italy. Villas flourished above all in central Italy and Campania. Pliny the Younger held estates both in northern Italy and close to Rome, adopting different strategies for each of them.[50] Suitable tenants for the Tifernum estate, located on the Tiber with good access to transport and markets in Rome, were farmers who were secure enough to carry the risk of market production. Tenants of the remote estate at Comum in northern Italy tended to be subsistence farmers of lower status. The distinction qualifies a rigid model according to which the Italian economy was divided into an urban monetary sector specializing in production for towns and Roman markets, on the one hand, and a rural sector with little market exchange, on the other. Instead, rural monetization varied considerably according to location and costs of transport.[51]

---

[47] E.g. Duncan-Jones (1982): 33–55; de Neeve (1990); Kehoe (1997); further literature in von Reden (2002): 148–52.
[48] Hitchner (2005): 215.   [49] De Ligt (1990); cf. Spawford (1988) for comparative evidence.
[50] De Neeve (1990).   [51] De Neeve (1990); cf. Morley (1996).

A third stimulus was financial activity itself. As Andreau notes, 'it encouraged monetization in all social circles in which the elite financiers moved,
but above all within the elite itself. An aristocracy whose wealth remains
constant flourishes with all the more brilliance when it has the means of
procuring liquid cash – liquid cash which, in its turn, stimulates purchases
and, as a result, encourages the commercialization of merchandise.'[52]

The growth of a monetary economy affected coin production. Access
to new mines and precious-metal resources accelerated the process. For a
century the interdependent processes of monetization, military expansion
and metal supply seem to have been fairly balanced, as governments managed to hold both silver and gold coins stable in weight and fineness until
the mid-first century AD.[53] Yet with an ever increasing demand for coinage
in the military sector, and growing monetization in terms of coinage in the
provinces, the Roman government began to stretch its financial resources
by manipulating the weight and fineness (silver content) of precious metal
coins.[54] This reduction happened in the first century AD temporarily, but
regularly from the mid-second century onwards. Nero in AD 64 had reduced
the weight of the gold aureus from 1/40 of the Roman libra (pound) to
1/45, and that of the denarius from 1/84 to 1/96. The fineness of the latter
was dropped from 98 to 93 per cent. Under the early Flavians (late first
century), fineness decreased further to 80–89 per cent, was restored to
98 per cent in AD 82, but declined to less than 80 per cent by AD 161. In AD
215 a double denarius ('*antoninianus*'), introduced by Caracalla at 1.5 times
the weight of the denarius but twice its value, soon had to be abolished
because it drove into hoards the 'good' denarii of the old weight. In AD
238 the *antoninianus* was re-introduced, this time in connection with the
demonetization of the single denarius, and was further reduced in weight
and fineness. Provincial currencies were adjusted accordingly, while the
growing number of cities producing local bronze coins suggests, among
other things, that the increase of Roman coins in circulation increased the
demand for small change in local economies.

By the third quarter of the third century, monetary manipulation
combined with increasing political disintegration had reached a scale that
made the population lose their trust in the Roman silver coinage.[55] After a
period of massive price inflation, the introduction of a gold standard fixing
the value of monetary units, and further reforms under the emperors

---

[52] Andreau (1999): 28.   [53] Harl (1996): 97–124 for the following.
[54] For cases of monetization in the provinces under Roman rule Woolf (1998): 40 ff.; Katsari (2005);
     (2008).
[55] For a plausible down-dating of the third-century price inflation, Rathbone (1996b).

Diocletian (AD 284–306) and Constantine (AD 306–37), which aimed at stabilizing a monetary system which had become impossible to stabilize, many users turned away from coinage and established their own methods of exchange.[56]

MONETIZATION UNDER ROMAN INFLUENCE:
CELTIC GAUL AND BRITAIN

The territories that later formed the provinces of Roman Britain and Gaul were part of the Celtic world that by the time of the late third century BC comprised most of temperate Europe from Galatia in the east to Galicia in the west, and included Northern Italy, large parts of the Danubian region and the Southern parts of the British Isles (map 4). Despite great diversity in social organization and political development, Celtic society shared visible signs of cultural unity regarding language, artistic articulation and religious practice.[57] The degree of cultural cohesion was sustained by a high degree of geographical mobility and expansion that from the fifth century BC onwards (the so-called early La Tène period) moved Celtic populations around Europe. Belgic Gaul and Britain had particularly close contacts among themselves, and parts of each tribal group settled on either side of the Channel. It is therefore useful to treat Britain and Gaul in common as well as looking at the monetary development of the Celtic world more generally before focussing on its Western parts.

Greeks had deplorably little knowledge of Celtic society despite the fact that from the fifth century BC onwards the Celts encroached on their borders, and the Greek city of Massalia (Marseille) had been settled in their immediate vicinity since 600 BC. There were, moreover, innumerable contacts between the Celts and their Mediterranean neighbours. Mercenaries were hired both by Celts from the Greeks and by Greeks from members of Celtic societies. Massilia was a place of cultural interaction with signs of mutual acculturation, despite the city's effort to remain distinctly Greek.[58] In the eyes of the Romans the Celts were a society of enemies rather than neighbours. Yet as Roman conquest progressed from Spain into Gaul in the second and first centuries BC, the Romans had to learn 'to govern the Celts rather than to extinguish them'.[59] When they began to

---

[56] The complex process of demonetization and monetary transformation in late antiquity and the early Byzantine periods are beyond the scope of this book; see Hendy (1985) and Depeyrot (1991).
[57] Brunaux (1988).
[58] Momigliano (1975): 50–73 for the mixed feelings surrounding Greco-Celtic acculturation.
[59] *Ibid.*: 65.

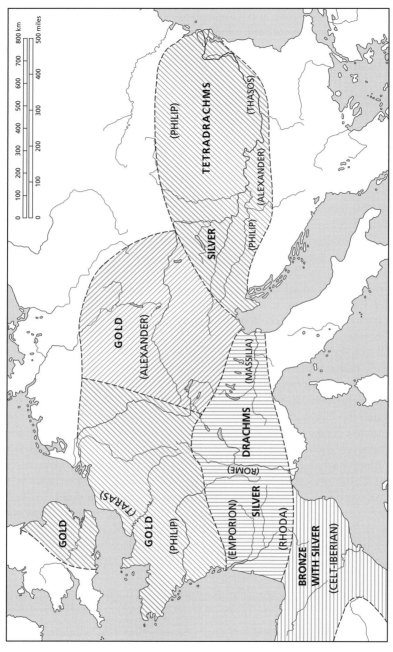

Map 4: Celtic coinages and their metals at the beginning of the first century BC

study their lands, they did so in order to find out how to rule what since Aristotle had been imagined as a warrior society.

Celtic society itself has left us with no written texts. Archaeological and numismatic evidence in combination with the ambivalent reports of Greek geographers and Roman writers, most notably Julius Caesar, are the major sources of information. The literary tradition about the Western provinces has been used by modern scholars to a variable degree, but still with surprising confidence. While the archaeological evidence lies at the centre of any research on Celtic society, some of the most influential historians of Celtic society have been unduly influenced by the tainted observations of Greco-Roman authors.[60] Literary scholars suggest, by contrast, that there is little historical information to be gleaned from ancient approaches to the foreign peoples in Central Europe.[61]

Given that material culture provides the major source for Celtic history, there is once again an unfortunate bias towards coinage in our understanding of monetization. Yet in contrast to other parts of the ancient world, where numismatic approaches tend to represent coinage as a phenomenon in its own right, archaeologists of Celtic Europe have the chance to contextualize the development of coinage more fully within a more general picture of material culture. Moreover, by using theoretical models of transactional systems and their political consequences archaeologists have provided a number of complex perspectives on the function of coinage in Celtic society, especially in its relation to pre-existing patterns of social interaction, metal use and the circulation of prestige goods. Abundant coin finds, which have increased exponentially in recent years, have created databases that help to locate very precisely the movement and circulation of particular coin issues.[62] The nature of the evidence and the models of explanation therefore offer an interesting contrast to the approaches of the previous sections.

The Celtic world was a rural society whose major communal organization was the tribe, called *tribus* by Latin and *phyle* by Greek authors. The territory (*pagus*) of one tribe extended typically over 60,000 to 200,000 hectares, which is roughly comparable to the size of small to mid-size Greek *poleis*. But in contrast to the social geography of Greece, Italy, Asia Minor or Egypt, there was little communal urbanized space. Dispersed settlement on isolated farms, occasionally clustered together in small hamlets or villages, was the pattern. Urbanization was low, and it has been asked

[60] E.g. Haselgrove (1987a): 108; Nash (1987).
[61] Again, Momigliano (1975): 50–73; and O'Gorman (1993). [62] De Jersey (2006b).

whether the large fortified sites which emerged in the late La Tène period (late second and first centuries BC), and which the Romans called *oppida*, can be regarded as towns.[63] *Oppida* exhibit a certain degree of clustered building and urban-style occupation such as iron working and exchange represented by the mixing of ceramics and coinage. But the sites identified as *oppida* tend to be extremely variable in size, and an 'urban' outlook appears also in unfortified settlements that have never been regarded as *oppida*. A model according to which increased urban living, urban pro-duction, urban exchange and an increasing use of coinage were related may therefore not be applicable to the Celtic development. Woolf (1993b) has suggested instead that the change must be envisioned more generally in terms of a transformation of social power going hand in hand with a greater degree of economic differentiation, more intense iron-working, and changing modes of exchange. This approach has been developed further by Creighton (2000) and will be looked at in more detail below. Yet the late La Tène also saw a rapid and significant transformation of social and political practice, which also involved coinage.

Greco-Roman authors emphasize, and the archaeological evidence of the middle and late La Tène seems to confirm, that wealth in precious metal on the one hand and warfare on the other were the most distinct characteristics of the Celtic aristocracy. Gold and silver ornaments, feasting implements, horses, arms, cattle and subsequently coinage were the instruments, and forms of self-representation, of aristocratic life, and as such under the control of the leading elite. Polybius attributed the Celtic preference for movable wealth to their quasi nomadic and primitive lifestyle:

They lived in un-walled villages, without any superfluous furniture; for as they slept on beds and leaves, and fed on meat, and were exclusively occupied with war and agriculture, their lives were very simple . . . Their possessions consisted of cattle and gold, because these are the only things they could carry around with them anywhere they chose. They treated comradeship as of the greatest importance, those among them being the most feared and most powerful who were thought to have the largest number of attendants and associates (Polyb. 2.17.11).

Both Polybius and other writers tell us that the Celts fought naked or clothed, on foot or on horseback, but always resplendent in gold.[64] The material culture from the middle to late La Tène onwards reflects this link between wealth, warfare and aristocratic culture. Warriors, horses, war-rior equipment, as well as warrior and hunting scenes on horseback are

---

[63] Woolf (1993b) against e.g. Collis (1984).
[64] Nash (1981): 13 f. with e.g. Strabo 4.4.5; Polyb. 2.29.7, 2.31.5; Caes. *BG* 7.47.5.

among the most frequent iconographic concerns and seem to have played an important role in the religion and rituals of local tribes.[65] The role of precious metal artefacts is thought to have been related to a ranked social structure that was produced and reproduced through religious ritual, on the one hand, and the support of groups of dependents paid and maintained by circulating precious metal objects, on the other. Both Polybius and Caesar emphasize that the power of a Celtic aristocrat was constituted by the number of his armed retainers who would remain with him only so long as he was successful at war and hospitable at home (Polyb. 2.17.12; Caes. *BG* 6.15.2).[66] Although the picture is derived from a debatable Greco-Roman perspective on an *interpretatio Graeca-Romana* of Celtic institutions, it represents the unchallenged scholarly consensus about the principal structures of Celtic society, which in turn forms the background to the interpretation of Celtic coinage.

Coinage was adopted at different times and in different metals in various parts of the Celtic world. Coinage spread locally, circulation patterns were local, and minting depended on local metal resources and social practices, while individual tribes adopted coinage in consequence of their individual contacts with the Greco-Roman world. In his major work on Celtic coinage D. F. Allen identified three numismatic zones of Europe according to the metal of their basic currency (see map 4).[67] The gold zone comprised northern France, Belgium, Britain, western and southern Germany, northern Switzerland, and Bohemia. The silver zone stretched from the Atlantic coast line along the south of the Loire to the mouth of the Danube in Bohemia. And a bronze zone, very small, developed in north-eastern Spain under the influence of the Greek colony Emporion (modern Ampurias).

The first Celtic coins are attested in two parts of the gold zone where Macedonian coins of Philip and Alexander were imitated by the mid–late fourth century BC. In Gaul the gold staters of Philip II were adapted, while in Bohemia and adjacent areas Alexander staters were used as a model. It is possible that genuine Macedonian coins had circulated before the first imitations were struck, but very few specimens have been found in Celtic territory.[68] Coins in the silver zone were adopted first by the Cisalpine Gauls who imitated silver drachmas of the Greek colony of Massilia by the early third century BC. Different kinds of imitations were used in different localities. A century later they were given legends in Italiot letters, but in the whole area the coinage was rather resistant to change for over two

[65] Nash (1987): pl. 2 and 3; Brunaux (1988): 99–112; Creighton (2000) *passim*.
[66] *Ibid.* with Athen. 4.36; Strab. 4.2.3; cf. Diod. 5.26.2; Polyb. 2.19.3–4; 11.3.1; Amm. Marc. 15.12.4.
[67] Allen (1980): 9–23.   [68] Nash (1987): 17; Allen (1980): 68.

centuries. In the East, Macedonian silver coins were adopted in the Danube basin during the mid-third century whence they slowly spread to adjacent areas. At first these Celtic coins were good copies of the prototypes and may well be categorized as imitations of Macedonian staters rather than genuine Celtic coins; but soon they acquired their own individuality.

In Britain coins are not attested before the late third or early second century BC, whereas in other parts of the Celtic world native coins already flourished before then.[69] The first coins appearing in Southern and south-eastern Britain were imported from Belgic Gaul. These gold coins and the first genuine British series that followed in the mid-second century BC are so similar that they have been variably attributed to either region, or have been thought to be produced by Belgic chieftains occupying the southern parts of Britain.[70] As minting of coinage in Britain progressed, distinctly local patterns emerged and coinage spread further to the north of the Thames. However, regions with close ties to Gaul, such as Southern Britain and Kent, continued to use continental types and were also the first to adopt the Gallic potin coinage, which was cast from an alloy of copper and tin. The coins of the so-called peripheral tribes of the Northern Midlands, East Anglia, Gloucestershire and Avon followed continental developments less closely, although developing similarly to each other, and each tribal group shared a common design. The south-western tribe of the Durotriges around Dorchester in Dorset used gold coinage for a short period only, while – possibly for lack of gold resources – minting silver from about 60 BC and potin from *c.* AD 20. All areas of Celtic Britain, apart from the south-western region, had distinctive gold coin series during the last 100 years before their conquest in AD 43 under the emperor Claudius, and some included silver and potin fractions as well.

The interpretation of Celtic monetization (as reflected in the adoption of coinage) has taken various directions. Particular emphasis has been put on distinguishing why the Celts came into contact with coinage in the first instance from why contact was so successful. Two reasons for contacts with the Mediterranean world are usually brought forward: mercenary warfare and trade, especially in slaves and wine *via* Massilia from and to Italy and southern France. Of the two, mercenary warfare provides a chronologically fitting and more compelling reason for the early contacts of Celtic people with coinage in the gold zone.[71] In the second half of the fourth century BC, the expansion of the Macedonians under Philip II and Alexander in

---

[69] Haselgrove (2006a): 24; Sills (2003); Creighton (2000): 224 for a slightly lower chronology.
[70] Nash (1987): 119; see, however, de Jersey (2006b).
[71] For a balanced view of the significance of trade, which all too commonly is adopted as an explanation for coinage, see Woolf (1993a).

the Eastern Mediterranean, and in the West the conflict between Carthage and the Greek cities of Sicily and Magna Graecia, gave rise to an unprecedented demand for mercenaries who were recruited from the Celts as the single most important ethnic group. The Macedonian design of the Celtic prototypes in the gold zone, the prestige attached to military activity, and the lure of metallic riches gained in the form of spoils and payment in coin provide ample support for the mercenary hypothesis. Some ancient authors suggest that under exceptional circumstances mercenary leaders were rewarded with gold coins. According to Livy, King Perseus of Macedonia (179–168 BC) offered Claodicus of the Danubian Bastarnae 5 gold staters for each infantry soldier, 10 for each cavalryman and 1,000 for the king himself (Liv. 44.26). Polybius has the leaders of the rebels during the mercenary revolt at Carthage in 241 BC receive one gold stater each to meet their expenses (Polyb. 1.66.7). Some scholars suggest that gold coins were minted by the hiring states to meet the general preferences of the Celtic mercenary market.[72] But day-to-day subsistence was paid in bronze from the second half of the fourth century BC onwards, which may explain the finds in France and southern Britain of third-century bronze coins struck by Carthage and Syracuse, the most important employers of Celtic mercenaries in that period. But the finds of bronze coins in Britain long before British tribes adopted their own (gold) coinages show clearly that mercenary payment cannot serve as a general explanation for the influx of coinage into Celtic society.

The notable predilection of the Celtic warrior elite for ostentatious ornamentation in the form of metal objects provides a better context.[73] It is generally assumed that not only gold and silver, but also potin coinage, served as gifts and valuable tokens in social and political transactions.[74] The archaeology of Celtic Britain and Gaul is in the fortunate position of being able to ascertain find spots of many of their coins and thus to plot depositional patterns of individual coinages. Although deposition does not reflect usage directly, the fact that depositional practice changed over time, as well as differing according to coin material among different people, suggests that coinages served variable functions in the Celtic communities over a period of three centuries. What is more, they are likely to have played an active role in the transformation of Celtic society under Roman influence in the late La Tène period.

The nature of these changes, and the part played by coinage in them, are controversial. Nash argued that coinage was linked to a process of state formation, reflected not least in more centralized living and interaction,

[72] Nash (1987): 15 f.   [73] See esp. Gruel (1989): 111–37.   [74] Haselgrove (2006a).

which marked the archaeology of central Gaul and southern Britain in the century before the Roman conquest. Late La Tène coinages were more distinct from neighbouring ones and had a more distinct circulation pattern, thus reflecting a new degree of political identity and bounded territorial interaction.[75] Haselgrove (1987a) rejected this view, regarding the notion of state formation as anachronistic and overstated.[76]

Creighton (2000) links the circulation of gold coinage in Britain to changing forms of political authority in Iron Age Britain. Avoiding any speculation on the reasons for the adoption of coinage, he describes a revolutionary process affecting Britain from the late second century BC onwards. There was change in the design and location of settlement space, change of pottery styles, increasing continental imports, increasing emphasis on horse equipment and equine ritual, as well as the emergence of gold as a symbol of power. British gold coins were linked to golden torcs that arrived on the island at around the same time. Torcs, weighing up to 100 times the mean weight of gold denominations, but often hoarded together with them, could be seen as high-value insignia of kingship or paramount lineage. Coinage represented the more portable and transferable counterpart of torcs, and was distributed as a means of social payment rather than stored. Its appearance was closely linked to the nature of authority which acted upon its users. So, for example, the serial transformation of the Macedonian prototypes could be interpreted as trance imagery that referred to the leaders' religious role and connection with an outer world. The value of coins, moreover, depended on the aesthetic value of colour rather than our notions of metallic value, which place gold above silver and silver above base metal. The gradual reduction in gold content of the Gallo-Belgic and British staters should be understood not in terms of debasement, but in terms of an attempt to create a more lasting form of the preferred colour. Changes of alloy occurred in connection with changes in serial imagery and so might reflect deliberate attempts to enhance the aesthetics of a series. Late Iron Age Britain saw the emergence of a new kind of kingship with a new degree of individualized authority, individualized political space and representation of power. The emergence of this new form of authority was reflected in coinages which in their final phase bore the names of individual chiefs.

The exploding amount of numismatic and archaeological evidence is likely to keep discussion alive for some time in the future.[77] The idea

---

[75] Nash (1981); (1987): 51–5.   [76] Further approaches in Creighton (2000): 225 f.
[77] De Jersey (2006b).

that monetization in Celtic Gaul and Britain did not result from economic changes in the first instance is attractive, although there is no reason to deny any function to Celtic coinage in trade and commercial exchange. There was, as we mentioned above, a notable absence of Mediterranean-type markets, towns or central places. We must first rethink our notions of trade and its connection with social exchange, power, authority and ritual before social purposes of Celtic coinages are separated from economic functions.[78] The fact that after the conquest Roman coinage was at first imitated in Gaul, and only gradually replaced local issues in the course of time, suggests that coins, however different their social function, were convertible.[79] In Britain, moreover, Roman images and imperial themes had been adopted on local coins since the first encounter of individual kings with Julius Caesar, and more thoroughly in the Augustan period, suggesting a gradual absorption of Roman values into local ideology.[80] However, the degree of social unrest and debt that was created in Gaul by Roman monetary taxation during the first century of provincial exploitation suggests that the nature of monetization here was minimally compatible with its Roman counterpart.[81] It is likely that the Celts applied their coinages to a larger range of transactions, as well as combining transactions in ways which are unfamiliar to us.[82] But while we have to remain susceptible to uncomfortable explanations, we should perhaps not go entirely the other way, constructing the Celts, in Polybian fashion, as a strange society that did things in opposite ways to the ones we prefer.

MONETIZATION: A TENTATIVE FRAMEWORK

The degree of overall monetization in antiquity is impossible to assess, but any approach must consider the following five factors. (1) There was, within 100 years of the adoption of coinages in either Greece or Rome, a trend towards thorough monetization in the places that are documented by Greek and Roman written evidence. Barter, gift-exchange and any other form of pre-monetary commerce were relegated by Greek and Roman authors to the distant past, or were associated with foreign peoples, so as to make them a threatening vision of civilization undone.[83] General use of money in the form of monetary units is also presumed in local inscriptions (usually related to urban culture and frontier towns), papyri (related to Hellenized and Romanized parts of Egypt) and wax tablets

---

[78] Thus Woolf (1993a).   [79] Nash (1978); Haselgrove (2006b) for Gaul.
[80] Creighton (2000): 80–125.   [81] Woolf (1998): 44.   [82] Haselgrove (2006a): 25.
[83] E.g. Strab. 3.3.7; 7.5.5.

(extant from garrison settlements), as soon as they throw light on provincial economies. (2) There is a similar archaeological presence of Greco-Roman coins in places of Greco-Roman settlement. It would be surprising to discover a site with developed urban structures, but no coins. Degrees of monetization cannot be inferred from individual coin finds or texts, but it can be assumed that Greek and Roman influence went along with some use of coined money. (3) Money use went beyond the use of coins. Comments like that of Gaius quoted in the first chapter (p. 26) demonstrate a highly variable supply of coins against a background of widespread monetization. There was an increasing demand for money that was not always met by an adequate supply of coinage. This led to a thriving culture of credit, and any increase in the supply of coinage had a high chance of being absorbed into economies insufficiently supplied with it. From the late second to the third century AD the increasing demand for coinage by the Roman government led to increasing amounts of coin use in local economies and eventually to massive problems of regulating the monetary system. But it is unlikely that any increased quantity of coinage in circulation led directly to price inflation. (4) There was a considerable degree of interaction between the use of Greek and Roman coinage on the one hand and native money on the other in the areas of Greek and Roman conquest. Hybrid monetary cultures in which coins functioned in connection with other means of payment, such as grain, bullion or tools, are most likely to be expected in places of cultural interaction as a result of conquest. (5) Despite the rapid expansion of Greco-Roman coin use alongside conquest and trade, monetary cycles in which coinage circulated could remain tiny and monetization limited to a few transactions. Public payments on the one hand and fiscal demand on the other stimulated the circulation of coinage. But it cannot be taken for granted that this led automatically to coin use in a wider range of transactions. Depending on the size and frequency of the payments demanded in the form of coinage, it may have caused just a bilateral movement of coins to and from the local administration.

Some of these observations will be substantiated further in chapter 4. In the following chapter, we will look at the expansion of monetary networks, as these provided a further condition for monetization and coinage becoming an increasingly powerful medium of exchange.

CHAPTER 3

Monetary networks

INTRODUCTION

According to Moses Finley, the great number of weight standards and individual coin designs used throughout the Mediterranean impeded proper circulation of money, and in particular coinage. The fact that states showed little interest in removing these boundaries demonstrated that local rather than broader economic principles guided their monetary policies. What is more, the economic impact of coined money remained limited because of the political boundaries created by local weight standards and coin designs.[1]

We know, however, that many cities adopted common weights and measures, or made their coinages more easily exchangeable by using the same weight standard for their principle coin. Every precious metal monetary system is based on a principal unit of weight (normally slightly lighter than the unit of metal weight itself). There is also a standard coin (stater) which represents a specific number of these units. In Greek *poleis*, for example, the stater could represent two, three or four drachmas of a different size.[2] It is highly significant, therefore, that the Athenians in the sixth century seem to have changed their metal-weight system from the Aiginetan standard to one that scholars identify with the island of Euboia (Arist. *Ath. Pol.* 10.3). The change was not related to coinage, for coins were not minted in Athens at the time of Solon to whom the change was attributed in the fourth century BC. It did, however, affect the monetary units on the basis of which monetary exchange was conducted. It seems that it was deemed important to facilitate transactions among people who used the Euboian rather than the Aiginetan monetary weight system and thus avoid negotiation and conversion charges. In this chapter I wish to explore weight standards as a reflection of monetary networks developing within the tension of local

[1] Finley (1985): 166 f.
[2] Thus the numismatic terms 'didrachm' (two-drachm-piece), or 'tetradrachm' (four-drachm-piece) which are not used in ancient texts.

65

and inter-regional systems of exchange and identity.[3] In their capacity to reduce the costs of transactions, monetary networks represent the attempt to enhance monetary integration and circulation, which in turn increases the power of money.[4]

Monetary networks are the result of a complex interplay of political, ideological and economic factors. National or 'territorial' currencies that are valid almost exclusively in their country of issue belong to the history of the European nation state that peaked in the last two centuries.[5] Many countries nowadays share a common currency or use a combination of local and international currencies to satisfy their various monetary needs. The spread of the dollar, euro and yen is an expression of the globalization of the international financial economy, the internationalization of politics, and the dissolution of national identities and boundaries. Ancient currencies, too, were embedded in particular political and economic systems which in turn they symbolized. Plato suggested for moral reasons that a state should have a local ('epichoric') coinage alongside a general 'Hellenic' one that was valid outside the *polis* (*Laws* 5. 742a–b). This imaginary coin system aimed at preventing the influx of luxury goods through trade and controlling the relationships which the members of an ideal city entertained.

In practice, the boundaries of monetary relationships ran somewhere differently. The transition from bullion money to stamped coinage in the archaic period can be regarded as reflecting a changing balance between civic relationships and the contacts which individuals entertained across *polis* boundaries.[6] Similarly, the continuing tension between local coinages, on the one hand, and the attempt to lock these coinages into larger networks of common weight standards, on the other, reflects the particular kind of 'connectivity' which marks ancient Mediterranean history. As Horden and Purcell have argued, the Mediterranean was characterized by 'dense fragmentation complemented by a striving towards control of communications'. Connectivity refers to the 'various ways in which micro-regions cohered, both internally and also one with another', while 'micro-regions ranged in size from small clusters to something approaching the entire Mediterranean'.[7] In the classical Greek period most of the approximately one thousand known *poleis* were

---

[3] The weight standards of coinages are discussed in any general numismatic introductions; e.g. Kraay (1976) for the Greek world; Crawford (1985) for the Roman world. But the monetary implications of weight standards have rarely been explored; see however Schmitz (1986); and Meadows (unpublished).
[4] B. Cohen (2004): 46 f., for the effects of non-territorial monies on the reduction of transaction costs.
[5] *Ibid.*: 7–14.   [6] Thus Kurke (1995); cf. (1999).
[7] Horden and Purcell (2000): 25 and 123; see also Erdkamp (2005).

small, politically autonomous units controlling territories not larger than 100 square kilometres; a handful only were as large as Athens, Sparta, Syracuse or Miletus. Even the wealthy *polis* of Corinth occupied an area of 90 km² only. Yet common language, religion and culture created a network of competitive relationships and exchange. This pattern, crossed by the attempt of some *poleis* to dominate politics and exchange, is the background of the local production of coinages on the one hand and their competitive inter-regional spread on the other.

What were the motivations for creating monetary networks of common weight standards? In principle, different weight standards did not prevent monetary communication across political boundaries. Herodotus translates the Babylonian weight system into the Euboian for his Athenian listeners (Hdt. 3. 89). Xenophon tells us that a Lydian *kapithe* cost four Lydian *sigloi*, while one *siglos* was equal to 7½ Attic obols and a *kapithe* equal to two Attic *choinices* (*Anab*. I. 5. 6.). In the Greek cities of Sicily there was even a regular conversion rate of 1:1 between the standard bronze unit (the *litra*) and the silver obol of the Aiginetan standard.[8] An inscription listing the costs of the building of the temple of Asclepius at Epidauros in the fourth century BC shows how a city using the Aiginetan standard accounted for wages and purchases from Athens where a different standard was in use. The relationship of weight between the coins was seven to ten, and so 400 Aiginetan drachmas were paid for Athenian marble costing 600 Attic drachmas. A commission charge (*epikatallage*) of a further 25 drachmas was charged by the moneychangers in addition.[9] The Romans, too, exchanged denarii into Greek-standard silver coins at fixed conversion rates (see below). Traders were well-known for their skills in reckoning with different currencies (e.g. Athen. 6.225a–b). They also assembled caches, using each currency where it was most acceptable (Lys. 12.11). Many hoards representing the savings of individuals or households contain a variety of current coinages, suggesting that the use of particular currencies was not confined to the town or country of their origin.[10] But different weight standards of local monetary systems added costs in terms of negotiation and uncertainty. Common weight standards facilitate trade.[11]

---

[8] Carradice and Price (1988): 92.
[9] *IG* IV² I 103 A and B, 35 f; 41 f. and 126 with Burford (1969): 126 and Carradice and Price (1988): 91–7, who also argue that the profit derived from currency exchange was the major incentive to maintain local currency systems; Maresch (1996) for commission charges in Ptolemaic Egypt where they were called *alage*.
[10] For example, *IGCH* 1637 (Demanhur, Egypt, *c*. 500 BC; *IGCH* 1639 (Sakha, Egypt *c*. 500 BC)); *IGCH* 1166 (Bairakli, Turkey, *c*. 500 BC).
[11] E.g. Wallace (1984).

Inter-*polis* relationships, however, in combination with the interests of
political elites, are more likely than the interest of traders to have affected
the decision of Greek governments. Greek settlers abroad, for example,
made their currencies compatible among each other and with those of
their mother cities. Examples are the cities of the Chalkidike founded by
Chalkis on Euboia, and several Euboian settlements in Sicily.[12] Military
leagues, short-term alliances, and imperial taxation provided further reasons for the adoption or imposition of common weight standards (see
below).[13] Some temporary allies, such as towns in Asia Minor and the
Propontis, periodically adopted common weight standards. The need to
choose a standard in which payments to heterogeneous troops or subsidy
payments to states were made is known from several examples in Thucydides (e.g. 5.47; 8.29; 8.45.2). In Euboia coin series are known which were
not minted on the Euboian but the Aiginetan standard and are likely to be
related to a time when Euboia changed temporarily its political and military affiliations.[14] Part of more long-term interaction, including economic
links, was the reversion of many Cycladic islands from the Attic to the
Aiginetan standard after the dissolution of the first Athenian confederacy
(see below). Members of the political elite and kings moreover frequently
had financial stakes in trade. Olives, wine and grain were in regions of
high productivity cash crops produced on large estates owned by leading citizens.[15] In the Eastern empires kings were either directly involved
in export, or their treasuries profited from harbour taxes and tolls. The
kings of the Bosporan kingdom, the pharaohs of Egypt and their Greco-
Macedonian successors are all well-known for their control over grain-
resources supplying Mediterranean cities in the classical and Hellenistic
period.[16] In the case of archaic Athens, it is thus not unlikely that the
switch of weight standard in the sixth century BC was in the interest of
a land-owning elite who sold their surplus within an exchange network
dominated by the Euboian rather than Aiginetan weight system.

An important motivation for keeping standards apart was competition.
Although all precious metal coinages represented the same degree of bullion
value, some coinages became superior to others.[17] Xenophon, emphasizing
the benefits of Athenian coinage, writes:

[12] Kraay (1976): 206.
[13] There is some controversy over the question of why empires brought with them a certain consol-
     idation of the coin systems in their realm. See further below in this chapter and Martin (1985);
     Howgego (1995): 9–61; Figueira (1998); and Kallet-Marx (2001): 213–25.
[14] Schmitz (1986): 82 f.   [15] Hollander (1999).   [16] Garnsey (1988): 151–4.
[17] For the general principle of currency hierarchies, B. Cohen (2004): 14–26.

At most other ports merchants are compelled to ship a return cargo, because the home currency has no circulation in other states, but at Athens they have the opportunity of exchanging their cargo and exporting very many kinds of goods that are in demand. Or, if they do not want to ship a return cargo of goods it is good business to export money. For wherever they sell it, they are sure to make a profit on the sum paid (*Por.* III, 2).

Xenophon wrote at a time (*c.* 350 BC) when Athenian coinage dominated the Mediterranean despite the decline of Athenian political power. It was a superior currency because of its acceptability and trust in the wake of the former power of Athens. The competition of currencies and weight standards began in the early history of Greek coinages. The Aiginetan weight standard spread rapidly across the southern Aegean, Boiotia and Thessaly soon after Aigina had adopted coinage. At the beginning of the fifth century local coin production peaked but monetary units were clustered into a handful of weight standards.[18] The Athenian/Euboian weight standard and the coinage based on it began to dominate the Aegean from the mid-fifth century onwards, eventually leading to an Athenian imperial decree stipulating that only Athenian coins, weights and measures should be legal tender in the markets of the allies. In the fourth century many issuing authorities, including Egypt, imitated Athenian coins so as to have available the most acceptable coinage. Fifty years later, the posthumous Alexander coinage produced in most areas of the Hellenistic kingdoms (yet still based on the Athenian standard) for the first time transcended the identification of a coinage with a particular state, and dominated inter-regional exchange in the Hellenistic world. A fully unified imperial monetary system, though still supplemented by subordinate local currencies, developed under the Roman empire even after 296. In AD 296 the Egyptian drachma-system, which had been the last bastion of a purely local currency under Roman rule, was abolished, and the Roman denarius became the only inter-regional currency throughout the Roman empire. While monetary networks facilitated transactions in a political economy of taxation and public finance, they also affected trade. More difficult to answer is the question of how we can measure this effect.

LOCAL COINAGES AND INTER-REGIONAL EXCHANGE

The first coins attested in Asia Minor were based on some highly localized weight system. They were made of electrum, an alloy of silver and gold

---

[18] Osborne (1996): 253–5; Parise (1997); Kim (2001b): 17 f.

that occurs naturally in the area of Mount Tmolos and could be panned
out of the river Paktolos in Lydia. The use of a local metal and the localized
weight system explains both why coins were invented in the first instance
and why they remained at first such a local phenomenon. Electrum has
variable proportions of silver and gold. In order to make pieces of the same
size and weight equal in value, the ratio of silver and gold has to be tested
and certified. Since this made the certification stamp an indispensable part
of their value, these coins did not travel well across the boundaries of the
cities in which they were issued. A fourth-century compact shows that
extensive regulation was necessary when two states wished to make their
electrum coinages interchangeable (*GHI* 2.112.14–16).

The spread of coinage began with the emergence of gold and silver coins
under the Lydian king Croesus, or a little later when Lydia was incorporated
into the Persian empire (*c.* 545 BC).[19] The new coinages were produced
in Sardis, but the variety of designs suggests that their production was
influenced by many cities in Asia Minor. But despite their association with
individual cities, coins were interchangeable because they were minted to
a common weight standard which modern scholars relate to the Greek city
of Miletus. Once electrum was replaced by gold and silver, and once coins
were used in Greek cities, the idea of coinage rapidly spread to mainland
Greece. Aigina was the first city which minted silver coinage almost at the
same time as the first coins were minted in silver and gold in Asia Minor.
The Aiginetan didrachma (2-drachma piece) of 12.1 g, however, was hardly
compatible with either the Milesian weight standard or the Persian daric
that replaced the coinage of Croesus at the end of the sixth century.[20] It was
also different from that of the island of Samos which began to mint coinage
at around the same time. It was the idea of coinage, rather than the Lydian
coin system itself, that travelled to Greece where coins were used for local
or regional purposes. The Aiginetan standard was adopted by most cities
in the Peloponnese, of the Southern Aegean (with the notable exceptions
of Delos and Melos), and for the federal coinages of Phocis, Thessaly and
Boiotia in Central Greece, when they began to mint coinages in the second
half of the sixth century BC.

Soon after Aigina, Athens began to mint coinage on yet another weight
standard. The Athenian stater (at first a didrachma as in Aigina) had the
same weight as the stater of Euboia, Samos, and Corinth, although in these
weight systems the coin represented three drachmas. A generation later,
the Athenians doubled the weight of the stater to a tetradrachm piece, as

---

[19] Carradice (1987).   [20] *Ibid.*

well as creating a new design for their coinage. Tetradrachms of this weight and value had already been minted by Chalkis before the reformation of the Athenian currency and may represent an attempt of the Athenians to assimilate their system to that of Chalkis and its foreign settlements.

In Magna Graecia either common weight systems or exchangeable coins were adopted for local transactions. In Southern Italy, where minting was begun in Sybaris and Metapontum by the middle of the sixth century, the local weight of 8 g per libra was used for the stater here called *nomos* (Lat. *nummus*). It was divided into thirds, in turn divided into sixths. Although the subdivisions of the Greek drachma are recognizable, the preference for a local weight system, combined with a peculiar mint technology and very little intrusion of foreign coinages, represents an insulated monetary network, rather than extensive monetary connections with mainland Greece. This contrasts with the Greek colonies in Sicily which generally adopted the weight system of their mother cities.[21]

In Macedonia minting began in the last quarter of the sixth century with a complex mix of different standards in the Chalkidike, the tribes and cities of Macedonia, and various areas in Thrace. In the Chalkidike the largest denomination was compatible with the stater in the Attic-Euboian system and was divided at first into half-pieces and then into thirds, sixths and twelfths. In the tribes and cities of Macedonia, by contrast, alongside some smaller fractions unusually large pieces were produced. Specimens are found more frequently in the Persian empire than in their area of origin itself which suggests that they were struck for a special range of external transactions.[22]

By 480 BC over 115 different mints, some of them closing after a short period of activity, can be identified.[23] The speed with which the idea of coinage spread in Greece on the one hand, but the fact that many large economies in the Mediterranean, most notably the Phoenician cities and Egypt, did not adopt coinage at all until the fourth century BC, on the other, shows that coined money was related to particular exchange networks. Despite the potential exchangeability of many coinages, and despite the domination of certain weight standards in some regions, the circulation pattern of individual coinages was normally a local one.[24]

Yet the relatively wide dissemination of the Aiginetan weight standard was an exception and gives Aigina a pioneering role in the growth of monetary networks in mainland Greece. Not only do archaic and classical

---

[21] Crawford (1985): 344 f. [22] Kraay (1976): 139. [23] Osborne (1996): 251–5.
[24] Figueira (1998): 31–46; Kim (2001a): 47 f.

hoards show that coins of the Aiginetan standard tended to be stored together, but also that Aiginetan coins travelled earlier and further beyond the Aegean than others.[25] The prominence of the Aiginetan weight standard is usually attributed to Aigina's dominant role in trade during the late archaic period. According to the logic of the argument suggested here, however, the Aiginetan standard created a degree of monetary consolidation which in turn increased its role in trade. The effect of Aiginetan currency domination is as important as the fact that hostile states, most notably Corinth, Athens and some large cities of western Asia Minor, chose not to participate in this network.

ATHENS

Monetary networks were created regionally as a result of political alliances and the hegemony of one state. At the same time, the mostly political origin of currency networks is likely to have become an economic dynamic as soon as certain currencies became more acceptable to users than others. As we suggested above, the connectivity of the Mediterranean was based on bonds and communications between places that were separated by exclusive citizen rights and local economies, but united by language and culture. Social mobility, religious interaction, aristocratic friendship and the advantages of Mediterranean shipping routes were reasons for relationships with a monetary dimension as much as were warfare, tribute payments, and trade. It would be misleading to approach monetary consolidation in exclusively economic or exclusively political terms. Not only did fiscal pressure lead to an increasing demand for the currency in which taxes and tributes were paid, but markets in turn were dependent on the conditions created by inter-state relationships and their influence on monetary production.[26]

The dominance of the Aiginetan weight standard was outgrown by a much more powerful monetary network following the Delian League founded by the Athenians in 478/7 BC. The degree of consolidation that came along with the military alliance of the Athenians is reflected in the composition of hoards from the first quarter of the fifth century onwards and confirmed by the Athenian Tribute-Quota Lists that survive for several years from 454 BC until 430/29 BC. The lists recorded the sixtieth part of each contributor's payment that was reserved for Athena in Athens, and

---

[25] Figueira (1998): 37 f.
[26] Morley (2007): 64–70; Hopkins (1980) for the connection between tribute payments and the need for coined money.

Figure 2: Athenian stater of the fifth century BC. By permission of Classical Numismatic Group, Lancaster, PA [www.cngcoins.com].

from 413 BC the income from the 5-per-cent harbour tax that was raised by the Athenians in the allied cities.[27] The tribute was levied at first in the form of either ships or money paid in any currencies. By the time of the first Tribute-Quota List, however, the allied treasury had been transferred from Delos to Athens. All payments were noted down and, with a few exceptions, paid in Athenian coinage.[28]

Some figures can illustrate the speed and extent of monetary consolidation. Over 280 cities belonged to the Delian League at one time or another; between 140 and 180 allies contributed in any given year. According to a recent assessment, only sixty-nine of the known contributors minted their own coinage either continuously or intermittently during the time of the League, and an additional twenty-three coined fractions below the stater only.[29] A measurable increase in Athenian coin production during the early years of the League was most likely related to the increase both in Athenian mining and in monetary transactions consolidating the empire.[30] The transformation of the League treasury into a fund of Athenian coinage by 454 BC increased still further the production of Athenian coinage. Although the absolute volume of coin production is notoriously difficult to ascertain, it can reasonably be argued that from the mid-fifth century onwards Athens produced a substantial proportion of the total coinage in circulation. By a conservative calculation, somewhere between one and nine million tetradrachms were annually produced in Athens from around 450 BC onwards.[31] The consequences of this scale of coin production for the coin supply in the Aegean were massive.

---

[27] Most recently, Kallet-Marx (2001): 195–222; see also Figueira (1998): 266–95, with earlier literature.
[28] Eddy (1973). [29] Figueira (1998): 563–76. [30] Rutter (1981). [31] Meadows (unpublished).

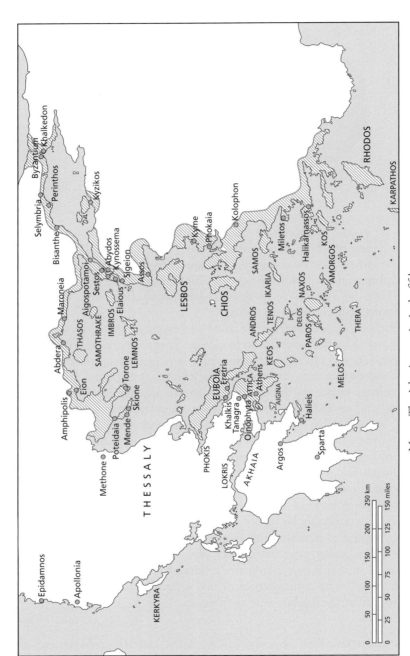

Map 5: The Athenian empire in the fifth century BC

Fifty per cent of the minting members of the alliance ceased minting between 478 and 445 BC. A further 10 per cent can be added if cities are included which had minted denominations smaller than the drachma.[32] By 445 BC the proportion of minting states among the allies had dropped from about 35 to 20 per cent. Among those which maintained minting were Aigina until its destruction in 430 and the autonomous members of the Athenian alliance, Chios and Samos, which did not pay money tribute to Athens at all.

Monetary consolidation becomes even more apparent if the closure of mints is related to the weight standards. No allied city which had used the Aiginetan standard produced denominations larger than the drachma by the time of the Peloponnesian War. Only one city that had previously minted on the Attic standard continued to mint after that time. Those allies which continued to mint after 445 BC were tied into other weight systems, such as the Phocaean or the Persian which dominated the Northern coast of Asia Minor. Apparently, states that in the pre-League period had belonged to a regional monetary network not linked to Greece and the Western Aegean were more likely to maintain their insulated position than those participating in the major Greek exchange networks. This meant that many of the highly monetized Aegean islands minting on the Aiginetan standard discontinued their coinages in the earliest years of the League, while the member states in Ionia and the Hellespont which minted on the Persian and Eastern Greek standards, or in electrum, rarely gave up minting their own coins.

The dominance of Athenian currency in mainland Greece and the Aegean islands had effects on the desirability of Athenian coinage beyond the members of the Athenian military alliance. Imitations of Athenian tetradrachms were minted from the beginning of the fifth century onwards, increased in the middle of the century and are particularly common in hoards from Syria and Egypt.[33] Since the latter did not use coins for their internal transactions, it is likely that they were minted because of their attractiveness to Greek mercenaries. It has been argued that Athenian imitations were produced in greater quantities after 413 when the supply of genuine Athenian coins fell short of the demand for this coinage.[34] Particularly noteworthy is a special issue attributed to a Persian king or satrap in the late fifth century BC. The three letters AΘE ('[coin] of the Athenians')

---

[32] Figueira (1998): 58 f., 62 f., 576. The chronology of coinages, and thus any attempt to date their termination precisely, is open to discussion. It is therefore better to argue with the help of a general picture rather than on the basis of precise figures and dates.

[33] Robinson (1947); Buttrey (1982); van Alfen (2002).   [34] Kraay (1976): 73; Figueira (1998): 530.

of the Athenian tetradrachms were replaced by the letters BAΣ ('of the king'), notably in Greek letters. The obverse of the coinage bore a bearded portrait of a Persian noble instead of Athena. It has been suggested that the coinage was issued by the Persian satrap Tissaphernes subsidizing a Spartan fleet against Athens.[35] If this is the case, it appears that the acceptability of Athenian coinage by the end of the fifth century had moved beyond the boundaries of its own monetary network.

Some time during the height of Athenian currency domination the Athenians legislated about the use of Athenian silver coinage, weights and measures.[36] According to the so-called Athenian Standards Decree (*ATL* II, D 14), issued any time between 445 and 413 BC, all members of the Athenian alliance, apart from those using electrum coinage, were forbidden to produce their own silver coinages but had to use Athenian coinage instead. They were to bring their old coinage to the mint of Athens and have it re-minted for a fee. Heralds were sent to the cities where the decree was to be published in the market place and members of the Athenian Council had to swear that they would enforce the decree. It is the first time we hear of an ancient city attempting to establish its coinage as exclusive legal tender.[37] Unfortunately, we have no evidence that the Athenians were successful. Regardless of the date of the decree, which we do not know, there is no numismatic evidence for a sudden break of local coin production or of non-Athenian coins disappearing from hoards at any time in the fifth century. As we just saw, many independent mints either had ceased minting by 445 BC. The best explanation available is that, despite heavy penalties imposed on negligent magistrates, the law was unenforceable.

The motivation for the decree is as uncertain as its success. Arguably, the Athenians introduced it for their own convenience, since the administration of the empire, especially the maintenance of the fleet, involved many purchases and payments. There may have been special reason to unify the coinage when Athenians switched the obligation of tribute payment to raising a harbour tax in each allied harbour between 413–410 BC.[38] The

---

[35] Kraay (1976): 74, with Thuc. VIII, 29.
[36] Wartenberg (1995): 25–7; Howgego (1995): 44–6, for discussions and further literature; the term Standards Decree is preferable to the common title 'Coinage Decree', because it referred to Athenian weights and measures as well as to coinage.
[37] Another example is an inscription from Olbia in southern Russia, which decreed that within the city only the city's own silver and bronze coinage was allowed to be used. Sales and purchases in other coinages were restricted to take place 'at the stone in the Assembly building'. (*SIG³* 218, mid-fourth century BC); cf. Carradice and Price (1988): 96 f.; Figueira (1998): 57.
[38] Thus Kallet-Marx (2001): 195–226.

Figure 3: Imitation of an Athenian tetradrachm of the fourth/third century BC
issued in Arabia

Athenians may also have hoped to gain silver, and make money from the fee
charged for re-minting foreign coins into their own species. Many scholars
have emphasized the hegemonic aspect of the decree.[39] Such a policy would
have fitted the early 440s, when Athens was popular and successful, or the
420s when its assembly was dominated by imperialist politicians such as
Cleon. The attempt to make a profit from the fee, or to consolidate the
coinage for administrative purposes, would have been more typical for the
last ten years of the empire.

Scholars who emphasize that the Standards Decree curbed monetary
sovereignty among the allies against their will argue that local mint production re-emerged soon after the loss of the empire.[40] But there is equally
compelling evidence that, despite the revival of some mints in the Cyclades,
Athenian currency continued to dominate the Aegean after the Peloponnesian War. In the passage quoted above, Xenophon stressed the exceptional
desirability of Athenian coinage in the mid-fourth century (*Por.* III.2; see
above). Athenian coins dominate fourth-century coin hoards by a notable
margin.[41] The production of valid imitations peaked in the first quarter of
the fourth century with more, and more remote, issuers producing staters
in Athenian style.

Figueira (1998) has argued that already in the fifth century Athenian
coinage was extremely popular so that the Standards Decree consolidated
rather than enforced Athenian currency domination, greatly to the benefit
of the allied cities themselves. By establishing Athenian coinage as legal tender in local markets, these markets became more attractive to traders and

[39] For a discussion of these views, Howgego (1995): 45 f.
[40] For example, Kraay (1976): 48; 73.   [41] Ober (2008): chap. 6: 240.

thus more highly frequented. Although Figueira's textual reconstruction of the decree has been rejected, his emphasis on the currency dynamics in the fifth and fourth century adds an important aspect to the discussion.[42] Whatever the motivations for the Standards Decree, and however successfully it was enforced, it would have confirmed rather than imposed Athenian currency domination.

In 375/4 BC the Athenians once again legislated about Athenian coinage. According to the law of Nicophon, the money testers sitting beside the bankers' tables in the agora and the Piraeus should test all coins brought forward to be deposited or exchanged. They should make the bankers accept any genuine Athenian coins; foreign silver coins with the Athenian stamp should be approved, but returned to their owners, while imitations with a base-metal core or counterfeit coins should be confiscated and destroyed.[43] Money testers (public slaves) are known to have tested Athenian coins as early as the mid-fifth century BC. Yet now there seems to have been a new need to distinguish clearly between genuine Athenian coins, imitations of pure silver, and counterfeit coins. Many scholars believe that the law was made to control exchange in the market; in fact it instructed bankers how to deal with a variety of different quality Athenian coins. It shows a collective concern for the trust to be put in coins that purported to be Athenian. Good imitations were permitted as legal tender. Although they were not exchanged by Athenian bankers into genuine Athenian coins, they were returned to their owners who could use them for transactions wherever they wanted. Athenian coinage had ceased to be a token of merely local identity and ownership. It had turned into a widespread economic medium that was controlled by the Athenian government in order to increase trust in it, which meant more security in the market and thus more efficient exchange. As Ober suggests, 'Athens was extremely productive in comparison with rival *poleis*. For much of the fifth century, Athenian productivity is at least in part a function of coercive imperialism and violent (or at least potentially violent) resource extraction. But in the early democracy that preceded the imperial period and in the post-imperial fourth century, Athens had no empire from which to extract major resources. During these pre- and post-imperial eras, high Athenian productivity depended primarily on domestic production and exchange.'

---

[42] Figueira's re-reading of section xii of the decree prescribing that Athenian coins, weights and measures should be valid *alongside* local coinages, rather than exclusively (1998: 392–410), has been rejected for epigraphical reasons; see the review by H. Mattingly *AJA* 103 (1999): 712.

[43] *RO* 25 with ed. comment p. 118 and Stroud *Hesp.* 43 (1974): 158–88; see also Ober (2008): 220–39 for the impact of this law on the efficiency of the Athenian economy.

The law [of Nicophon] revealed much about the design of Athenian legal institutions, suggesting that the Athenians explicitly sought to facilitate market exchanges by using government institutions to lower transaction costs.[44]

BEYOND ATHENS

The expansion and contraction of ancient currency networks cannot be adequately understood, if only the top currencies are taken into consideration. Beyond the Athenian currency network Taras dominated Southern Italy, as Syracuse dominated Sicilian weight standards in Greek, Phoenician and native towns. In the Achaemenid empire, there was no standardization of coinage, weights and measures, and so individual satrapies, dynasties and cities had the chance to integrate themselves in any monetary network most suitable for them. Among the cities that opened, or re-opened, local mints in the fourth century were the Aegean islands which adopted neither the Athenian nor their former Aiginetan standard, but a new one related to Chios or Rhodes. Chian-standard coins were prevalent along the coast of Asia Minor, and in the Black Sea and Hellespontine area where electrum coinage retained a dominant influence.[45]

The somewhat curious spread of the Chian weight standard in some parts of the Aegean in the first half of the fourth century throws further light on the interplay of political and economic factors, and of weight-standard and coin design in the formation of monetary networks. Through the experience of the Athenian imperial coinage, the advantages of a united weight system, and coinage, must have become generally recognized. Chios had been a rich island from the archaic period onwards, drawing its wealth from the substantial wine production which was distributed all over Greece. It was highly monetized by the fifth century because of its production of one of the most important cash-crops.[46] As a non-tributary ally of Athens, Chios minted substantial local coinage. But only in the fourth century did the Chian weight-standard spread. This is an interesting development, since there is no evidence for a notable growth in the Chian economy, or change in its trading pattern. One advantage of the Chian coinage may have been that its weight was compatible with the Aiginetan standard, which continued to play some role in the Aegean during the fourth century. According to Thucydides, forty Chian tetradrachms were equal to one

[44] Ober (2008): 215 and 217 ff.   [45] Carradice and Price (1988): 92 f.; Kraay (1976): 249.
[46] Horden and Purcell (2000): 216, for the link between Chian wine production and monetization.

Aiginetan mina (Thuc.VIII 99). However, temporary political conditions triggered the particular attractiveness of the Chian standard.

Shortly after the Peloponnesian War some towns on the mainland and islands along the coast of the Eastern Mediterranean produced a common coinage marked with the letters ΣΥΝ ('[coin] of the *syn[machoi]* (allies)').[47] The obverse had a common design – Heracles strangling snakes and the letters ΣΥΝ – but on the reverse each city chose its own type. The coinage was probably the result of a brief alliance formed under the command of the Spartan admiral Lysander at the end of the Peloponnesian War. The weight of the stater was carefully chosen, for it was equal to three Chian drachmas as well as two Persian sigloi. Apparently the coinage was intended to be compatible in both adjacent systems. Yet it also reflects and affected the new importance of the Chian weight standard. Before the federal coinage, the Chian standard had been current only locally in Chios, Ephesus and Rhodes. Immediately after the minting of the alliance coinage, it was adopted by Cos, Caria, Smyrna, Colophon, Iasos and Idyma, Aenos and Thasos. By 375 Abydos, Miletus, Assos, Tenedos, Erythrai and the Persian satrapies joined in; twenty-five years later it had been adopted by the Achaemenid royal mint. Of the over 1,000 coins which have been found in hoards deposited in Halikarnassos *c.* 341/0 BC, all were struck on the Chian standard.

Apart from making the Chian standard more popular, the temporary alliance coinage marks a turning point in the way ancient cities resolved the tension between local and regional identities in terms of coinages. For the first time the alliance coinage was a locally produced coinage, allowing for some local identification with the stamp on the reverse, while transcending local meaning and function by a common type and by its deliberate compatibility with more than one weight standard. The alliance coinage, moreover, was among the first that were produced in combination with civic coinages in the same city; the cities that issued the federal coinage retained their home issues. These civic issues were not even linked to the federal coinage by a shared denominational structure, but circulated independently in what must have been a two-currency system in the cities in which they were produced. In the fifth century, some towns had produced small change while using a more powerful coinage as inter-regional currency. Now, however, even larger communities (such as Rhodes) combined their local with an inter-regional coinage. By the mid-fourth century BC

---

[47] Examples are known from Cyzicus, Ephesus, Samos, Cnidus and Rhodes; see Meadows (unpublished) also for the following; the material and examples can be found in *CH* 9 co-edited by the same author.

Philip II adopted Attic-standard coinage for external transactions, while local Macedonian mints continued to produce coinages on various local standards for internal purposes. Such bi-monetarism, which became the pattern in the Eastern Mediterranean from the fourth century onwards until well into the Roman period, reflects two important developments. Firstly, local monetary networks based on small civic coinages and weight standards continued to exist side by side with inter-regional networks connected through a top currency. Secondly, inter-regional transactions, whether commercial or political in nature, were increasingly conducted by means of such top currencies that were either related to the power of one state, or had some inter-regional political meaning. Examples of the former are the coinage of the Athenians and the denarius of the Romans; an example of the latter is the posthumous Alexander coinages that were minted in all Hellenistic kingdoms except Egypt after the death of Alexander.

CHANGING POLITICS AND CHANGING CURRENCIES

The fourth century saw the transformation of the Greek world from one dominated by independent *poleis* into a conglomeration of leagues and empires. Although civic identities were strongly defended and maintained, autonomy had become more precarious and beyond the control of civic governments. The decline in political autonomy of Greek *poleis* created favourable conditions for the circulation of money and the expansion of monetary networks. In addition, new cities and mints were founded by Alexander the Great, creating new places of production as well as use of the powerful Macedonian coinage. Still, the ease with which Alexander coinage by the end of the fourth century took over the role of an international currency needs explanation. The power of Macedonia is only one factor. Others were the wise decision of Philip II to adopt the Attic standard for his coinage, which made it compatible with the currency with which it competed most. Yet another factor was the great mobility of Greek troops, mercenaries and, eventually, civilians who created close-knit ethnic subgroups in the countries of conquest. The Hellenistic period also witnessed new degrees of monetization as a result of new degrees of monetary taxation, urbanization, mercenary warfare and access to new precious-metal resources.[48] The amount of silver captured by Alexander from the Persian treasury between 333 and 330 BC is said to have been worth 180,000 talents

[48] Von Reden (2007b).

of silver. To give an idea of the scale of this figure, it would have provided metal for 300 years of the estimated annual Athenian production of tetradrachms in the fifth century, which already had been comparatively large. Not all of this treasure was minted into coin; but its impact on coin production – constrained as that was by precious-metal resources – must have been massive.[49]

Let us digress briefly in order to look further at the scale of the change. It has been calculated on the basis of extant obverse dies that between 332 and 290 BC 240,000 tetradrachms of Alexander coinage were struck – with minor coinages, denominations below the tetradrachm and previous issues adding to that stock.[50] The annual revenue of Ptolemy II in Egypt was thought to have reached almost 90 million drachmas of silver (14,800 talents) and 1.5 million artabas of grain (Jer. *Comm. To Dan.* 11.5). The grain revenue is estimated by modern scholars closer to six million artabas, equivalent to a monetary value of roughly 20–30 million drachmas of money, while for the cash income even larger figures could be imagined in antiquity.[51] By comparison, the annual income of Athens from the entire Delian League is quoted by Thucydides as 6,000 talents (36 million drachmas) by the beginning of the Peloponnesian War (Thuc. 2.13.3).[52] Xenophon (*Anab.* 7.1.27) gives Athens' total external and internal revenue at the beginning of the war as 6 million drachmas (1,000 talents), which has been regarded as 'plausible as an approximation.'[53] Moreover, the income from the 2 per cent harbour tax (*pentekoste*) in second-century Delos, which from 314 BC onwards had taken over the role of Athens as the major port of trade in the Aegean, amounted to some one million drachmas (*c.* 170 talents) in the first quarter of the second century BC (Polyb. 30. 31.12). This was equivalent to a monetary value of trade passing through Delos of about 50 million drachmas (*c.* 8,300 talents). The comparable income from the *pentekoste* in late fifth-century Athens was a mere 186,000 drachmas (And. 1.133), equivalent to a trade volume of 9.3 million drachmas (*c.* 1,550 talents). An impression of the increasing volume of money in circulation can also be gleaned from the wealth of bankers in the Hellenistic period (discussed

---

[49] Howgego (1995): 50 with de Callataÿ (1989).

[50] De Callataÿ (2003): 87. De Callataÿ adopts a fairly positive view about the possibility of calculating coin production on the basis of extant dies. For the controversy, see the bibliography in von Reden (2002), n. 46.

[51] App. *Praef.* 10 (740,000 talents); Strab. 17.1.13 (12,500 talents under Ptolemy XII); Diod. 17.52.6 (6,000 talents); Manning (2007): 454–5 for a discussion of these figures.

[52] Thus also Plut. *Arist.* 24.4. Diod. 12.40.1 gives 460 talents, which Thucydides quotes (probably mistakenly) as income at the beginning of the League (Rhodes (1988) *ad* Thuc. 2.13.3 for further discussion).

[53] Rhodes (1988) *ad* Thuc. 2.13.3.

Figure 4: Posthumous Alexander tetradrachm of the late fourth century BC
issued in Miletus

in more detail below, chapter 4). The banking business at Delos flourished
in the third and second centuries BC. Bankers appear among the wealthiest
benefactors of the cities and were given great honours. Philostratos, a native
of Ascalon and banker in Delos around the middle of the second century
BC, was among those residents who subscribed towards the building of a
theatre. He offered two altars in the sanctuary of the gods at Ascalon and
dedicated the northern portico and adjoining exedra in the agora of the
Italians. In turn he was honoured with at least four statues.[54] The Athenian
banker Pasion in the fourth century, too, had been very rich, but no more
than one banker of his standing is known for the entire classical period.

To return to Hellenistic coins, not only the weight standard but also
Alexander's portrait proved so popular that it continued to be produced
on coins after his death. The so-called posthumous Alexander coinages
did not have standard types, but as a rule bore Alexander's portrait on
one side. Some kings started to mint it in Alexander's name, others in
their own. Cities added civic symbols to the field or dated each issue. Of
posthumous Alexander coinages 4,000 varieties are known to date, but all
are recognizably comparable in design and imagery.

Later kings replaced Alexander's portrait with their own, but maintained
the weight standard and general layout so as to facilitate their interchangeability. The posthumous Alexander coinage, though locally produced both
in civic and royal mints, represented an inter-regional currency that symbolized a new form of trans-local Greek identity and at the same time
created a new degree of monetary consolidation in a time of shifting power
relationships and boundaries.[55] It was imitated in Scythia and Arabia where

[54] Andreau (1999): 49, with further examples.   [55] Price (1991): 79.

tribes had a demand for 'good money' without being able to get hold of it in sufficient quantities by means of circulation.[56]

The importance of weight standard for the formation of monetary networks is once again borne out by the fact that Attic-weight coins circulated alongside the posthumous Alexander coinages, while those of other standards did not. The Seleucids tolerated Attic coinages in their sphere of influence, but those of a different weight standard, such as Ptolemaic and Rhodian coinage, are not found there.[57] Outside the Seleucid kingdom, too, the Attic standard dominated coin production. In Syria, Macedonia and the smaller kingdoms of Asia Minor it was continuously used until the end of their dynastic histories. Most cities in Greece and Asia Minor adopted it for their civic and royal coinages. The economic power of Attic-standard coins is illustrated impressively by the large number of Hellenistic coin hoards which are of very mixed composition, but contain exclusively coins of Attic weight.[58]

The posthumous Alexander coinage, in combination with the dominance of the Attic standard, created an unprecedented degree of monetary cohesion in a Greek world now spanning from the Eastern empires into the west. Other weight systems had a more limited circulation pattern. The Chian standard survived along the Western coast of Asia Minor, in the Aegean islands, and on Rhodes.[59] The Aiginetan standard continued to be used in various coinages of Central Greece, the Peloponnese and Crete during the early Hellenistic period. The weight system of the Persian *siglos* was used by Byzantium and other mints in the Propontis, and was adopted occasionally by Phaselis in Lycia and Aspendus in Pamphylia. In the Western Mediterranean the monetary system was dominated by Syracuse and the Greek cities in Southern Italy that now used the Attic weight system. The Carthaginians, controlling the Western Mediterranean economically and politically until the second half of the third century, had a weak monetary tradition and do not seem to have imposed any unified fiscal or monetary structure in their direct sphere of influence in North Africa or Spain.[60] Nor did Roman coinage at first compete with Greek currencies in the Eastern Mediterranean, despite increasing movement of Roman troops and expanding political influence of the Romans.

The Roman denarius began to spread in Italy, Sicily, Africa and Spain from the end of the Second Punic War (214 BC). Macedonia after the Roman conquest, which led to its division into four regions in 167 BC,

---

[56] Mørkholm (1991): 35 f.   [57] Howgego (1995): 52.   [58] Mørkholm (1991): 8.
[59] Ashton (2001) for Rhodes.   [60] Crawford (1985): 87, 138.

retained monetary autonomy. Yet the coinages of the coin-producing regions, though imitated in adjacent Romania and Bulgaria, did not spread into Greece.[61] The increasing re-fragmentation of the Hellenistic empires in the second century BC led to the fragmentation of currencies as well. The Attalid kingdom with its capital in Pergamon produced a new light-weight coinage, the so-called *kistophoroi*, circulating in a closed-currency system similar to, but much smaller than, that of the Ptolemies.[62] In Greece the so-called New Style Athenian coinage gained in influence, above all because of its use on Delos which in 167 BC had been made a toll-free harbour by the Romans. In the second half of the second century BC, New Style Athenian coinage was the only inter-regional currency in Greece, but unlike its predecessor it did not spread much beyond the Aegean.[63]

The re-emergence of regional monetary networks during the long decline of Hellenistc power in the Eastern Mediterranean during the second and first centuries BC once again demonstrates the interplay of local factors with larger political developments. The spread of the posthumous Alexander coinages and the resulting monetary network had been a consequence of Hellenistic empire-building in the late fourth and third centuries. Yet this had no long-term effects.[64] The dominance of particular currencies had been stimulated by the power and prestige of their issuing authorities, on the one hand, and by fiscal pressure, military needs and the demand of capitals and courts, on the other. Inter-regional monetary networks, however, did not last independently of the imperial structures which had sustained them. In particular, they do not seem to have had the capacity to transform economic behaviour in the long term, as the regional economy of Hellenistic Delos seems to demonstrate.[65]

However, Finley's claim that local coin production and idiosyn-cratic weight standards prevented economic integration and inter-regional exchange cannot be sustained. Rather than actively preventing economic integration, they were themselves part of economic patterns that could not be transformed simply by monetary policy. The fact that measures such as the Athenian Standards Decree were extremely difficult to implement or, conversely, that territorial 'closed'-currency systems could be maintained only under special political circumstances, shows the resistance of exchange patterns to top-down interference.

---

[61] Crawford (1985): 128 f.
[62] See above, chapter I; Le Rider (1989) for the currency system of the Attalids.
[63] Mørkholm (1991): 171.
[64] Meadows (2001) for the continuity of regional exchange networks that seem to have continued to exist even when the political situation changed.
[65] Reger (1994); (1997); see further below, chapter 5.

Figure 5: Silver denarius issued under the emperor Tiberius

TOWARDS A SINGLE CURRENCY

The monetary consequences of the Roman conquest and annexations in the Eastern and Western Mediterranean are the best evidence for the tension between local dynamics of exchange and imperial power fostering monetary cohesion. At the time of the Severan emperors in the late second century/early third century AD, the Roman historian Cassius Dio has Maecenas advise Augustus: 'Let no one have currency and weights and measures of their own, but let them use ours instead' (Dio 52. 30). If this was an imperative of the imperial policy of Augustus (27 BC–AD 14), or that of the Severan emperors, it had not been so from the beginning of Roman expansion.[66]

In Italy, Sicily, and Africa the Roman silver currency soon was the only precious metal currency after their conquest. Yet in Greece, despite the fact that the Romans became involved here from the end of the third century onwards, Roman silver coinage does not appear before the time of Sulla (80s BC). In Asia Minor, Roman denarii became current around the late first century BC and in Syria from the time of Augustus. In Egypt, the Ptolemaic tetradrachma continued to be the only valid coinage until AD 296. Down to the Julio-Claudian period the *kistophoroi* of Pergamon and Ephesus remained important in Asia Minor, the drachms and didrachms of Caesarea in Cappadocia, and tetradrachms in Antioch.

In other areas, denarii were the dominant currency, but coexisted with local issues. In Spain, Iberian denarii, which had been minted in a large number of local mints from the second century BC onwards, continued to be in use until the time of Augustus. In Western Macedonia, the denarius began to spread slowly, but was supplemented by silver coins of Dyrrhachium and Apollonia. In Gaul, natively produced silver coinages

---

[66] For a summary of the following, see the introduction in *RPC*: 2 ff.

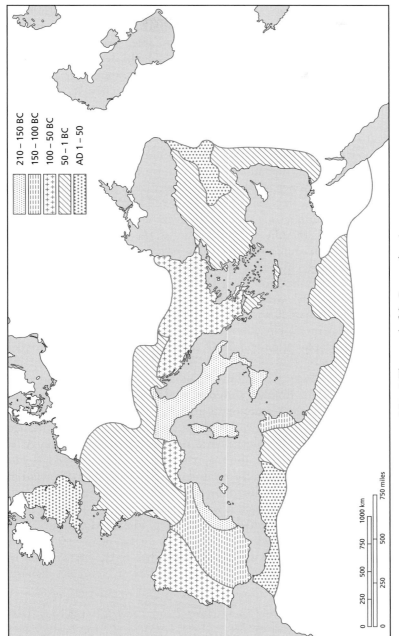

Map 6: The spread of the Roman denarius

210 – 150 BC
150 – 100 BC
100 – 50 BC
50 – 1 BC
AD 1 – 50

continued to play a role, as did surviving British issues in Norfolk and Southern Britain. In addition, many cities minted local bronze coinages, a practice which was both prestigious and profitable.[67]

Although other currencies circulated alongside the denarius, by the middle of the first century BC there was no real currency competition any longer. The Roman denarius began to constitute a top currency. Its exceptional role was due to the monetizing dynamics of Roman military movements, tax regulation, increasing imperial control over currency production, and above all a new degree of mining.[68] Whereas in the first 150 years of Roman expansion it seems to have been impossible for both economic and political reasons to interfere systematically with local production of coins, or centrally to produce money on an imperial scale, these possibilities emerged gradually during the first centuries BC and AD. Michael Crawford has estimated that the number of Roman denarii in circulation increased more than tenfold from the mid-second century to the first quarter of the first century BC.[69] In absolute terms, there may have been as many as 450 million denarii in circulation in *c.* 80 BC as against 40 million in 157 BC. This means that within eighty years more than 400 million denarii had been produced at irregular intervals, averaging 50 million per year. Although absolute numbers must be treated with caution, the figures support the impression that the massive increase in Roman wealth generated by successful warfare and provincial exploitation had direct effects on the monetary economy in the Mediterranean.

Where local monetary traditions remained strong, consolidation alongside the dominant Roman currency was achieved by monetary coordination, that is, the regulation of exchange rates, rather than the total suppression of the local currency. Official exchange rates were introduced in order to integrate old coinages into the new monetary system. As we saw in the previous section, the major silver currencies in the late Hellenistic period were based on three standards: the Attic, the Chian and the Ptolemaic. On the Attic standard, on which the Seleucid coinages in Syria were still based, one tetradrachm was equivalent to four denarii. On the lighter Chian standard, to which the *kistophoroi* in Asia Minor came close, a tetradrachm was equalled to three denarii. In Egypt, where the silver content of the tetradrachm was much diminished in the first century BC, 4 drachmas were reckoned at 1.5, and by the time of Nero, at 1 denarius.

---

[67] Burnett in Burnett *et al.* (1991).   [68] Hollander (2005); Katsari (2008).
[69] Crawford (1969); cf. Hopkins (1980); more recently de Callataÿ (2005a) and Wilson (2002); (2007), emphasizing the increase in Greenland ice core lead as a result of a significant increase in mining activity during this period.

Whether these rates were applied in practice, or officially prescribed, is not entirely certain.[70] In the course of the empire, however, these relationships were subject to frequent change and led to a great degree of uncertainty about the value of money in transactions.[71]

In payments by and to the state, the denarius was usually the official accounting standard even when payments were made in other currencies.[72] In some areas we know that reckoning in Roman units (rather than using Roman coins, as is often argued) was enforced by law. Thus an inscription from Thessaly in Northern Greece refers to a directive (*diorthoma*) of Augustus according to which customs and taxes had to be reckoned in denarii (*IG* IX.2 415, ll.52–60).[73] Similarly, Germanicus laid down for the customs stations in Palmyra that taxes must be reckoned *pros Italikon assarion* (in Italian asses, *OGIS* II 629, 16 ff.). In a subsequent reissue of that law under Hadrian, however, only larger dues were to be collected *eis denarion* (on the denarius standard), whereas those below the denarius were allowed to be exacted in local *kerma* (*ibid.* ll.153–8). Scholars tend to believe that this meant that local coins were unacceptable in the former case. But it is also possible that *eis denarion* and *pros Italikon assarion* simply referred to the monetary standard on which the tax was levied, whereas in practice tax payers could pay in any coinage, provided they paid an agio on top.[74] In some areas local coins were countermarked with Roman denominations in order to be valid for payment. This practice is known from Caesarea where a Greek coin has been found marked with a stamp stating its Roman equivalent of two quadrantes. In Chios, where at one time value marks were put on coins, pieces of the same size and weight were inscribed with either obolos (1 obol) or hemiassarion (1/2 as).[75]

The need of Roman emperors to incorporate, rather than extinguish, local monetary systems into their system, can also be inferred from the *kistophoroi* in Asia Minor. At times of independence, this coinage showed on the obverse the sacred chest (*kista*) encircled by a laurel wreath. In the early decades of Augustan rule, however, Ephesus and Pergamon produced *kistophoroi* with imperial iconography. Instead of the chest, coins now showed a portrait of Augustus and the Roman Pax on the reverse. The change may not even have been prompted by imperial directive but could

---

[70] Wolters (1999): 373, for the former; Harl (1996): 98, for the latter.

[71] Wolters (1999): 371–4.   [72] Christiansen (1984).

[73] Burnett (2005): 176, also for discussion of the following example. The Ephesian Customs Law, sections 25–6 (Engelmann and Knibbe (1989), AD 62), may refer to a practice of taxing the transportation of coined money across provincial borders, but the evidence is inconclusive.

[74] Maresch (1996): 121–7; Gara (1976) for agios in Roman Egypt.

[75] Burnett (1987): 46, for both examples.

represent some kind of voluntary acknowledgement of Roman rule. For the next 150 years, Roman-style *kistophoroi* continued to be minted locally while many other provinces used denarii imported from the Roman mints.

In Egypt, too, local currency was maintained. Since the introduction of the closed currency system under Ptolemy I, the Egyptian tetradrachm had been lighter than the Attic, although a high degree of fineness had been maintained well into the first century despite a perennial shortage of silver.[76] Ptolemy XIII (73–51 BC), however, took the step of reducing the silver content of the Egyptian coins. By the time of Cleopatra VII (51–30 BC), the tetradrachm contained less than 50 per cent silver. These coins continued to be used in provincial Egypt during the Augustan period. Under Tiberius minting of precious metal tetradrachms was resumed, but their silver content was further reduced and a distinctly imperial design adopted. Egypt occupied an exceptional position in the Roman economy, producing much grain for the capital as well as other parts of the empire but not receiving much of its monetary rewards. The economic exploitation of Egypt had worked for centuries on the basis of a currency that was regulated not by circulation but administrative control. There was no reason for the Romans to change this. On the contrary, they expanded exploitation by maintaining the local currency yet reducing its precious-metal content. Augustus is said to have stripped the capital and temples of their silver resources and prohibited any import of precious metal. By the time of Nero, the Egyptian tetradrachm contained a little more than 50 per cent of the silver of a denarius, but continued to be exchanged at the rate of 1:1.[77]

Coin circulation reached an unprecedented scale as an ever-increasing portion of the Mediterranean came under the control of the Romans and their coinage. But the degree of monetary consolidation that was achieved under the Roman empire cannot lead to the conclusion that the economy of the Roman empire was integrated in terms of market prices and production.[78] There has been much debate about the question of what economic integration might mean.[79] There is no unequivocal evidence that there were inter-regional markets for goods, labour, or credit. Even at the level of monetary circulation, the cash flow was interrupted by the limited degree of monetization of some regions where many taxes continued to be collected in kind.[80] The difficulty of policing an imperial currency across the geographical reach of the empire added further problems for a unified monetary system. The Roman government continually legislated against

---

[76] Hazzard (1984). [77] Christiansen (1984): 292–6.
[78] Bang (2008): 93–110; unconvincingly, Kessler and Temin (2008).
[79] Woolf (1992); Howgego (1994); Wolters (1999). [80] Duncan-Jones (1990); Rathbone (1996a).

counterfeit and adulterated coins produced both privately and officially by local mints.[81] On the one hand, official local counterfeiting shows the demand for Roman coins over and above their supply. On the other, it calls to mind that a tremendous amount of administrative energy and regulation is required to maintain a trustworthy currency.

A unified currency facilitated the collection of taxes and, in principle, benefited the flow of coins between Rome and the provinces. But arguably, imperial finance remained decentralized, with most taxes being spent where they were raised.[82] Moreover, local economies were to a large degree based on bronze coinages which were locally produced and accepted only in the area of their production. It has proved difficult to derive a general pattern of coin circulation from the composition of surviving hoards, but some consensus is emerging that, despite the existence of an imperial currency, the predominant circulation pattern of bronze and silver coins was regional rather than inter-regional. The monetary network that was created by the denarius in the first 250 years of Roman rule will have had effects on the economy of the Roman government itself, and on the 'private' economy of those who benefited from public infrastructures and communication lines. Yet it remains open to further discussion whether the Roman currency network was able to transform the Roman economy into a market economy with an empire-wide consolidation of prices affecting local patterns of production and consumption.[83]

---

[81] *Dig.* 48, 13, 1; Wolters (1999): 365–7.
[82] Rathbone (1996a); Wolters (1999): 233 f.; against Hopkins (1980).
[83] Thus most recently Kessler and Temin (2008); see further, chapter 6.

CHAPTER 4

Cash and credit

INTRODUCTION

The largest maritime loan known from Athens in the fourth century BC is 4,900 drachmas. The largest maritime loan attested in Roman Alexandria in the second century AD was equivalent to 1.75 million Attic drachmas.[1] Pasion, the richest banker in classical Athens, is said to have had 300,000 drachmas on loan, which was by the standards of his time an enormous sum (Dem. 36.5). But Seneca in the second century AD allegedly had just in one province an equivalent of 10 million drachmas (40 million sesterces) in debt claims (Dio 62.2.1; cf. 61.10.3).[2] Not only had the ancient economy expanded over the 600 years between the classical Greek and Roman imperial periods, but the financial resources that supported such expansion had also grown. In this chapter we will investigate the changing financial capacity of the ancient monetary economy, looking in particular at credit and other strategies that were adopted to increase the money supply.

For most of the last century scholars have insisted that the ancient economy was both dominated and limited by the use of cash. 'Money was coin and nothing else', Finley wrote in the *Ancient Economy*, and similar were the assumptions of leading historians of the Roman economy.[3] Legal historians regarded it as a fundamental principle that sale was an exchange of goods for cash and that an equivalent to the consensual contract, which constitutes an enforceable agreement without the immediate exchange of goods for money, was unknown until the Roman period. If one of the parties did not perform immediately, a loan agreement had to be drawn up

---

[1] Millett (1990): 189 for the Greek figure; Rathbone (2003) for the Roman figure.
[2] Regular inflation was not above 1 per cent in ten-year periods (Burnett (1987); Duncan-Jones (1994): 25–9; Beyer (1995): 31) so that the increase of the size of monetary loans can be taken as almost real increase.
[3] Finley (1985): 166; cf. Lo Cascio (2003); Harris (2006) for discussion and further examples of this established orthodoxy.

in order to circumvent the principle of cash exchange.[4] One of the most important economic opportunities afforded by money, consisting in the possibility to use it without the deployment of a monetary substance, was thus not much taken advantage of in the ancient world.

This orthodoxy has now been challenged. In contrast to earlier arguments, scholars have brought together many indications that the circulation of money was not just based on coinage. There were, first of all, forms of cash-less payments, ranging from a simple setting off of obligations against each other to the use of written debt claims that could be transferred to third parties.[5] There was, furthermore, a flourishing credit economy that made payments possible when cash was not in hand. The importance of credit for cash exchange had already been emphasized by Friedrich Pringsheim, in a cumbersome legal argument that largely ignored the social and economic significance of it.[6] But credit was not just a legal tool to overcome the complications of cash exchange but a ubiquitous practice that could increase the money supply, if there were proper procedures to recover loans. The fact that the law of debt was among the most advanced in ancient private law, and the great range of formal and informal credit institutions that developed in classical antiquity, suggest that the ancient monetary economy was highly dependent on credit. It became even more so when monetization and contractual security increased.

Credit, moreover, does not only refer to formal loans but also includes the various forms of accrual which might be either the payment of salary after a person has worked for a period, or the advance payment for goods and services that are delivered later (or in instalments). In the ancient world, this applies above all to the delayed or pre-payment of rents and wages, and loans of seeds and tools which were central to many agrarian systems. Construction and textile work, too, was quite regularly given to contractors who received payment in advance in order to purchase labour, material and tools in the course of their projects.[7]

There was, furthermore, a close link between cash and kind. Evolutionists might regard the use of kind for payment as a sign of an underdeveloped monetary or even barter economy. But this view is inapplicable to the ancient world. Payments in kind (especially grain) as well as grain loans had a particular monetary function and developed in close connection with the

[4] Pringsheim (1950).
[5] Harris (2006); Hollander (2007): 31–52; Rathbone and Temin (2008); and already Cohen (1992): 14–18.
[6] E.g. Finley (1951); Millett (1990).   [7] Burford (1969) and von Reden (2007a): 207–27 for examples.

cash economy.[8] Taxation and rent-extraction in kind continued to play a
role in many parts of the ancient world due to the nature of agrarian labour
organization and the high demand for grain as a staple.[9] The medieval historian Marc Bloch once called the distinction between an economy in cash
and one in kind a pseudo-dilemma, and a similar impression emerges from
the ancient world.[10] In Egypt, where we have best knowledge of day-to-
day economic practice in an agrarian setting, there are many examples of
cash obligations converted into kind according to fixed rates of exchange.
Although in principle contractual liabilities were clearly specified as to the
form in which they were to be paid, conversion into another medium
was possible and indeed frequent. There are also examples of accounting procedures which converted cash payments into payments in kind
and *vice versa* despite their different appearance in accounts. Such procedures are by nature under-documented, but occasionally surface in the
correspondence of business partners and accounting details of agricultural
estates.[11]

While there is a growing consensus that complex forms of credit and
cash-less payments were essential to the monetary economy at least from the
Hellenistic period onwards, their implications for the ancient economy are
more controversial. Scholars who have emphasized the importance of credit
and cash-less monetary instruments have done so in a macro-economic
context, wishing to draw out their impact on trade and productive enterprise. In this function cash-less payment was part of, as well as evidence for,
significant economic development especially under the late republic and
early empire. 'It seems that Rome did not miss industrialization for want of
adequate financial intermediation', Rathbone and Temin write; and similarly, Harris concludes that 'shortage of money was not to any important
extent a brake on growth.'[12] Others have been more cautious about the
function of credit and its impact on markets and trade.[13] Here we shall
begin at a more fundamental level by looking at credit and other monetary
strategies from the point of view of their capacity to sustain and increase
levels of monetization. I shall suggest that the normative imperative of
helping friends and neighbours, and an evolving law of debt, had significant effects on monetization. Credit and cash-less payment, while playing

---

[8] Preisigke (1910); Hollander (2007): 61 ff.; von Reden (2007a): 79 ff.
[9] Migeotte (2002): 105; Erdkamp (2005): 219–25; Duncan-Jones (1994): 47–63, for land taxation in
kind in Roman Egypt; (1990): 200 f. for first-century AD Phrygia; 189 f. with Cic. *Verr.* 2.3.174, 194
for first-century BC Sicily; see also Livy 43.2.12 (Spain under the republic); Dio Chrys. *Or.* 38.27
(Bithynia).
[10] Bloch (1967).   [11] Rathbone (1991): 318–32; von Reden (2007a): 118–31.
[12] Rathbone and Temin (2008): 371; Harris (2006): 24.   [13] Millett (1991); Andreau (1999).

their role in trade and commerce, increased the use of money where and when coinage was scarce. Greater legal security for the repayment of loans created favourable conditions for economic development, but an increase in size and number of loans cannot be taken by itself as an indication of economic growth.[14]

An emphasis on the impact of credit on monetization takes away the pressure from the question of the purposes of ancient loans. The problem of whether loans were made predominantly for productive or consumption purposes has dominated the discussion on ancient credit in the last century.[15] According to the neo-classical approach, credit has economic consequences only if it supports investment in productive enterprise such as production for markets and trade. Beyond this function it has limited economic significance. So-called consumption loans that are taken out to cover unexpected deficits, personal expenses or the profligacy of political elites are of little interest in this approach. Outside this approach, however, any credit has economic impact thanks to its capacity of increasing the number of monetary transactions and, in modern parlance, 'consumer spending'.[16] The economy of scale, in which the largest proportion of money must have circulated, will have profited most from the credit structures in which the ancient economy was embedded, but the availability of cash and cash-substitutes to peasants and small retailers increased the possibility and propensity to consume, that is, to satisfy desires via markets and monetary exchange.[17]

THE CULTURE OF CREDIT

The temporary transfer of goods and money was central to the functioning of ancient society. The mass of such transfers were oral agreements between neighbours, friends and relatives and therefore largely escape our evidence. Yet we can glimpse their importance from the discussions of moral predicaments about social behaviour, which have survived from the archaic period onwards:[18]

---

[14] As North and Weingast ((1989): 831) write, ' . . . we are convinced from the widespread contemporary Third World and historical evidence that *one* necessary condition for the creation of modern economies dependent on specialization and division of labour (and hence impersonal exchange) is the ability to engage in secure contracting across time and space.'

[15] Bogaert (1968): 356 f.; 411 f.; Millett (1991): 9–18; 229–32; Cohen (1992): 32–6; Tenger (1993); Verboven (2002): 116 f.; Gabrielsen (2003).

[16] E.g. Andreau (1999): 28.

[17] Morley (2007): 43; de Vries (1994) for consumption as an explanation for the significant economic growth during the course of the Industrial Revolution; see also von Reden (forthcoming).

[18] See above all Millett (1984).

Measure out carefully when you must borrow from your neighbour, then, pay back the same, or more, if possible, and you will have a friend in time of need. (Hes. *W&D* 348–51)

One of the earliest concerns of archaic legislation in Greece and Rome was the settlement of interpersonal debts, and the control over personal security and interest rates. While Solon abolished personal pursuit of debts in Athens (Arist. *Ath. Pol.*6), *nexum* was banned in Rome by the *lex Poetelia* of *c.* 326 BC (Liv. 8.28.18). The laws of the Twelve Tables also lowered interest rates in the fourth century BC (e.g. tables 8 and 12). In Crete, certain items that formed the basis for the survival of the *oikos*, such as looms, iron tools, ox yokes and hand-mill stones, were prohibited from being used as pledge.[19] The collective concern over debts and debt claims was certainly related to the attempt to establish a free citizen body. But within the context of these broader concerns, the mass of debtors constituted a real political force in the early stages of state formation, and cancellation of debts was a major factor in the establishment of social peace in the history of Mediterranean communities. In face of the high variability of yields, a high incidence of crop failure and recurrent food crises, the ideological and (later) political protection of debtors and creditors was the moral corollary of a scarcity of resources dependent on unpredictable factors.

As loans and payments can involve any substance, credit is independent of the development of either money or coinage. The earliest examples of loans refer to food, seeds and agricultural implements (Hes. *W&D* 396 ff., 453 ff.). Such loans could include interest in the form of fixed or agreed sums voluntarily or contractually added to the loan at the end of the lending period.[20] Important steps towards the moral regulation and contractual protection of creditors and debtors were taken before coinage was introduced. Aristophanes still uses *metrein* ('to measure out') in the sense of 'giving a loan' (Schol. Arist. *Ach.* 1021). The terms *daneion* and *daneizein* (loan, lending) were etymologically rooted in notions of gift-giving which encompassed every kind of generosity from the provision of food and hospitality to the transfer of objects and cash.[21] One of the many institutions of social support and shared financial responsibility in classical Athens, the *eranos* loan, had developed from a system of commensality where each diner had to contribute a share (Hom. *Od.* 1.226). In late fifth-century Athens it became a pooled credit system in which each contributor lent a sum of money to help a common acquaintance in need. Its original

---

[19] Willetts (1955): 221.
[20] Millett (1984) for archaic Greece; Menu (1982), (1998) for pre-coinage Egypt.
[21] Millett (1991): 28 f.

function in the context of hospitality remained alive, however (Xen. *Mem.* 3.14.1). By the Hellenistic period, *eranos* was regularly a loan of cash, stripped of its civic ethos, but still typical of friends (e.g. *P. Col. Zen.* I 41 (254 BC); *P. Tebt.* I 112 (112 BC).

Once a cash economy was fully established in classical Athens, money was among the most important things lent and borrowed. Monetary credit operated at all levels of society. Evidence extends from small loans exchanged between city dwellers in Athens (Theophr. *Charact. passim*) to substantial cash loans attributed to status expenses of the political elites (e.g. Ar. *Nub. passim*; Plut. *Mor.* 827 ff. for Athens). In his survey of the purposes of elite borrowing in Rome, Verboven lists warfare, *luxuria*, purchases of houses and estates, building projects, dowries, travel and accommodation expenses, repayment of debts, bribery, unforeseen deficits and business expenses among the most frequently mentioned.[22] While most of these loans were non-productive in the neo-classical sense, they mobilized coinage. The financing of houses, buildings, *luxuria* and warfare involved considerable labour input, transport costs, imports, use of materials and so on, which had a multiplier effect on the circulation of money. We mentioned the impact of Athenian liturgies and *eisphora* on monetization in chapter 2, and it is unsurprising that loans financing financial contributions to the *polis* are among the ones most frequently mentioned in the Attic orators, our main source for economic life in Athens. The nature of the evidence may create a certain bias towards lending for communal benefit, as forensic orators had to persuade a mass audience, but the rhetoric would not have worked if loans for these purposes were untypical.[23]

Athenian *horos* inscriptions provide further evidence for regular lending and borrowing in the city of Athens and Attica. *Horoi* were normally inscribed boundary stones used to circumscribe any kind of reserved space. In Athens between the fourth and early second centuries BC they were also used to give public notice of the encumbrance of property rights over a piece of real estate to which they were fixed.[24] A *horos* inscription usually recorded the name of the estate owner, the value of the debt, and the reason for which the land, garden, workshop or building had been mortgaged. The vast majority of the over 220 extant stones relate to the financial side of dowry provision and upbringing of underage orphans. Either an estate was mortgaged to secure a dowry payment ('dotal' *apotimema*), or it was leased out on behalf of an orphan or underage girl ('pupillary' *apotimema*). It is likely that the hypothecation of real estate served a limited range of

---

[22] Verboven (2002): 153 ff.
[23] Morris (1994) for a persuasive evaluation of the nature of the evidence in classical Athens.
[24] Finley (1952) with Millett (1982).

purposes and does not represent a cross-section of loan transactions in Athens. But it does show that in Athens dowry money of wealthy families often had to be raised by third parties. As dowries were not just saved but actively used as capital for financial activities in the hands of women and guardians, dowries and the assets of orphans played an active role in the circulation of cash in classical Athens.

It is typical of the monetary economies of Greece, Rome and their empires that there were always those who had too much and others who had too little cash. This was not just a question of wealth and poverty but of liquidity problems on the part of the rich. Cicero is known for both borrowing and lending large amounts of money. Thus he writes to his friend Atticus that if necessary he would be borrowing 800,000 sesterces to pay off a loan, since he did not wish to wait to receive the cash owed him by his own debtors (*Att.* 5.1.2). Credit was an economic strategy among the elite. The wealth of affluent Romans was always described in terms of land and debt claims rather than land and cash. Caesar's law of 46–44 BC provided that no more than a third of that part of a senator's property which was situated in Italy (that is, the part that qualified for registration in the census) should be in loans rather than land (Tac. *Ann.* 6.16). Scholars usually quote the law to illustrate political restrictions on lending; but other aspects are equally noteworthy: the relationship between the control over loan activities and the census; the link between land and loans, and the fact that the significant part of senatorial property was in land and loans. Eumolpos, a fictional character in Petronius' *Satyrikon* (first century AD), is made to pretend to have in the province of Africa 30 million sesterces partly in land and partly in debt claims (*Sat.* 117). Seneca describes a fortunate man as one who was 'sowing and lending a lot' (*Ep.* 41.7) and he himself was known for 'spreading estates and equally extensive lending' (Tac. *Ann.* 14.53). Pliny the Younger was more law-abiding, but thought in the same terms when claiming that he was all in landed property, while having some money on loan (*Ep.* 3.19.8). Monetary property was regarded as an asset of wealth only when it was used productively by being lent at interest.[25]

FORMS OF LOAN AND FORMS OF SECURITY

The variety of forms of loans and the way in which they were secured demonstrate the range of credit activities, as well as the concern of

---

[25] This form of productivity, however, must be distinguished from the notion of production loans which refers to loans invested into productive investments; see above, introduction to this chapter.

governments and collective citizen bodies to protect the property rights of a broad social spectrum of lenders and borrowers. A law of debt-redemption surviving from Ephesus in the first century BC distinguishes between several types of loans which may serve as a guide to the range of typical loan transactions (*SIG*³ 742 (85 BC)). We must note, however, that the host of oral arrangements for which no written documents were drawn up were not affected by the law and are thus not mentioned. Yet among the loans fixed in writing there were *cheirographa* (unsecured informal contracts, documented by informal note), *parathekai* (loans secured by pledge), mortgages (secured by land), maritime loans (secured by a cargo of trade commodities) and *homologiai* (loan agreements related to sale and purchase). As in most Western legal systems, there were two ways of securing a loan both in Greek and Roman law: personal security, where an individual or a group of sureties warranted a loan with their property, and real security in the form of an asset of economic value. Personal security was generally preferred by lenders, because of the standing of, and trust in, the economic power of the surety appointed. Yet for present purposes the categories of property deployed for the latter are more revealing.

One type of real security was, as we just saw, mortgage of land and real estate (*hupotheke*). Debtors had to be owners of land, houses, gardens or workshops and, as the size of the loans confirms, were relatively affluent proprietors above the status of landless citizens. The median value of *hupothekai* attested in the Athenian *horos* inscriptions is 750 drachmas, which, though appearing modest by comparison with senatorial loans, in Athens was equal to more than a two-year salary of an ordinary labourer. Possibly, those who mortgaged their land were never expected to pay back these loans, but simply backed up a monetary promise by this loan construction. Or they used it as a financial strategy, hoping to make a profit on the investment of that money. Alternatively, they had assets on loan themselves, or simply paid back in instalments from the surplus of a year-by-year income. Whatever the strategies of repayment, in Athens (though not in Rome) mortgage was a civic type of credit based on the most stable type of property as well as on the trust and communal ideology guiding civic relationships. Not accidentally, temples and demes when lending their funds insisted on landed security, despite the sums often being small.[26] Mortgage was part of a financial strategy backed up by the status of citizens and land as well as being subject to collective control.

[26] Davies (2001); Millett (1991): 171–80.

Related to the *hypotheke* was the *prasis epi lusei* – *fiducia cum creditore* in
Roman Law – which was a conditional sale (*prasis*) of real estate whereby
the seller (and recipient of money) retained the right of redemption (*lusis*)
when he returned the money.[27] It is uncontroversial that *prasis epi lusei* was
a form of loan rather than of real sale, but the motivations for borrowing
money on the basis of *prasis epi lusei* rather than mortgage are uncertain.
Both are attested by the *horos* inscriptions as well as Attic oratory; but
prasis epi lusei – accidentally or not – dominates the *horos* inscriptions,
while *hypotheke* occurs more frequently in oratory. In the *horos* material
sale *epi lusei* tends to involve larger sums (a median value of 1,100 drachmas
as against 750 drachmas for *hypotheke*), but it is likely that the transactions
were adopted in different social contexts of credit. *Prasis epi lusei* (like
fiducia cum creditore) contained some notion of the property actually being
transferred to the creditor (like in a real sale), although in practice it was
not. So the borrower of the money in *prasis epi lusei* could be asked to
perform work as a lessee of the property and pay the rent as interest.
Though keeping possession of the piece of land, and retaining valid claims
to its return, the legal title under which the debtor used the property
changed.[28] *Hypothekai* were more favourable to the borrower than *praseis
epi lusei* in that the borrower retained full ownership of the property despite
its encumbrance. In case of the debt's not being repaid, he did not lose
all claims to the property, but only that part that covered the debt. The
co-existence of mortgage and provisional sale in Athens might point to
different, as well as changing, power relationships between debtors and
creditors, and changing degrees of legal protection of each of the parties
involved.[29]

A third way of securing a loan was the pledge (*enechuron* in Greek, *pignus*
in Latin). In contrast to mortgaged land, pledges were usually transferred to
the creditor for the duration of the lending period. The rights the creditor
obtained over the pledge differed in the laws of Athens and Rome, but in
classical Athens and early Rome only movable property could be pledged.
There is a certain bias of our knowledge towards high-value pledges such
as jewellery, horses, slaves, precious-metal cups and crowns.[30] Anecdotal
allusions to the habits of the poor suggest, however, that it was regarded as
quite common for poorer people to pawn their modest possessions for small
emergency loans (e.g. Aristoph. *Ekk.* 746–55). In Rome, movables pledged

---

[27] Harrison (1968): 271 ff.; Phillipson (1968): 1,230; the contract was comparable to *fiducia cum creditore*
in Roman law.
[28] Finley (1952) [1985]: 25.   [29] Harrison (1968): 263–93 for further discussion.
[30] Millett (1991): 77; Phillipson (1968).

by tenants for unfulfilled rental obligations formed the background to the legal changes attributed to the *actio Serviana* of the mid-first-century BC, while the tablets of the archive of the Sulpicii from Puteoli (first century AD) contain examples of produce pledged by wholesalers and retailers for large and mid-size loans.[31] By the time of the late republic, houses and land could be pledged, whereby the lender received rights of use or usufruct during the period of the loan. The increasing frequency and role of pawning in an expanding range of transactions among an ever increasing social range of borrowers can be inferred from the fact that by the second century AD any *res* (property) that had a monetary value could be pledged (*Dig.* 20.1.9 (Gaius)).

Maritime loans (*nautika daneia* in Greek, *pecuniae traiecticiae* in Latin) were a special form of loan as they were secured by the cargo purchased by the money lent rather than any property extraneous to the transaction. Maritime loans were known in Athens by the late fifth century BC (Eup. *CAF* fr. 43), but details have survived in a number of Attic law-court speeches of the second half of the fourth century BC (Dem. 32; Dem. 34; Dem. 35 and Dem. 56). In Rome they were well established by the time of Cato the Elder (mid-second century BC) who was remembered to have invested substantially in maritime commerce (Plut. *Cat.* 21.6). The loan, made by a creditor to a merchant for a one-way or return trading journey, covered the purchase and transport costs of a trading journey and was repaid with interest from the proceeds of the sale of the cargo. Security for the loan was the cargo bought by the merchant. If the borrower was also owner of his ship, the ship could be part of the security as well. If the cargo (and ship) were lost en route through *force majeur*, the debt was extinguished. Thus the lender carried considerable risk, while the borrower was somewhat insured against the loss of his cargo. Interest rates were very high as a result, ranging well above those attested for ordinary loans (a lump sum of 12.5–30 per cent per journey as against *c.* 12 per cent per year in ordinary loans).[32] In Rome, maritime credit was regularly excluded from regulation of interest (Paulus *Sent.* 2.14.3).[33] In Athens, both citizens and non-citizens could contract maritime loans. The size of the transaction varied according to the size of shiploads and ships. Maritime loans attested from Athens range between 1,000 and 4,000 drachmas, with a median of 3,000 drachmas, while the largest loan, amounting to the equivalent of 1.75 million Attic drachmas, known from the Roman period is a maritime

---

[31] Andreau (1999): 74; Jones (2006): 198 f.
[32] Millett (1991): 189, also for the following.   [33] Millett in *OCD*[3] s.v. 'maritime loan', p. 924.

loan.[34] From the second century BC onwards, merchants are attested as having formed business associations (*societates, koinoniai*) that collectively could borrow more substantial sums (Plut. *Cat.* 21.6; see also *SB* III 7169 (early second century BC, Egypt)). The fact that maritime loans could be made to foreigners and slaves, that they were regularly based on formal written contract and, for some curious reason, rarely were made by bankers add to the special nature of the transaction.[35]

Maritime loans have received much attention in the debate over the ancient economy. Seaborne trade provided a large economic potential in the ancient Mediterranean, given the wide spread of resources and the network of communication created by Greek and Roman cities from the early archaic period onwards. But did it play the same role as maritime commerce did in early modern Europe? And were banks as crucial to the growth of maritime commerce and finance as they were in the late sixteenth and seventeenth centuries? The model of Venice and Amsterdam has long been abandoned for the ancient world. But this role within the total value of credit extended in the Greek cities or Roman empire is still most controversial, as is the involvement of bankers in the transaction.[36] At the root of the controversy still lies the controversy over the value of the neo-classical project according to which market exchange, trade and capitalist finance provide the clue to economic development. In the following I shall explore the possibilities of other approaches.

THE DEVELOPMENT OF CREDIT

We started this chapter by looking at some figures which represent no mere rhetoric: the quantities of money moving around the Mediterranean, in the form of both cash and credit, had increased substantially between 400 BC and AD 200.[37] Compared with the operations attested in Rome some 500 years later, lending and borrowing in classical Athens appear rather simple. Millett's concept of Athenian credit, despite being deliberately anti-modernizing, is still the most faithful to the evidence:

[One] characteristic of Athenian credit operations is the relative simplicity of individual loan transactions, with goods or money being borrowed and repaid in the same way. Obligations arising out of credit sale – deferred payment of goods and services – are rare. Also absent from Athenian sources are undisputed

---

[34] Rathbone (2003).   [35] Rathbone (2003); Cohen (1992): 53 ff.
[36] Millett (1991): 188–217; Cohen (1992): 53 ff; Andreau (1999): 54–6; Rathbone (2003), each with further literature; see also below.
[37] Duncan-Jones (1994): 25–9; Beyer (1995): 31.

examples of credit instruments in the form of promissory notes, cheques and bills of exchange: all transactions were carried out on the basis of cash or kind. One result was the physical transfer of cash and valuables over considerable distances, with all its inconveniences and dangers . . . From the whole of classical Athens, we hear of only three occasions on which arrangements were made to avoid the actual transference of cash (Lys. 19.25–6; Isoc. 17.35–7; Dem. 50.28). In each case, arrangements were *ad hoc* and on an informal basis without any direct involvement of banking institutions. Absence of credit instruments also meant that there could be no creation of credit by banking institutions operating on a limited cash base and issuing paper credit. There was instead a straight transference of resources of purchasing-power direct from lender to borrower.[38]

The reasons for the financial development between the classical Greek and Roman periods are partly external to trade and the monetary economy itself. The expansion of empires and the exploitation of imperial possessions, population increase, population movements, urbanization, changing nature of military recruitment, and the development of larger political units linked by better lines of communication are among the most important factors fostering economic development from the beginning of the Hellenistic period onwards.[39] Access to new precious-metal resources, increasing monetization in the areas conquered by the Greeks or Romans, decreasing costs of regional and inter-regional exchange as a result of larger monetary networks, and probably also changing attitudes to monetary wealth can be regarded as some of the internal factors encouraging monetary development (see previous chapters). Rome began to profit from these dynamics when it came to be engaged in the Mediterranean from the time of the Second Punic War onwards. As Harris writes, Rome, while retaining its agrarian-military economy, had:

become part of a larger Mediterranean Hellenistic-Carthaginian economic system which was different in kind from the economy of Greece before 400 BC and from that of pre-Hellenistic Italy. The links between this world and that of Rome grew steadily stronger as Rome asserted its control over the Greek areas of Southern Italy and over Sicily . . . and even more of course as Roman power spread into the Aegean and Asia Minor. Among the many symptoms of this linkage are the eastwards movement of Italian amphoras, the commercial settlement of Romans, Italians, and their freedmen established on Delos from 166 BC, and the presence of Italian merchants at Alexandria. The most important result of all these Hellenistic ties was arguably the spread of Greek financial sophistication to Rome and Italy.[40]

[38] Millett (1991): 8.
[39] E.g. Morris, Scheidel and Saller (2007); Reger (2006); Davies (2006); von Reden (2007b).
[40] Harris (2007): 513.

Direct evidence for the nature and scale of Roman credit becomes available only from the time of Cicero in the first century BC, but memories of the financial dealings of Scipio and Cato in the second century BC suggest that Roman finance had changed its pace already in the previous century. Cato the Elder was known for having spread credit among an association of fifty traders to reduce risk and accumulate profit (Plut. *Cat.* 21.6). Scipio Aemilianus is said to have had more than 1.2 million sesterces on deposit with a single banker (Polyb. 31.27.6). Details of Roman banking, financial intermediation and credit during the late republic and early empire have thoroughly been re-assessed in a recent analysis by Rathbone and Temin (2008), as well as being the subject of Jean Andreau's excellent volume in the same series as this volume.[41] Instead of rehearsing their results, I shall confront their observations with some material from Egypt in the third and second centuries BC. This will yield important insights into the nature of both legal and financial developments from the Hellenistic to the Roman period. There is a certain leap in time and context of the material we shall be comparing, but many of the financial strategies and legal practices that supported the Roman economy from about the second century BC onwards are well-attested in Egypt a century before.

EGYPT

Egypt has been approached very differently by legal scholars, on the one hand, and social and economic historians, on the other. Greek papyri offer a wealth of insights into contractual law and legal practice, which legal historians have exploited unconditionally as evidence for classical Greek and Roman law. Social and economic historians, by contrast, have been more hesitant to use the evidence from Egypt for Greco-Roman history. In the wake of nineteenth-century categorizations of land and labour regimes, they emphasized the very difference of Egyptian agrarian organization, the lack of private property rights over agrarian land, and the predominance of semi-free tenant labour. Both extremes are ill-founded. From a socio-economic point of view, the difference between Greco-Roman and Near Eastern agrarian organization is much less articulated than was postulated in the distinction between an Asiatic and Ancient mode of production, which was very popular in early twentieth-century social sciences.[42] There was much greater diversity of agrarian organization, land- and labour

---

[41] Andreau (1999); see also Rathbone (2003); Harris (2006); Hollander (2007); Rathbone and Temin (2008).
[42] Introduction in Morris, Scheidel and Saller (2007).

regimes within the ancient (Mediterranean) world, while any presumed Asiatic (including the Egyptian) mode of production was no more different from the ancient than this was heterogeneous itself.[43] It is true that neither royal tenants nor temples and military settlers (cleruchs) endowed with a piece of land enjoyed full property rights over their land in Egypt and the Seleucid empire, which made some difference to economic behaviour and goals. But not only are the forms of land-holding on Egyptian temple estates nowadays regarded as nearly private, but also cleruchic property rights became increasingly stable as well as inheritable in the course of 300 years of Ptolemaic rule.[44] Land planted with vines, oil plants and other fruit trees had always been fully conveyable by means of interpersonal contracts of sale. Under Roman occupation, all royal land became private land, which was a confirmation of the status quo rather than an agrarian revolution. Although the Ptolemaic economy was focussed on royal rather than strictly 'private' wealth accumulation, to the extent to which both were intertwined, there were institutional and legal frames for personal enterprise.

As far as legal development is concerned, both Greek and Roman occupation introduced Greek and Roman law into Egypt without an extinguishing of previous legal practice.[45] Thus although the contractual forms, terminology and legal procedures documented in Greek papyri from Egypt are recognizably Greek or Roman, particular types of contract are known only from Egypt. If they were not invented to accommodate new forms of transaction in a particular social environment and tradition, they received a new degree of significance, and increased in frequency, in the particular context of Egypt. It is not accidental that many credit operations that Pringsheim observed in the papyrological evidence from Egypt are little or hardly at all attested in Greek and Roman law.[46]

The most important difference between Egypt, Greece and Rome is the nature of the evidence that is available. Papyri have survived in the dry conditions of the Nile valley, but not in Athens, Rome or the Greek capital city of Alexandria and the harbours of the Mediterranean coast. One area of intense Greek settlement (and papyrological finds) was the Fayum, an artificially irrigated rural area to the south-west of Memphis. The Fayum was well-connected with the Nile harbours, the cities in the Delta, the capital, and the harbours opening up into the Mediterranean and Red Sea. It was a particular focus of agrarian development, designed

---

[43] Rathbone (1989).
[44] Manning (2007): 451 f.; Vandorpe (2000); Rupprecht (1994): 171 f., for the legal categories of land in Egypt.
[45] Rupprecht (1994): 94 ff.   [46] Millett (1990): 176 f.

to supply the capital and local markets with grain and Greek products, especially wine. So while it was an area of intense foreign immigration and settlement, cash-crop production and marketing, it was not comparable to the urban settings of Alexandria, Athens and Rome. It offers abundant evidence for local economic activity under foreign influence, but illustrates its rural rather than urban development. It would be surprising, however, if practices in the Fayum, so closely linked to Alexandria and maritime sea routes, would not reflect in some ways practices of the capital and harbours as well.

From about the second quarter of the third century BC onwards, when the papyrological record becomes substantial, we find a wide range of well-established credit arrangements. For the present purpose they may be divided into three different categories: (a) monetary loans based on written or oral contract, (b) pre-payment of rents, and (c) credit related to commodity sale.

(a) Best documented, but probably by no means the most frequent form of credit are loans based on written contract (*sungraphai;* compare with the *homologiai* in the previous section).[47] Written loan contracts were formal documents, sealed in the presence of six witnesses, deposited with a *syngraphophylax* (keeper of contracts), and were subject to a fee. Such loans were legally enforceable on production of the written document, and it was this document which secured the loan. Greek military settlers (who often were resident in the local *metropoleis* or the capital of Alexandria), first- and second-generation immigrants, as well as their wives and sisters (represented by a male relative), occur most frequently as contracting parties. The size of the sums lent ranges from as little as 20 to up to 1,000 drachmas. The purpose for which they were used is rarely known. Lender and borrower tended to be connected by neighbourhood, service in the same troop, or country of origin, which, however, did not prevent lenders from charging interest, usually at the official rate of 2 per cent per month, or 24 per cent per annum.

Similar to the formal loan contract were less formal arrangements contracted by *cheirographon* (informal note, see above). The transaction was recorded in an account, but it depended on the nature of the agreement whether the contract was secured further by real or personal security.[48] In some cases, borrowers offered pledges for the period of the loan, in others,

---

[47] For the following, see von Reden (2007a): 151–252.
[48] A particularly good example of an account serving as a record of loans is *P. Cair. Zen.* III 59326 *bis* + *P. Lond.* VII 202 (249/8 BC) with von Reden (2007a): 248–50.

the transaction was made in the presence of witnesses (e.g. *P. Köln* VIII 346 (third century BC), for several different kinds of informal loans). But many such loans are known only through the receipts issued on repayment, letters requesting repayment, or entry into account. Smaller loans up to 100 drachmas dominate the evidence, and they were typically exchanged between members of the same household, employer and employee, business partners, or friends.

A third type of loan was extended by professional money lenders (*tokistai*) and private bankers (*trapezitai*) who acted as pawnbrokers. Records were kept by both lender and borrower. Examples range from small sums borrowed against blankets or everyday clothing to large amounts taken out on security of jewellery, precious-metal containers, gold coins or high-value cloth. The largest loan against pledge attested in the third-century Fayum was based on security of silver articles pledged for 900 drachmas (*P. Lugd. Bat.* XX. 31). Interest rates were high (4 per cent per month, or 48 per cent per annum) even after the interest rate for loans based on written contracts was fixed at 2 per cent by royal decree. Pawn seems to have been the most flexible and in many ways most convenient form of loan, although its costs for the borrower were high.

Only occasionally were loans based on mortgage. A few examples are known from the entire Ptolemaic period, and it seems that they served very specific purposes. For example, any tax-farmer had to provide sureties, who in turn had to provide real security to back up the sum guaranteed by the tax-farmer to the tax revenue office. The sureties had to stand in for any default noticed in the monthly audit, and if they themselves became insolvent their land was confiscated and auctioned off at the end of the taxation period (e.g. *P. Petr.* III 57 (a) and (b)). In other cases, mortgage appears as a fiction in the case that the ownership of a piece of real estate which could not be sold was conveyed as the result of an unfulfilled obligation (e.g. *P. Ryl.* IV 584).

(b) Many loan agreements in Egypt appear as pre-payment in lease and labour contracts. One such type was similar to a mortgage, but constructed as a pending sale (compare *prasis epi lusei* in Athenian law; but there were Egyptian antecedents as well).[49] Two parties agreed to exchange the property of real estate, but in addition to the sales agreement the buyer drew up a contract about the purchase price being held as a loan until the certificate of purchase was provided and the sales tax paid.[50] In the

---

[49] Manning (2001).   [50] E.g. *P. Hib.* I 89 with Rowlandson (1998): 247 f.

case of real sale, this was a plausible way of dealing with the period of insecurity during full payment and transfer of property. But the contract could be used as a loan agreement with the pending sale providing the security for the loan. In this case, the 'seller' held a loan until the notional buyer requested repayment of money or completion of the sale. As in the case of *prasis epi lusei*, it is difficult to understand why the construction of provisional sale was so much more popular than mortgage. It can be assumed that legal tradition and the relationship of the contractual parties are likely to have influenced the choice.

Loans, furthermore, could be combined with a lease contract.[51] Part or all of the rent was advanced in the form of a pre-payment (*prodoma*) and considered a loan repayable when the rent was due at the end of the agricultural year. If the lessor did not repay the loan, the lessee was permitted to continue the lease and retain the yield up to the monetary equivalent of the loan. Loans of this kind were usually contracted for one year, but could be extended for one more if the parties so agreed (e.g. *P. Frankf.* 1). Interest was usually included in the sum repayable at the end of the year rather than being a monthly rate. Most interestingly, this type of contract could be deployed as a financial strategy by people not engaged in agriculture at all. In some of the extant contracts, the lenders were typically second-generation immigrants with no landed property but some financial means. In some cases they can be identified as entrepreneurs specializing in financial activities as well.[52] The borrowers, on the other hand, were normally landowners (*cleruchs*) and prospective soldiers of the Ptolemaic army. Whatever their actual occupation before military enrolment, they were landowners not primarily engaged in agriculture. But neither did the lenders cultivate the land for which they paid rent as a loan in cash or kind. Aristolochos, son of Stratios, for example, is known from several papyri, leasing land and prepaying rents, sometimes individually, and sometimes in partnership with others. He then sublet the land to others who cultivated it and paid rent in return.[53] It is likely that men like Aristolochos acted as intermediaries in several capacities, providing cash as well as grain for sale to estate holders who were commercially active in local towns and the *metropoleis*. Pre-payments of agrarian rents were thus not motivated just by the need of cash; they could have functioned as a financial strategy in the cash economy of Greek immigrants.

---

[51] Geginat (1964): 22–52; Herrmann (1958): 229–335; and Kramer in *CPR* XVIII, pp. 40 ff.
[52] Bingen (1978b).   [53] *P. Hamb.* II 188 and 189; *BGU* VI 1265 and 1268; with Bingen (1978b).

(c) Several forms of pre-payment are known from the context of rural commodity exchange. A frequent practice was the payment of 'earnest money' (*arrha, arrhabon*).[54] The down-payment ensured that buyer and seller stood by their promises, since, when a down-payment had been made, both were required by law to deliver and accept what had been purchased. It may also have served in practice to pay for the costs of transport, tolls, and purchase of material, for example, if a coat was to be made. *Arrha* varied from a small percentage to up to a third of the purchase sum (e.g. *P. Cair. Zen.* 59769, 3). It occurs in connection with a wide range of goods and services, both home-produced and imported, and seems to have been quite a regular institution both in small- and large-scale exchange.

Buyers and sellers could also agree that the price for goods delivered immediately was paid later. Written or formal oral loan contracts were agreed together with, and at the moment of, the sales transaction and regulated what nowadays would be called a credit sale. Conversely, a buyer could pay the full price of a commodity to be delivered later. From a legal point of view, these were ways of dealing with credit sale or sale with deferred delivery, devices that bridged the gap between payment for, and transfer of, the commodity purchased.[55] The latter may have been used to secure produce before the season in which it was available, or buy it at a better price before the harvest. Thus a merchant could buy up wine or grain out of season, or wool still on the sheep (*P. Ent.* 3 and 35). But if we look at the whole range of extant examples, a much wider spectrum of motivations can be identified. In one contract the payment of money against a quantity of wheat looks like an ordinary *prodoma* in a tenancy contract in which the pre-payment was secured by part of the yield (*P. Hib.* I 84). In another, a simple loan of money was made against security of wheat, which was delivered only if the loan was not repaid (*P. Corn.* 2). In yet another case, a large monetary loan was repayable in grain to be delivered at the borrower's expense (*P. Heid.* VI 383). This is not to say that this type of contract could not be used as pre-payment for a commodity. Rather, extant examples suggest that the strategy helped in a number of situations involving both money and produce.

In the wake of Pringsheim's *Law of Sale* the origin and function of credit sale, *arrha*, and sale with deferred delivery has been much debated. Pringsheim argued that they evolved in the context of advanced commerce,

[54] Pringsheim (1950): 355 ff.; Geginat (1964): 15 ff.; von Reden (2007a): 200 ff.
[55] Rupprecht (1994): 119–21.

most notably in Athens, where some equivalent to the consensual contract (a contract not requiring immediate performance by both parties) had to be invented.[56] Millett argued instead that examples of *arrha* and credit sale were almost absent from classical Athens, and rare in Greece as a whole.[57] The very broad range of loans constructed as pre-payment, which we know from Egypt both before and during the Hellenistic period, suggests that the economic significance of these contracts, if not originating, at least considerably increased, in Hellenistic Egypt. They are attested at first not in the context of international trade and urban markets, but in the world of rural exchange where one of their purposes was to compensate for the endemic shortage of ready cash. Just as much as both city and countryside were sites of financial innovation, a wide range of transactions could be regulated by a few principal contractual forms.

ROME

There were two principles of the financial world that seem to have remained unchanged from the classical Greek to the Roman period. The state, apart from providing, testing and regulating the coinage, interfered little with the money supply for markets and individuals. An important exception was the control of interest rates which the Ptolemies limited to 2 per cent per month in Egypt (24 per cent per year), and the Romans to 1 per cent per month (12 per cent per year). Ancient governments also promulgated laws cancelling debts at moments when debt became a political issue. The other principle was that the state provided a legal infrastructure in terms of legislation, prosecution and jurisdiction. Written and oral agreements were subject to rules and regulations as well as being enforceable by public procedures and law courts. In improving procedures of recovering loans, ancient governments created greater security for monetary transactions and private property.

Roman finance, as we mentioned above, owed much to the Greek monetary economy with which they had come into contact from the fourth century BC onwards. Several Latin financial terms were borrowed from the Greek. The early term for bank, *mensa*, was directly derived from the Greek *trapeza*, both meaning table. Other Greek institutions, such as written loan

---

[56] Pringsheim (1950): 268–86; cf. Rupprecht (1994): 119–21.
[57] Millett (1990): 176, with Theophr. *Nom.* fr. 5–6 (Szegedy-Maszak); and Arist. *Pol.* 1259a 3–19. Harrison (1968): 139, for a more optimistic assessment including the evidence from Roman comedy as a reflection of Athenian practice.

agreements (*chirographum* and *sungrapha*) were adopted by the Romans for dealings with foreigners (*Dig.* III.134 (Gaius), though increasingly the distinction between civic and peregrine transactions became irrelevant in practice).[58] In early Hellenistic law *sungraphai* were witnessed loan contracts, while *cheirographeia* were their less formal written counterpart. In Rome, by the time of the first century BC both *chirographa* and *sungraphae* referred to debt claims transferable to third parties. The meaning seems to have been developed from the fact that in Greek *sungraphai* the so-called *kuria* clause stipulated that the document itself, rather than the transfer of money, was proof of the debt.[59] This had gone so far that in Rome loans based on *sungraphae* could be reclaimed by the heirs of a deceased creditor on production of the loan document (e.g. *IG* XII 5, 860, *c.* 75 BC). Yet in a letter to the jurist Gaius Trebatius Testa, Cicero alludes to the possibility that *sungraphae* were also a means of cashing money (Cic. *Fam.* 8.2.2, 8.4.5; 8.8.10 and below). Criticizing Trebatius for his eagerness to exploit financial opportunities in the provinces too hastily he writes:

For you were in a hurry to snatch the money and return home, just as if what you had brought the commander-in-chief was not a letter of recommendation, but a *sungrapha*; and it never occurred to you that even those who went to Alexandria with *sungraphae* have never yet been able to bring home a single penny. (Cic. *Fam.* 7.17.1)

This and some other passages in Cicero suggest that *sungraphae* were used especially for transferring money to provincials who in turn repaid the loan on production of the document to a third party. Thus Cicero alludes in a brief fragment to *sungraphae* which he had written to Greek *negotiatores* (businessmen) who seem to have been able to cash them in the province of Achaia.[60] According to a letter to Atticus, an official envoy of Salaminians from Cyprus in 56 BC had borrowed some 100 talents from Brutus in Rome, a loan for which a *sungrapha* had been written (Cic. *Att.* 6.2.7). In 51/0 BC, Brutus' *negotiator* M. Scaptius wished to reclaim the money on the basis of the *sungrapha* he held as proof of the loan (Cic. *Att.* 5.10–12). Some quarrel arose over the rate of interest, as the *sungrapha* contained an interest rate of 48 per cent per annum, which had become illegal when Cicero had become governor of Cilicia and Cyprus in 51 BC and introduced the usual *usura centesima* of 1 per cent per month. Only through Cicero's intervention, and

---

[58] Rathbone and Temin (2008).
[59] Nelson and Manthe (1999): 516–23; Rupprecht (1967): 42 ff. (*kuria* clause), and 50–8.
[60] Non. 334. 1 L; for the provincial function of *negotiatores* Andreau (1999): 137.

by some good will of the Salaminians who felt obligated towards Cicero, did Scaptius receive the sum he claimed.

The typical form of credit among Roman citizens was the *mutuum* registered in an account under the name *(nomen)* of the borrower/lender. This made the term *nomen* a metonym for *mutuum*. As we saw the Greeks doing in Egypt, Romans recorded loans by entry into accounts of all income (*accepta*) and expenditure (*expensa*) arranged in chronological order. Borrowers could either do the same or take a witnessed statement (*testatio*) of the transaction. Both accounts and *testationes* were valid evidence for a loan in court.[61] Already by the mid-second century BC, it was recognized that *nomina* could be transferred by *delegatio* or *transcriptio* from one creditor or debtor to another (Cat. *De agr.* 149.2). Thereby obligations could be settled without money changing hands. At the beginning of the Civil War in 49 BC Quintus Cicero tried to pay off a loan to Atticus by assigning to him a debt owed to Quintus by Egnatius (*Att.* 7.18.4). In 45 BC Faberius wished to pay off a debt by assigning to Cicero several of his *nomina* some of which, however, were not acceptable to Cicero (*Att.* 13.3.1).

Delegatio referred to the order of a creditors to his debtor to pay the debt to a third party to whom he himself was the debtor. The *nomen transcripticium* was, conversely, a written order of a debtor to transfer the debt to another person.[62] It could also be applied to clear an obligation between principal and agent if the latter had made a payment on behalf of his principal (in this case the reason for the out-payment changed from loan to expense, rather than from one debtor to another). In all cases the transaction required the consent of all parties involved, as the transfer of claims from acceptable to unacceptable debtors/creditors was to be avoided (see above). As the order of *transcriptio* was always made in writing (*litteris*), the creditor did not have to be present, rendering it a convenient paper transaction between exchanging partners. A passage in Cicero's letters to Atticus suggests that *nomina* could also be sold, that is, traded for cash rather than transferred in order to meet other obligations (*Att.* 12.31.2). Harris suggests that by the mid-second century AD the serial transfer of *nomina* was standard practice.[63] In a Dacian document, the transaction is referred to by mere abbreviation (*CIL* III, pp. 934–5, no. V).

A third type of cash-less transfer of money was the *permutatio*, literally meaning the exchange of one thing for another. The transaction has been variously translated as 'barter' or 'written order of payment between banks'

---

[61] Rathbone and Temin (2008): 382.   [62] Gai. III 128–34 with Nelson and Manthe (1999): 198 ff.
[63] Harris (2006): 15.

or 'bill of exchange'.[64] Andreau suggests that it originally involved an exchange of currency.[65] Cicero alludes to the practice several times without explaining it.[66] In all cases, *permutatio* had the function of transferring money over distance and of using money that was in the place where it was needed. Thus Cicero travelling to Cilicia stopped over in Laodicea to collect money owed to him by the government. He refers to the operation as a *publica permutatio*, a transfer of public funds, and the money was handed over to him by the tax-collectors. Subsequently he paid to the *publicani* 2.2 million sesterces, which he had 'earned' during his proconsulate in the province (Cic. *Fam.* 3.5.4).

When sums were transferred for private purposes, no tax-collectors would be involved and other channels had to be used. So Cicero, not in Rome at the time, asked Atticus to give to his son Marcus, who happened to be studying in Athens at the time, his stipend by *permutatio*. Atticus, who had many contacts in Greece, found a creditor who advanced the money to Marcus. The creditor in fact owed money to Atticus, so, by paying the cash to Marcus, he paid off his debts to Atticus. Cicero, on his part, paid over to Atticus rents of houses that he leased in some quarters of Rome.[67] *Permutatio* was thus a procedure, rather than a document or legal claim, involving a network of relationships and obligations built up within the multilateral activities of the Roman administration and its personnel. Although its primary context seems to have been the movement of public resources between Rome and the provinces, and between provinces, there was no reason for individuals not to make similar arrangements if their economic activities had reached a degree of complexity.

Let us pause for a moment and compare Roman with Ptolemaic practice. As in Rome, loans and debt-claims were transferred to third parties, and cash payments were reduced by the use of geographically diverse sources of income. Payments were made on the basis of several arrangements rather than just by the use of cash. Transfers of money could be made by written order, dispensing with the need for all parties to be present. Agents of various kinds created a physical link between monetary resources in different locations, and a sophisticated law of debt created a large degree of security for any of these transactions. There was, however, some development between and within the two periods. First of all, the geographical radius within which these activities took place increased. As has been pointed

---

[64] G. Kießling in *Pauly-Wissowa* suppl. IV *s.v.* Giroverkehr: 696–709; Lewis and Short *s.v. permutatio*.
[65] Andreau (1999): 132; see also Cic. *Att.* 11.1.2.   [66] Hollander (2007): 40 f., with examples.
[67] Cic. *Att.* 12.24.1, 27.2, 32,2; 13.37.1; 14.7.2, 16.4, 20.3; 15.15.4, 17.1, 20.4; 16.1.5; for which Andreau (1999): 21.

out a long time ago, the nature of Roman provincial administration supported giro-transfer of money over huge distances without generating its
full equivalent.[68] Although Roman law provided no security for such transactions, and in no case do we have examples of money being moved or
traded anonymously, money in practice did move across political borders
without the physical movement of coinage. As the radius of the Ptolemaic
administration was smaller, any advantage the administrative infrastructure
provided for commercial business was also more limited. In Egypt cash-less
movement of money was confined to the modest number of closer imperial possessions, which in the third century comprised Syria, Cyprus and
Cyrene, and which in the second century contracted dramatically.

The second fundamental change must be seen in the increasing
anonymity of cash-less transfers of money and credit. Examples of debt-
claims and other cash-less transfers of money in Ptolemaic Egypt extend to
the dealings between administrative offices, banks in adjacent areas, members of the same household, principals and agents in economic enterprises
or agrarian estates, as well as their most trusted associates. Formal loan
documents do not seem to have been transferred until well into the second
century BC.[69] In Rome, by contrast, debt claims could be transferred to
any third party, provided all parties consented. Entry into account, which
in Egypt represented a simple record of loan transactions for creditor and
debtor, became valid proof for enforceable loan contracts in court. With a
greater degree of legal security and abstraction from social contexts operating on moral principles, cash-less payments increased in frequency and
economic impact. In the next sections we shall turn to banks as credit
institutions. We shall begin with some general considerations, returning to
the comparison between Egypt and Rome in the subsequent sections.

BANKING

Banks through their functions of both exchanging and testing coins and
providing credit lubricated the flow of cash. Once again, most scholars
have discussed ancient banks against the commercial background of modern and early modern European banking, thereby obscuring the particular
functions of ancient banks. Ancient bankers fulfilled multiple tasks. They
exchanged and tested coins for a fee, took money, valuables and legal documents in deposit, and discharged from, as well as accepting payments
to, monetary deposits. They extended and mediated loans, most likely by

---

[68] G. Kießling in *Pauly-Wissowa* suppl. IV *s.v. Giroverkehr*, p. 699 f.   [69] Rupprecht (1967): 51.

means of money they borrowed themselves. In Rome, they also mediated the transfer of money from buyer to seller on the occasion of auctions, and in both this and other contexts extended loans against either a pledge or written contract.[70] There may have been further banking services of which we do not know. Conversely, not all banks provided all the services just outlined. Some were specialized in money changing, others in the management of deposits and credit, yet others were present when auctions were held. In Egypt royal banks (*basilikai trapezai*), which were part of the administration rather than private organizations, stored tax money, managed the accounts of tax-collectors and tax-farmers, as well as keeping safe all tax-farming contracts. In the early republic public bankers (*quinqueviri mensarii, tresviri mensarii*) were appointed to deal with emergency situations. Whether the different tasks of banks were as neatly distributed among different types of banks, as Jean Andreau has suggested, is open to question.[71] In Egypt, there are clear indications that some functions of banks overlapped, while others were exclusive to one particular kind of bank.[72]

Banks differ from private creditors in so far as they take funds on deposit for the purpose of making payments to, and accepting them from, third parties. The question of what else ancient bankers were entitled to do with the deposits of their clients is crucial to the question of their economic power. Possibly, bankers were authorized to make loans from any deposit entrusted to them. But more likely, they could lend out only those for which they paid interest themselves.[73] In other words, bankers enjoyed no advantage over other creditors who used their own wealth to advance loans. Quite the contrary in fact; because bankers were normally of moderate to reasonable social and economic standing, their major function was to support the business of people equal to their own standing. It has been asked how bankers could compete against private creditors if they had to pay interest for the money they lent.[74] Considering the transaction costs of private lending and borrowing (finding a trustworthy lender or borrower, mediating and recalling loans, etc.), and the advantage of the reputation, trust and professional skill of a banker, these advantages justified the costs of higher interest rates. Herein lay the major role of ancient bankers in the competitive world of ancient credit.

[70] Andreau (1999): 30–50; Millett (1991): 197–217.
[71] Rathbone and Temin (2008) against Andreau e.g. (1999): 1–8.   [72] Bogaert (1998/9).
[73] Bürge (1987) for the former view; but see Andreau (1999): 41; Millett (1991): 205 against Thompson (1979).
[74] Thompson (1979).

The limited role of bankers in maritime finance adds to the impression that the major function of bankers lay in the provision of a greater degree of security in depositing, transferring and lending money. In Athens, bankers provided to foreigners those services which citizens could regulate through their social ties. Traders' deposits form the majority of bank deposits known from classical Athens.[75] The banker Pasion, moreover, not only looked for sureties to back up loans for traders, but himself stood surety for foreign merchants (e.g. Isoc. 17.43). But no Athenian maritime loan comes from a banker. Millett argued that both the limited financial means of most bankers and the high risk of loss in maritime loans explained the limited role of bankers in maritime finance. Eduard Cohen has contested this position, arguing that the lack of bankers' involvement in maritime finance is an accident of the evidence. There are instead explicit examples of bankers mediating maritime loans between clients, keeping the documents, organizing sureties, and so on.[76] This may well be the case, but it is noteworthy that still in the archive of the Sulpicii of first-century AD Puteoli there is not a single case of a maritime loan, despite the fact that they lived in a harbour town and most of the sums they lent were quite large. The Sulpicii made loans to traders, wholesalers and foreigners, but the particular form of maritime loan was not advanced by the members of the banking clan. Only in one instance was one of the Sulpicii involved as an intermediary in a maritime loan.[77]

A papyrus from mid-second-century AD Theadelphia has also been brought to bear on the question. In this document a banker mediates part of a maritime loan for a journey from Alexandria (*SB* XIV 11850). But the banker, Marcus Claudius Sabinius, or his son of the same name, was also priest and chief civic magistrate in Alexandria. He was a member of the Romanized elite of Egypt and ran the bank for it.[78] It cannot be compared with the majority of ancient banks run by first- and second-generation freedmen. Although the example qualifies a notion of banks never being involved in the big business of maritime finance, it cannot serve to illustrate that they typically were. The large, risk-laden loans necessary for seaborne trade were not normally provided by bankers, although they filled an important function in mediating, and providing safe procedures for settling, the transaction.

---

[75] Millett (1991): 211, also for the following.
[76] Cohen (1992): 160–85, with Dem. 32.4; 32.14 and Hyp. *Dem.* 17 for examples where bankers' involvement in a maritime loan is 'likely'.
[77] Andreau (1999): 74; 71–9 on the Murecine tablets more generally; Jones (2006).
[78] Rathbone (2003): 218.

In order to understand the role of banks, it is important to disaggregate the banking profession in antiquity. Banks were what bankers did. Some co-operated with wealthy private financiers either by mediating between potential lenders and borrowers, or by sharing in loans.[79] Others facilitated payments at a distance by guaranteeing payment to third parties so as to make monetary transactions more reliable, especially when they took place in distant locations. This was important despite not being an equivalent to an early modern bill of exchange, or cheque. In the *Trapezitikos* of Isocrates, for example, we hear that a resident of the kingdom of Bosporus once secured a loan with money deposited at the bank of Pasion. At the same time he wrote a letter to his father at home to repay the loan to the creditor who was about to travel there. The creditor thus had the chance to cash the debt in the local currency of the Pontus region, and not to have to ship any cash for making purchases there. However, he would not have trusted in the letter of credit to the debtor's father, had not the banker issued a guarantee of payment in the case the lender would not be able to redeem the loan.[80]

Bankers operated in various economic and social milieux on which the nature of their business depended. Not all bankers moved in the circles of Marcus Claudius Sabinius, or of the banker of Scipio Aemilianus who in 162 BC paid out from Scipio's account 25 talents (2.4 million sesterces) in one instance (Polyb. 31.27.7). At the most basic level, banks formed a network of trustworthy monetary resources and an alternative to social financial networks. Their wide distribution in cities and towns, their high reputation of honesty, their money-testing facilities, and their superior possibilities of transferring money from one location to another facilitated and thus increased the opportunities for complex monetary transactions.

BANKING IN EGYPT

Banks in Egypt were royal institutions that had the primary function of collecting taxes, royal rents and fines, as well as providing money for administrative and military purposes.[81] Intermittently there existed other types of banks, run by private individuals who were not authorized to manage

---

[79] Thus also the case of the Athenian banker Herakleides in Dem. 33.4 ff. with Cohen (1992): 154–7.
[80] Isoc. 17. 34–5. Cohen's interpretation (1992): 15 f., overstates the case. This is not a 'bank-guarantee of payment' carried to the kingdom of Pontus. Similar cases are described in Lys. 19.25 f.; and Dem. 50.28.
[81] Greek banking in Egypt has been explored in a number of articles by Bogaert collected in Bogaert (1994); see also Bogaert (1998/9), and von Reden (2007a): 253–95 for further comment.

royal income. Evidence for private banks is fairly limited throughout the
Hellenistic period, and their role in the financial life of Egypt seems equally
limited. In the third century, when private bankers needed a royal licence,
their primary role was that of money-changing and collecting the fees from
that exchange. Both types of banks held private accounts and provided
loans to their personal clients. Yet according to the evidence available,
it seems that private bankers were pawnbrokers only, while royal banks
offered loans against personal and landed security. Banks were densely distributed in the tax districts and towns of Lower Egypt, but their number
was dependent on the degree of Greek involvement in the administration
of taxes and rents throughout Egypt.

Royal banks played an important role in the money supply of local
administrations. In particular, they kept tax-farmers' deposits of tax money
which facilitated their monthly audit. In managing the accounts of tax-
farmers and officials, transfer of money from one account to another, as well
as between banks of different tax districts and towns, was regular practice.
Another important task was making authorized payments to contractors of
public work and employees in the administration who drew their salaries
from royal banks in the district. Payments could be made by written order,
meaning that bankers could be advised in writing to pay out from, or accept
money for, an account of a client. Since, however, there is no indication
that payers and payees needed to identify themselves, it is certain that
written orders of payment depended on the personal acquaintance of all
parties involved.[82]

All banking services were available to private account holders. From these
accounts money could be drawn or paid out, and bankers could be advised
by written order to pay out money to an agent or any other authorized
person named in the document. By implication, bankers must have been
entitled to transfer money of their clients from one account to another if
these held money in several banks. Tenants and employees, furthermore,
could either receive wages from or pay rents into accounts at the local
bank, which became important not only when a large number of payments
were made and accepted at a time, but also when payments were made
for, or on behalf of, an absentee landlord. Royal banks also provided loans,
but unfortunately the evidence is scarce. In one case, 100 drachmas were
borrowed from a bank because the sale of wine had not generated enough
money to pay for some honey (*PSI* V 512). Little can be inferred from
this instance, but loans quite clearly were extended by bankers. Another

---

[82] Bagnall and Bogaert (1975).

banker's loan was used to make up a temporary tax deficit in order to satisfy the tax-collector until the arrears were collected. (*P. Mich. Zen.* 32). The most revealing case is a series of communications Zenon exchanged with his banker in Athribis in the Delta. When attempting to borrow 2,000 drachmas for the purchase of donkeys, his agent found that the bank had been emptied by Antiochos, the military commander, when needing money for rations. Zenon sent to a subordinate banker who scraped together the requested sum in a mixed bag of silver and bronze coins. In turn, that banker asked for a favour, endorsed by his superior confirming how difficult it had been to get hold of money. We cannot be sure, but it is most likely that the banker borrowed the sum himself, or acted as broker for the money raised (*P. Lond.* VII 1938, 1942, 1943). What is more, Zenon was well acquainted with all bankers involved, who also did other business for him in the local markets.

There is no indication that banking was an anonymous business making money available to anyone who showed sufficient credentials. More typical than the credit function of banks was their role in handling payments by written order. The bank *diagraphe*, which is also known from classical Athens, referred to the order to receive money only, while *chrematismos*, not attested before the Hellenistic period, was the corresponding term for paying out money.[83] Their most important aspect was that payments made and received in this way were subject to legal execution. Payments had to be acknowledged by a written receipt which in combination with the order served as legal proof for the transactions having taken place. Written orders were a prerequisite for payments at a distance. Absentee landlords as well as other kinds of principals could thus keep control over payments made and received on their behalf in a commercial or agrarian context. A particularly noteworthy example dates to the year 261/60 BC and is mentioned in a letter written to a banker in Syria who appears to be supervising income from grain bought in and exported from Syria, which at that time was an imperial possession where both the king and some of his officials held landed estate. Apollonios, the *dioiketes* (financial minister of Egypt), thus advised Hikesios, the banker:

If any of those exporting grain from Syria advise in writing (*diagrapsousin*) its price or the *parabolion* (?surety payment) to you, please receive it through the bank and for us provide double receipts stating the name of the payer, the amount of money paid, and whether it has been paid in through someone else. (*PSI* IV 324)

---

[83] Bagnall and Bogaert (1975); Cohen (1992) for the *diagraphe* in Athens.

The aim of the instruction seems to have been to keep control over the income received from the sales by various traders. The bank, in combination with the written orders and receipts, functioned as a central place where payments were recorded without the account holders having to be present. The development of this particular role of banks was closely related to an economy in which production and marketing were in the hands of managers and agents rather than primary producers. It supported a system of absentee landholding and business management in which income was entrusted to bankers rather than the agent in charge of the holding. One can see how this function of banks in Egypt developed out of their function as treasuries of the local administration. They provided to personal clients the same services of storing and dispensing money, which was collected and spent by others than the account holder himself, as they did for the royal treasury represented by its local administrators.

BANKING IN ROME

Despite our relatively good knowledge of banking in Rome, Italy, Roman Egypt and some other eastern provinces, its scale both in absolute terms and vis-à-vis elite social networks and professional money lenders (*fenatores, negotiatores*), is difficult to assess. Andreau (1999) suggests that banks contributed substantially to the diffusion of monetary transactions, deposit and credit facilities in places and circles with little access to other social and professional credit facilities. But with some notable exceptions, banking was 'for people of no more than average means'. He concedes that some banks were involved in larger scale finance through their participation in auctions which could involve considerable sums.[84] Harris (2006), by contrast, emphasizes that at least some bankers participated in the affairs of the wealthy. For example, the governmental relief of the credit crisis of AD 33, affecting above all senatorial wealth, was paid out through banks (Tac. *Ann.* 6.17.3). When Herodes Atticus paid 500 drachmas to each citizen of Athens by virtue of his father's will, he too used bankers (Philostratus *Vit. Soph.* 2.1.549). The same bankers also held written records of un-repaid loans advanced by Herodes' father and grandfather. We should add that wealthy landlords in Egypt managed their affairs through banks both in Hellenistic and Roman Egypt, and that the nature of their complex business strategies involving transport and marketing of produce at widely dispersed places relied on bankers' credit.

[84] Andreau (1999): esp. 49.

Rathbone (2008) points to the increasing professional advantage of bank-ing over one-to-one financial intermediation.[85] Bankers, rather than *fena-tores* or non-professional lenders, spurred innovation by adjusting legal principles to financial reality. Ordinary deposits, for example, were used in practice for credit purposes, and subsequently were recognized legally as such. This increased the financial flexibility of those bankers in com-parison to others who left deposits untouched. Paper transactions from one deposit to another, moreover, came to be recognized as loans, since bankers and clients did not record every deposit through a proper con-tract of *mutuum*.[86] Bankers could also by convention make payments on a client's behalf without the client having sufficient funds in his account. The so-called *receptum argentarii* (responsibility of the banker) foresaw that legal claims of the beneficiary lay against the banker rather than the payer.[87] Many bankers, furthermore, were individuals, but some formed *societates* (partnerships) consisting of a group of associates or family mem-bers and appointed agents (e.g. *Rhet. Her.* 2.19; *Dig.* II.14.25 pr.; 14.27 pr. (both Paulus)). Already by the first century BC partners could contribute and profit asymmetrically, and a principal could by verbal or written order give an agent unlimited or restricted competence over transactions, thereby limiting his own liability. Conversely, claims to recover deposits and loans could be made against any partner of a bank set up as a *societas*, not just the one with which the client had dealt (again *Rhet. Her.* 2.19).

Banks, finally, were densely distributed in Rome, Italy and probably beyond, forming in practice a banking system either by the co-operation of different banks, or by the outreach of one firm. The Sulpicii, for example, are known to have been based in Puteoli, but may have had a branch in Pompeii, and were active in Capua, Volturnum and Rome. They also seem to have used another banker, Aulus Castricius, to handle an auction in connection with a debt, because the property of the debtor was in another town. The co-operation of bankers and banks made possible cash-less transfer of money and credit within and between towns, as well as across borders. The jurist Paulus even envisages a loan being advanced by two banks in common (*Dig.* II.14.9).

Comparison between Egyptian and Roman banking, however, is prob-lematic, as the most important type of bank in Egypt, the *basilike trapeza*, combined fiscal, administrative and economic purposes. Bankers were paid officials rather than entrepreneurs working for their own profit. Yet if one

---

[85] Rathbone and Temin (2008): 391–407.
[86] E.g. *TPSulp.* 60–5; and Rathbone and Temin (2008): 400.   [87] Andreau (1987): 597–602.

focusses on their services alone, one notes some significant similarities and differences. Firstly, bankers in Egypt, just as in Italy and Rome, transferred money from one account to another, and between banks, by written or verbal order. Clients, secondly, who held accounts in different banks could draw money in different locations, and it is likely that their bankers, frequently known to each other, co-operated in facilitating out-payments where needed. It is also likely that bankers executed payments for clients by temporary loans, but such will have been friendly arrangements rather than matters of routine.

The credit function of Ptolemaic royal banks was limited in comparison to what seems to have been the case in Rome. Private bankers in Egypt extended loans against pledge but charged exorbitant interest rates. Royal bankers, being public employees rather than private entrepreneurs, had little incentive to concentrate on risky business. It is possible that there were legal restrictions preventing private bankers from making loans against personal security. In no case, moreover, do we hear of banking partnerships during the Hellenistic period. Although partnerships sharing tasks, risk and profit were common in large tax-farming contracts, they were not typical for bankers. There was also some co-operation between bankers for administrative purposes, but not for entrepreneurial reasons. Personal connections between bankers did exist, and helped their clients' affairs, but the majority of business in the Nile valley relied on local monetary resources.

CONCLUSION

A deeply rooted culture of credit, by which the social imperative of helping one's friends, neighbours and fellow-citizens was transmitted, formed the background of an extensive monetary credit economy throughout classical antiquity. Already before money developed into coinage, there was some notion of a shared responsibility for the economic status of individuals as members of a community, while the resolution of debt-crises and settlement of interpersonal disputes remained a political issue from the archaic Greek to the Roman imperial period. Lending and borrowing took place at all levels of society and stimulated the circulation of money where cash was in short supply. The macro-economic impact of such widespread lending and borrowing is controversial. Most scholars in the past have emphasized that ancient exchange was cash exchange, while loans served above all consumptive rather than productive purposes. More recently, it has been argued that credit, cash-less forms of payment and monetary transfers increased the money-supply, especially as forms of contracts and their effective enforcement provided increasingly greater legal security.

In a celebrated article, North and Weingast (1989) suggested that for economic development (or growth) to occur, governments must not merely establish legal security but make a 'creditable commitment' to its institutions. We have seen that there was a considerable degree of legal development in the law of debt from the classical Greek period onwards. A detailed analysis of the question concerning in what ways contractual rights and their enforcement were improved in the course of the Greek and Roman periods must be left to historians of ancient law. It is certain, however, that the legal culture of the Roman republic and empire from the second century BC onwards improved the contractual conditions of credit. In the Hellenistic period, royal law courts may have provided safer procedures than the mass-courts of untrained jurors in classical Athens. Litigation in Athens, as David Cohen has argued, was predicated on long-standing traditions of feud; conflicting parties appropriated the courts to their own ends rather than obtaining a final settlement of the differences between them.[88] Security of property rights in financial affairs was a function of the parties' social standing and the possibility of asserting this standing in front of a mass audience.[89] The question of whether the monarchical regimes of the Hellenistic kingdoms provided a fairer system of private litigation than the democratic procedures at Athens is a field for further investigation. But *prima facie* it seems that, since jurisdiction in royal administrations was entrusted to a small circle of magistrates, contractual rights became less dependent on public negotiation. In the early third century BC, *dikasteria* were established in Egypt for the immigrant Greek population, while native Egyptian cases were treated in special courts (*laokritai*). In the second century BC *chrematistai* ('circuit judges') were established in local districts, dealing with cases of all members of the population in common. In addition, local administrators responded directly to letters of appeal (*enteuxeis*), formally addressed to the king, especially when oral agreements were in dispute.[90] New rules were created by royal ordinances and decrees (*prostagmata* and *digrammata*). The extent to which judges adhered to proper procedure and rules of jurisdiction is difficult to ascertain – individual outrage over unjust treatment is certainly attested – but the establishment

---

[88] D. Cohen (1995): 118.

[89] This was especially so in cases which involved invisible property, such as financial assets; a banking account, rather than assets kept at home or lent out, enjoyed some superior status and thus adds to the intangible services bankers offered to clients; see further Cohen (1992): 191–4.

[90] Rupprecht (1994): 143 f.

of *dikasteria*, local judges, and the right of appeal displayed some concern of the public authorities for the enforcement of private contracts.

The formulary system of Rome, sustained by expert advice of professional lawyers, created a new degree of legal security for contracting partners. The system of appeal that emerged in the early years of the Augustan period and the extraordinary jurisdiction of the emperor and his delegates – which was part of the public display of imperial power – showed that the emperor, more than provincial governors was committed to the principles of justice. It is a question deserving further investigation whether in the *cognitio* system of the imperial period the Roman government displayed the kind of 'creditable commitment' to contractual principles that North and Weingast postulate as a condition for economic development.

CHAPTER 5

Prices and price formation: issues

INTRODUCTION

The amount of price information which has survived from the ancient world is substantial. Although spreading over a great number of commodities and services, and scattered over a number of centuries and locations, in total it forms a considerable lot. In recent years it has been compiled into electronic databases too large to print out or make sense of by cursory reading. Yet what kind of economic information do prices render? The information, for example, that trumpets cost 60 drachmas in Athens at the end of the fifth century BC is as useless in itself as the question of how far a flea can jump.

Several approaches have been adopted in recent decades. On the one hand, scholars have used prices as an index of standards of living. Comparing per capita income and subsistence costs with estimated nutritional needs and the work-capacity of individuals or families has provided some idea of the financial balance-sheet of ancient households.[1] Another project has been to understand the nature of price formation. According to the neo-classical market model, prices settle at 'market' price (i.e. the intersection of supply and demand) and the market for a good is cleared. Were prices in antiquity, too, formed mostly by the market mechanism, or were they more strongly influenced by other factors, such as state intervention, custom or vague notions of normal or 'just' price? What exogenous factors affected prices, such as wars, conquest, army movements, political alliances, questions of upper-class power, or the formation of empires?[2] And were markets 'integrated' at a regional or inter-regional level so that the price of at least some goods settled at a similar level within or across a region?[3]

---

[1] Jongman (2007); Loomis (1998); Rathbone (2009).   [2] Andreau *et al.* (1997).
[3] The question was raised by Hopkins (1980) and was subsequently much debated; see von Reden (2002): 160–5 for a brief summary of the literature. See now also Erdkamp (2005). For a recent, though pessimistic, approach to the question, see Bang (2008).

Scholars have also asked whether ancient authors understood the nature of price formation. Aristotle, for example, suggested a theory of prices, but only within an ethical theory of justice. In order to determine justice in exchange, he defined prices as the monetary expression of the relative utility of the exchange of a good to buyer and seller.[4] Roman authors discussed prices mainly when there were sudden fluctuations in prices and interest rates. Did they understand reasons for inflation, and did they recognize the impact of money in circulation on prices and interest rates?[5] Were governments able to influence the movement of prices?[6] The fact that price rise was discussed only at times of crisis may suggest that there was generally no attempt to manipulate market prices through money supply and interest rates.[7]

The most ambitious investigation of ancient prices was published in 1930, just one year after the Wall Street Crash. In little more than 100 pages Fritz Heichelheim compared prices, wages, rents and interests rates across the Mediterranean and the Near East from the third century BC to the first century AD in order to explore structural change in the ancient economy (which he assumed to exist as such) from Alexander to Augustus.[8] He argued that there was considerable market integration between the Western and Eastern Mediterranean as well as the Near East, as could be shown in contemporaneous price fluctuations and a comparable development of local currencies. Heichelheim's argument was influenced by contemporary debates and especially the neo-classical project of relating prices to the interdependence of markets. Like Michael Rostovtzeff, he pre-supposed that by the Hellenistic period the Greco-Roman world was linked by an international supply and demand mechanism that had spread with the expansion of Greek settlement and culture from Greece and the Near East via Egypt into Africa and the Western Mediterranean. The demand for specialized goods increased, in his view, while the efforts of the Hellenistic kings and courts to intensify production created a tendency for prices to fall.[9] But more than Rostovtzeff, Heichelheim attempted to identify economic cycles, that is, fluctuations in the economic growth trend. At the end of the second century BC, there was a marked, though temporary, recession caused by a combination of political and economic factors, leading to an increase of the overall price level throughout the Mediterranean.[10]

---

[4] *NE* 1121a 21–34 with Meikle (1995); most recently, Amemiya (2007): 151–3.
[5] Nicolet (1971); Howgego (1992); Verboven (1997).   [6] Lo Cascio (1981).
[7] Nicolet (1971); Verboven (1997).   [8] Heichelheim (1930); cf. (1954/55); and (1970 [1938]).
[9] E.g. Rostovtzeff (1935/6): 235–40.   [10] Heichelheim (1930): 74 f; 77; cf. (1970): 39.

Heichelheim's approach has rightly met with criticism in more recent years. Neither his modernizing approach to the ancient economy, nor his conceptualization of markets and comparison of prices across different currency systems matches up to more recent methodological standards. Thus Reger (1994), dealing just with the price data from the accounts of the Apollo temple of Delos, demonstrated that local and regional supply mechanisms, rather than Mediterranean-wide market conditions accounted for price movements in his data set. The island of Delos was not a large-scale importer of grain from distant locations, such as the Black Sea or Egypt, but drew most of its grain from the immediate neighbourhood in the Cyclades; only in exceptional circumstances was grain imported from further afield. Long-term price histories that reveal significant change in the level of prices of olive oil in the late third and mid-second centuries BC do not correspond to Heichelheim's model of economic transformation caused by changing patterns of consumption and production in the Eastern Hellenistic kingdoms. They could more plausibly be explained by changing political alliances of the island with nearby Athens and Rhodes. The price rise in 304 BC, for instance, seemed immediately related to the siege of Rhodes by Demetrios Poliorketes in that year, and prompted the Delians to look for closer sources for their supply of oil.[11] Much price fluctuation, moreover, could be explained by seasonal conditions. Prices of different goods on Delos also did not climb and fall at the same time and thus did not suggest that they were a reaction to economic cycles in the first instance. Prices of olive oil and perfume, for example, had different peaks and falls. As for the price of frankincense, that was not regulated by the market at all, but supplied by other mechanisms which guaranteed a stable price.[12]

To answer questions about market integration and price formation we need to know the nature of our price data. In addition, we need a model that accounts for the nature of price formation, that is, whether production, distribution and consumption levels or some other factors influenced the level of prices. In this chapter I shall first look at the kind of ancient evidence we have in order to be able to explore the possibilities this evidence offers for long-term economic analysis. I shall then outline a tentative model of ancient consumption and production to gain a better understanding of the radius of the supply and demand mechanism at a local, regional or interregional level. Once the conditions of ancient price formation and our

---

[11] Reger (1994): 163.   [12] Reger (1997): 56–8.

data are roughly understood, we may be able to make some sense of price stability and movement in the ancient world.

Despite the large amount of extant price data, any historical interpretation is marred by their uneven distribution in time and place. Equally disturbing is the predilection of ancient authors for certain commodities and services, as well as particular numbers.[13] Literary texts tend to revolve around the social implications of prices, the social power and extravagance of elites illustrated by the cost of luxury goods, prostitutes and fish. Prices of ordinary foods and staples, especially grain, occur mostly when they are noteworthy or abnormal. Thus Scheidel expresses a justified warning about the economic value of price material:

> Owing to authorial ignorance and pervasive number stylization, many of these sources are of little or no use to the economic historian. Their main value lies in their capacity to shed light on ancient practices of symbolic quantification, and on the instrumentalization of numbers for rhetorical purposes.[14]

Documentary evidence offers more reliable information, but carries its own problems. From classical Athens, we have inscriptions recording prices in public sales of confiscated property, prices of sacrificial animals, and prices of pots. As such contexts show, these goods were either sold under special circumstances, or provide evidence for only one commodity within a total price structure that we do not know.[15]

The only places that have left us with a certain amount of usable data are Hellenistic Delos during the time of its independence, and Greco-Roman Egypt. On Delos a board of commissioners (*hieropoioi*) responsible for the financial management of the temple of Apollo recorded on marble *stelai* the annual income and expenditure of the temple for about 145 years (314–167 BC).[16] They gave the rents of houses and estates under the control of the temple, interest payments on loans, income from sales of concessions to farmers, some other regular and irregular revenues, as well as expenditure on payments to contractors, wages to hired labourers, and purchase of goods. The latter were not everyday necessities, which were procured in

---

[13] Scheidel (1996); Duncan-Jones (1997).
[14] www.stanford.edu/~scheidel/NumIntro.htm (30.6.2008).
[15] The literary material of Athens is accessible through www.nomisma.uni-bremen.de, the epigraphical evidence is considered by Loomis (1998), and von Reden in *Der Neue Pauly, s.v.* 'Prices'.
[16] For editions, Reger (1994): 7.

some other way, but supplies for the rituals and maintenance of the temple. This material provides minute detail and, as Reger has argued, reflects ordinary market prices rather than special contractual or social arrangements, state interference, or 'customary price'.[17] Yet the information also raises many problems since the *hieropoioi* published total sums expended rather than prices per unit or wages per man-day. They also tended to omit specifications of quality, volume, size or weight per unit. Moreover, because of the chance survival of the *stelai*, the price data are not spread evenly over the period they cover. Some years are represented by monthly data, while some years or even whole decades are not represented at all. Within the period of 145 years, ten years are represented by three or more usable prices per year in the case of oil (eighty-one in total), eleven in the case of firewood (seventy-five in total) and eight in the case of pigs (ninety-nine in total). For four, perhaps six, years we have prices for almost every month in the year, allowing analyses of seasonal development of prices as well as their annual average. This is a lucky situation, but cautions about the possibilities of generalization. Thus thirty-three of the eighty-one oil prices known by date give exactly the same price; fifty-nine prices deviate from the norm by less than 15 per cent. This suggests considerable price stability. However, five years are represented by fewer than three oil prices per year, providing just ten additional figures in total. Of these only four give the 'normal' price or deviate by less than 15 per cent. The remaining 60 per cent deviate substantially from the picture of stable prices. Statistically therefore, fewer data privilege a picture of greater price fluctuation. Yet it is the normal situation of ancient historians to have fewer rather than many data.

Greater in bulk but less homogeneous is the price material from Greek and Roman Egypt.[18] In contrast to the Delian records, public and private accounts, letters and receipts (many of which surviving on ostraca (shards of pottery)) provide a haphazard assortment of prices from the areas of Greco-Roman settlement over roughly 600 years. Many papyri belong to the dossiers and archives of local administrative offices and private estates, but in total the documentation provides a broader perspective. This is both an advantage and a disadvantage. On the one hand, we are less dependent on the behaviour of one economic agent, such as the boards of *hieropoioi* at Delos. On the other, there is less coherence in the data. Some figures represent or reflect market prices, others are prices paid by administrations for state purchases which may have differed from market prices in ways we

---

[17] Reger (1994): 11f.   [18] Drexhage (1991); Rathbone (1997); for Ptolemaic Egypt, Maresch (1996).

do not know. Some are so-called farm-gate prices, that is, prices for goods at their place of production and thus reduced by the costs of transport and other costs which were added in the markets and harbours. Yet others are internal estate prices granted by landlords to their tenants, labourers and staff. Some represent conversion rates, that is, the rate at which liabilities in kind were commuted into cash or *vice versa*. Indeed, both consumers and producers tried to circumvent market prices wherever possible, so that the majority of our information represents alternatives to any market price. Accounting practices, too, varied from place to place so that the data we have rarely are comparable figures. As in the Delian set, prices for transport come without specifications about the distance covered or the conditions of travel. Rental payments tend not to reveal the quality of the land, the total size of the plot, the amount of additional payments incurred, or the number of taxes added to or subtracted from the rental bill. What is more, although documents were normally dated by day, month and year, in many cases the date is lost, making attribution to any particular year or month a matter of guesswork.

A fundamental problem is posed by the use of different measures of weight and capacity. Grain measures were relatively uniform throughout the Greco-Roman period, but wine and oil were traded in containers of varying capacity. In the Ptolemaic period we have the additional problem of currency changes that make price information across decades difficult to translate into comparable monetary value.

Moreover, large total numbers of data do not mean that they form a usable sample. The fact that 150 prices of wine are known from Roman Egypt means that, at best, one is known for every two years.[19] Wheat prices are represented by forty-five pieces of data for the same period, meaning one in every five years. Yet only two wheat prices are attested for the entire Augustan period (over forty years), and only 35 per cent of the total wine data come from the first two centuries of Roman rule. What is more, seven of the twelve wheat prices known for the first 100 years of Roman occupation, and twenty-two of the thirty-four wine prices from the same period, come from the accounts of one village official. How representative are these data for the economy of Roman Egypt or the economy of the Roman empire, as a whole?

We glean some qualitative information about mechanisms of price formation from the comments by ancient authors. As mentioned in the previous chapter, Plutarch tells us that Cato the Elder encouraged the formation

---

[19] See the sample in Rathbone (1997).

of *societates* of fifty shipowners and moneylenders to spread the risk of lending money for maritime trade (Plut. *Cat.* 21.6). Plutarch represents these partnerships as doing purely financial business on an equal basis. Taking account of a much earlier story, we may argue, however, that they were organized on a hierarchical basis, and that they combined financial with other forms of co-operation, including the spread of information about foreign markets. According to an Athenian law court speech of the late fourth century BC, a certain Dionysodoros and his partner Parmeniskos were prosecuted for violating the conditions of a maritime loan that had been granted in Athens on condition that the cargo was brought there (as was required by city law). Yet instead of fulfilling the contract, they had allegedly taken the money to Egypt and used it for trading grain between Egypt and Rhodes. If the plaintiff tells the truth, they were agents (*huperetai*) of Kleomenes, the governor of Egypt between 332 and 323 BC and in charge of the entire Egyptian grain revenue. In order to profit most from its export, he had set up a consortium (*koinonia*) of business agents who funded, shipped and sold Egyptian grain around Aegean markets:

I would like to have you know that [Dionysodoros and Parmeniskos] were agents and operatives of Kleomenes who was in charge of Egypt. Since the time he took over the office, he has done no little harm to our city, and even more to the other Greeks, by selling and manipulating the prices of grain, both himself and those with him. For some of them send money to Egypt, others sail to the ports, and others who stay in them distribute the import. Moreover those who stay put send letters about the current prices (*kathestekuias timas*) to those who are away so that, if grain is expensive among you, they convey it here, but if it becomes cheaper, they sail down to some other port. Hence not least, gentlemen of the jury, has the grain business been price-manipulated by means of such letters and co-operation. Now when they sent the ship out from here, they left with grain being relatively expensive. That is why they allowed it to be written in the contract that they were to sail to Athens and not into any other port. But afterwards, gentlemen of the jury, when Sicilian imports came and the price of grain dropped and these men's ship arrived in Egypt, [Dionysodoros] straightaway sent somebody to Rhodes to report to his associate Parmeniskos the current conditions at home, knowing that it would be necessary for the ship to put in at Rhodes (Dem. 56.7–10).

As in Cato's *societas*, part of the aim of the consortium was to finance trade. The association was organized similarly in that a wealthy individual was in control of the group. But in addition, the traders under Kleomenes used their social information system for cornering markets. The power of merchants to control prices when acting as a group is well known from Lysias' speech *Against the Corn Dealers* (Lys. 22, 386 BC): corn dealers (resident aliens) combined in groups could buy up more corn for retail than individuals and thus controlled prices in the market of Athens. Was such behaviour, which retailers adopted in local markets, typical of larger business associations, and could they influence effectively the mechanism of supply and demand? Did such companies create a viable network of market information and power across the Mediterranean? We will return to this question in the next section.

SUPPLY AND DEMAND

Goods were distributed throughout the Greco-Roman Mediterranean by a variety of means.[20] Some goods passed through the hands of several intermediaries. Some goods never entered the market at all but were moved directly from the place of their production to the place of consumption. Some goods were requisitioned by the state to be redistributed to urban populations at a special price. What is more, a substantial amount of goods is likely to have been both produced and consumed at home.

Ancient markets were extremely complicated distribution mechanisms, and the fragmentary evidence makes them even more difficult to understand. Only a small proportion of the ancient population satisfied most of their needs regularly via markets. Larger was the number of people who turned to the market for some goods, at certain times of the year, or in exceptional circumstances. This applies to individuals as much as to communities. As the Mediterranean was an agglomeration of ecologically diverse micro-regions, most goods were produced in some variety in all regions, but only particular regions produced special varieties.[21] While most places were self-sufficient in most of their regular needs, local climatic variation, cultural predilection, and taste promoted trade at various levels. Moreover, massive amounts of meat, grain, oil, building materials, clothing, animals and manpower were needed on military campaign, and when festivals took place, buildings were erected and fleets were extended. When the Roman army operated against the Macedonians in 167 BC, for example, private contractors supplied instantly 6,000 togas, 32,000 tunics and 200 horses (Liv. 44.16.4). The value of the supplies has been calculated at 1,150,000 denarii, equivalent to the minimum census of about twelve Roman *equites* (knights).[22] But such extraordinary demand dropped away

---

[20] For the following, see above all Morley (2007); Rickman (1980); Garnsey (1988); Reger (1994); Horden and Purcell (2000); Erdkamp (2005); Bang (2008). Not all these authors would fully agree with the model I am outlining here.
[21] Horden and Purcell (2000).   [22] Badian (1972).

as soon as war preparations were over, festivals or building projects were completed, or funds exhausted.

Historical ecology suggests that one to three times in a five-year period rainfall during the growing season falls below the minimum required for wheat.[23] However, not every crop failure meant a food crisis, and not all crises were relieved by foreign imports. Climatic problems could be highly localized and could even be relieved by dispersed farming, with small plots being located in different micro-environments. Storage and substitute foods helped to buffer against fluctuations of yields, and are regarded as an important response to the vagaries of the Mediterranean climate.[24] Even so, food imports, preferably local but sometimes from more distant locations, became a viable option at least from the archaic Greek period onwards. They increased as seaborne transport became safer during eras of peace, in particular under the rule of one imperial power. Under these circumstances, demand (need satisfied by markets) was a highly variable, unpredictable and politically dependent factor that behaved differently in relation to different commodities, different political situations and different social groups.

It is just as difficult to generalize about the nature of supply. Local supply was dependent on agricultural seasons, weather and sailing season in the short term. In the long term it was dependent most of all on the expansion of urban hinterlands. Both factors were largely beyond the influence of private producers. Responses to changing levels of demand were slowed down by an inflexible production process that could not easily be intensified. Short-term responses to scarcity rather took the form of increased foreign imports on the initiative of governments and private benefactors. In the long term, the productive area of the hinterland could be extended, new areas brought under cultivation, populations resettled; but once again, it required collective – rather than private – initiative. Inter-regional connections of markets across the Mediterranean existed only in the case of 'mega-cities' such as Antioch, Alexandria and Rome.[25]

Markets, moreover, provisioned only a certain proportion of ancient households. Despite some justified criticism of Finley's subsistence model of the ancient economy, it is still reasonably agreed that between 60 and 80 per cent of the ancient population were either rural peasants, or rural tenants and serfs who produced their daily needs at home, or were supplied by their landlords or overseers with necessities, raw materials or seed corn. Exchange was built into all of these agrarian systems, but social support,

[23] Reger (2006): 333 f.; Reger (1994): 102–4; Garnsey (1988).
[24] Garnsey (1988): 43–68; Erdkamp (2005): 155–64.   [25] Erdkamp (2005): 155–96.

loans in cash or kind, long-term storage, etc. were better forms of response to irregular or unforeseen needs than purchase.[26] The quasi self-sufficient, barely monetized household is more characteristic of remote farmsteads than of places close to towns and roads. Form and levels of taxation also affected the economic pattern of rural households. But the just partial involvement of the majority of ancient households in monetized distribution processes provides the backdrop to the more eloquent picture of market exchange that our written sources present.

The situation was different in cities and towns. The fact that, in contrast to early modern and modern cities, ancient capitals and urban centres were sites of consumption and exchange rather than production renders direct comparison of ancient with modern urban markets problematic.[27] And yet, even in the case of the most peculiar town-like structures in Britain and Gaul, material culture points to a notable difference between patterns of production and consumption there in comparison to those in the surrounding areas.[28] At the other end of the scale, large cities, but in particular capitals such as Alexandria, Antioch and Rome, could not be sustained by the resources of their immediate hinterland.[29] The demand of urban elites, civic religious life, imperial governments and administrations, located in urban areas, stimulated the monetized distribution process in the Mediterranean, and provided a dynamic for increasing market exchange.

Armies, temples, and large rural estates cut across the dividing line between city and countryside. Armies on campaign, large estates and temples controlling substantial resources and land were islands of economic behaviour that tied the countryside to cities and promoted urban forms of exchange in rural areas. They provided occasions for large-scale consumption of not just domestic produce, but also goods procured through market exchange. It can be taken for granted that both Greek and Roman armies on campaign supplied their needs partly or fully via local markets, some of which were established just for the time of the military presence.[30] Those armies that were permanently stationed in occupied territory and frontier zones created new levels of demand. At first they may have been supplied by administrative regulation but, as time went on, they created new levels of production and exchange in the areas in which they were stationed.

---

[26] See above, and Gallant (1991): 34–60.
[27] Although Finley's (1981c) model of the ancient 'consumer' city has been qualified in important respects (Hopkins (1978); Osborne (1991); Morley (1996); cf. Morley (2007), any comparison of urban markets must consider the difference rather than the similarity of the economic role of towns and cities before and after the industrial period.
[28] See chapter 2, with Woolf (1993a).   [29] Hopkins (1978); Morley (1996); Manning (2005).
[30] Hollander (1999); Katsari (2008).

Mass imports in the early years of occupation were followed by a gradual shift towards local supplies as domestic production developed.[31] Temples, too, were centres of consumption and exchange independently of their location close to cities or in remote places. They could be large economic units with a differentiated apparatus of staff, a high degree of division of labour, and both land and money to control (see further, chapter 7). For ritual and festive purposes they supplied their needs via regular and, more frequently, temporary markets which distributed both local produce and foreign imports.[32] Large estates also affected rural markets and can be regarded as a major economic dynamic in the countryside. On the one hand, they had an internal payment structure which diminished their effect on local markets. Permanent residents, guests, staff, tenants, employees and friends received free handouts of food from the estate's resources, or set off their monetary wages and rents against payments in kind.[33] On the other hand, estates were centres of cash-crop production as well as consumption of goods that were not home-produced. Surpluses were marketed in the periodic markets of local villages and towns, and via middlemen reached the markets of major cities and harbours.[34] Marketing strategies of large estates could differ substantially, but there is little positive evidence that they by-passed the local markets close to where they were situated.[35]

State interference in the prices of staples suggests that markets were not regarded as reliable distribution mechanisms under all circumstances. Officials in charge of market control (*agoranomoi* and *aediles*) under normal circumstances were concerned with law and order rather than fair prices in the market place. However, governments and private benefactors who at times of crisis subsidized the import and sale of staples, especially grain, could temporarily fix prices and thus interfere with the supply-and-demand mechanism. In fourth-century Athens, there was the general rule, enforced by a board of *sitophylakes* (grain wardens) in the Piraeus and the city, that un-milled grain was to be sold fairly (*dikaiôs*) in the market, and that both miller and baker sold flour and bread in a fixed proportion to the price they had paid for the wheat (*Ath. Pol.* 51.3; cf. *SEG* XXVI 72.18 ff.). Interference with the supply-and-demand mechanism could be intensified in times of crisis, as was the case in 386 BC when no retailer in Athens was permitted

[31] Morley (2007): 576; Thompson (1999).
[32] Migeotte (2004): 109–10; de Ligt and de Neeve (1988) with e.g. *LSCG* 67, 26 f. (fourth century BC), I.Ilion 3 (third century BC); *SEG*³ 38, 1462 (AD 124/5).
[33] E.g. Rathbone (1991): 160–4; Erdkamp (2005): 114–18; von Reden (2007a): 138–44.
[34] Shaw (1981); Rathbone (1991): 278–318.
[35] Morley (1996): 159–80; de Ligt (1990); Erdkamp (2005): 118–34.

to add more than one obol per *medimnos* to the wholesale price of grain, or buy up more than 50 *medimnoi* a day (Lys. 22). During the severe food crises which affected most Aegean cities between 330 and 326 BC, traders were forced by law to bring their grain to Athens in order to keep prices down.[36] In addition, both Greek cities and the city of Rome supplied grain to urban consumers either regularly or in case of emergency. Some Greek cities in the fourth century BC established special funds and officials (*sitonai*) who ensured that emergency grain was purchased quickly for resale at an acceptable price. The Roman government fixed the price of grain sold in the city of Rome under the scheme known as the *frumentatio* or *cura annonae* (corn dole). Monthly rations were distributed in reserved places to a fixed number of recipients on production of a ticket of entitlement (*tessera*).[37] Despite its recognized indirect effect on food prices in the markets of Rome – emperors were under pressure to compensate merchants and farmers if they changed the scheme – the *cura* was sold at a price not made in the market.[38] The Ptolemies, moreover, controlled the distribution and price of oil in Egypt. *Nomes* which had a high productivity had to export surplus oil to *nomes* with insufficient local production, while differential prices were fixed for different *nomes* and for Alexandria.[39] Governments or market officials could also fix prices in order to influence tax income and their own profit. Thus, once again, the Ptolemies held the monopoly of the right of distribution of certain products (oil, beer, linen, lentils and many more), which were sold to licensed retailers at a fixed price (*P. Rev.* 38–56 = Austin (2006): no. 297). A Delian law of the second half of the third century BC, moreover, forbade selling wood and wood products at a different price than had been declared to the officials in charge of the 2 per cent harbour tax.[40] It is thought that, rather than protecting consumers, the law aimed to prohibit undervaluation of imported goods at customs, which would have led to a reduction of the city's income. Several official schemes collected in the Ps.-Aristotelian *Oikonomika* are related to the manipulation of retail prices for the benefit of public or royal treasuries (e.g. 2.33; see also 2.7, 2.17). Price controls are also known in relation to temporary markets held in connection with festivals and games. Here, too, tax revenue must have been at least one motivation, as it was in the interest of market officials and tax collectors to fix retail prices. According to a famous inscription from Oinoanda in Lykia, the *agoranomoi* in charge of the market set up on the occasion of a festival endowed by a benefactor were given the right, by

---

[36] Garnsey (1988): 16; and 154–62, also for the following.
[37] Rickman (1980): 156–97; Erdkamp (2005): 240–4.   [38] Suet. *Aug.* 42 (Augustus); Tac. *Ann.* 2.87.
[39] P. *Rev.* 60–72; Sandy (1989).   [40] *Syll.*[3] 975, with Reger (1994): 173 f.

the benefactor, to fix the price of any merchandise which was sold (*Syll*³ 1462.60 (AD 124)). In Andania in Messene, by contrast, the *agoranomoi* of a festival market held in AD 92 were forbidden to fix prices. But they were asked to control weights and measures.[41]

There were thus different distribution mechanisms in capitals, in cities, in rural areas, in places where armies were stationed regularly or temporarily, and so on. There were different degrees of state interference, depending on the nature of the commodity as well as on the status of consumers and producers. Different degrees of monetization and the variable degree to which households relied on markets must also be taken into consideration, if one wishes to understand the conditions of price formation in the ancient world. Important distinctions must be drawn between local, regional and inter-regional price mechanisms. As we saw in chapter 3, monetary networks were predominantly regional, rather than local or inter-regional. Prices fluctuated temporarily for local climatic reasons, because of the movement of armies and troops, and because of a range of political reasons that affected maritime transport. While it remains an important task for research to explore the capacity of ancient markets, our current knowledge suggests that other conditions than inter-regional economic cycles affected the level of prices in the ancient world.

INFLATION

Well into the third century AD there was little real increase of general price levels in any part of the Greco-Roman world.[42] Between the time of our first evidence of payment in monetary units in Rome and the mid-third century AD, annual inflation is reckoned to have been no more than around 1 per cent. The figure is calculated on the basis of the prices of wine and wheat, army pay, public wages for building, private wages for harvesting and digging, as well as the hire of transport donkeys in Egypt.[43] Occasionally governments decided to make an upward adjustment of taxes and public fines, which seems to have been a response to an increase in general levels of prices. We will see below that at the end of the third century BC the level of penalty prices in Egypt was increased by a factor of two and a half, which reflected a combination of currency change and (possibly) some additional change in the grain prices. In Rome a whole series of fines which had been expressed in asses during the fourth century BC were in the second century

[41] *Syll*.³ 736; Migeotte (1997): 40 ff. for both examples.   [42] Duncan-Jones (1994): 34.
[43] *Ibid*.: 25–8; Rathbone (2009).

Table 1: *Wheat prices in Rome, third century* BC *to first century* AD[44]

Date	Price per modius	Grs silver/ton	Reference
250 BC	1 as	66	Plin. *NH* 18.17
210 BC	25 asses	1,650	Polyb. 9.11a.3
203 BC	4 asses	264	Liv. 30.26.5–6
201 BC	4 asses	264	Liv. 31.4.6
200 BC	2 asses	132	Liv. 31.50.1
196 BC	2 asses	132	Liv. 33.42.8
123 BC	1.6 HS	226	Cic. *Sest.* 55
c. 100 BC	2 dr = 8 HS	1,130	DH 12.1.12[45]
64 AD	3 HS	424	Tac. *Ann.* 15.39

BC reassessed at the same number of sesterces. As the sestertius was then worth 2.5 asses, this meant an increase of 250 per cent.[46] At the same time the monetary property qualifications for Roman citizens entering the class of senators or knights were adjusted in the same way. Normal wheat prices in Rome, if we can judge from the few data available, might also have doubled in the second century BC and doubled once again between the mid-first century BC and the mid-first century AD (see table 1).

A certain degree of regular inflation can also be inferred from the disappearance of small coins within the Roman monetary system. In the second century BC the smallest coin was the sextans (one sixth of an as); by the first century BC it was the quadrans or one quarter of the as. By the second century AD this denomination was replaced by the semis valued at one half of an as. The shift from one sixth to one half of the as roughly confirms the three-fold increase of normal prices of wheat suggested by the price data between the second century BC and mid-first century AD. During the same period there was also a shift in the coin unit most commonly used from the as to the sestertius (a four-as piece), representing a four-fold loss of purchasing power of Roman coinage.[47] Although price inflation of 400 per cent may seem high, a four-fold price rise over a period of 400 years renders the annual rate negligible.

Increasing military pay (both per soldier and in aggregate terms), the outflow of precious metal in subsidy payments and trade, combined with a notable decrease of mining activity in the Roman empire, led to massive

---

[44] Rathbone (2009) with Szaivert and Wolters (2005).
[45] Inferred from DH's report of a fifth-century BC grain crisis in Rome; Rathbone (2009).
[46] Burnett (1987): 108.
[47] Burnett (1987): 109. In *c.* 130 BC the number of asses per denarius was changed from 10 to 16.

pressure on Roman coinage from the third century AD onwards.[48] By 270 AD the silver content of the imperial silver currencies had declined to about 1 per cent. Yet the effects of this debasement on prices in the Roman empire, and whether it had any effects at all, are still highly controversial. It has been argued that the continuous debasement of coins led to an increase in the supply of coinage in circulation, and thus to an increase in prices and military pay, which in turn affected prices. Others have suggested that, when the government debased the coinage in order to increase its quantity, it simply aimed at maintaining the amount of money needed. Local economies became increasingly monetized under Roman rule and demanded silver coinage.[49] In Egypt prices of wheat, wine and donkeys remained largely stable up to the 270s.[50] Price inflation followed eventually because the population lost trust in the currency, rather than because of an oversupply of coins.

What could cause price increase and inflation in the monetary economy of antiquity? Many scholars have developed their arguments either implicitly or explicitly against the Quantity Theory of Money. According to this theory – also formulated in terms of the well-known Fisher Equation – prices rise when the stock of coinage and the speed of its circulation increase, while at the same time the amount of goods in supply remains constant, or declines.[51] In a simple application of the Quantity Theory, disregarding the supply of commodities as well as changing speeds of circulation, prices are expected to have risen whenever large amounts of coinage were poured into circulation. This may have happened, for example, when Alexander captured the Persian treasury, or when the Romans siphoned off the gold coinages from Macedonia, Carthage, Egypt and Gaul in the course of the first century BC.[52] Even a one-off donation of money to 50,000 soldiers after the battle of Raphia in 217 BC has been made responsible for price rises by more than a factor of 60 at the end of the reign of Ptolemy IV in Egypt (222–204 BC).[53] But such arguments ignore important factors in the equation, which cannot be assumed to have remained stable. For example, it is quite likely that aggregate demand (in terms of needs satisfied by the

---

[48] Burnett (1987): 112–21; Howgego (1995): 121–31; Harl (1996): 125–37; Rathbone (1996b); most recently Katsari (2005); for further literature, see also von Reden (2002): 158 f;

[49] Katsari (2005) and (2008).

[50] Rathbone (1996b) and Wolters (1999): 409 f. against Corbier (1985).

[51] According to the Fisher Equation, it is P (Prices) × Q (quantity of goods) = M (money) × V (velocity of its circulation). The quantity theory underlies Corbier's (1985) explanation of the third-century crises in the Roman empire, as well as Cadell and Le Rider's (1997) explanation of the monetary crisis in Egypt during the third and second centuries BC.

[52] Howgego (1992) for some of these examples.   [53] Cadell and Le Rider (1997).

market) tended to respond to an increase of money available, which in turn increased together with the demand for coinage and the supply of goods distributed via the market.[54] The stability of prices over long periods of time suggests that local demand and supply kept pace with increasing monetization and coin supply. From all that we know about ancient monetary economies, a lack rather than an oversupply of species was the more endemic problem, leading – as I argued in chapter 4 – to a certain degree of under-monetization met by lending and borrowing or a combination of cash and kind as media of exchange. In local areas, governments returned to local minting of small change, or countermarked coins, henceforth circulating at a new value. This could lead to a confusion over exchange rates and the 'true' value of legal tender, and thus to a loss of confidence in its stable value.[55]

For the price inflation of the late third century AD an all-encompassing monetary explanation is so far not possible, and probably also not the way forward.[56] What is needed is a convincing model of the interdependence of politics, the nature of various local and inter-regional economies, and the currencies circulating in the Roman empire. There is still no consensus about whether the inflation was due to the political transformation of the empire, to the impossibility of controlling a single Roman currency against local bronze coinages, to an empire-wide economic crisis, or to the particular manipulations of the central Roman currency that had been taking place in the last half of the century. In particular, we need to know (a) whether the political transformation led to increasing monetary disintegration and difficulties of controlling a single currency; (b) what changes affected the supply-and-demand mechanism in local and regional markets so as to make prices rise, and (c) whether a decreasing amount of goods were distributed via markets, as currency value, credit and market conditions became unattractive to traders.

---

[54] Meissner (2000); also Hollander (2008): 132, within the context of an alternative approach to the conditions of coin circulation in the late republic.

[55] Katsari (2005): 274, for Roman Asia Minor; Wolters (1999): 410, for the loss of trust in the exchange value of gold coins.

[56] For a summary of debates until *c.* 2001, see von Reden (2002); and Hedlund (2008).

CHAPTER 6

Prices and price formation: a case study

INTRODUCTION

In order to substantiate both the propositions and reservations I have
expressed in the previous chapter, I wish to present in the form of a case
study the price developments in Egypt from the third to the first centuries
BC. In the case of grain prices, a reasonable amount of information has
survived, which permits investigation in serial form.[1] The corpus of wheat
prices from Ptolemaic Egypt comprises some 100 figures. Most belong to
the period between *c.* 275 and *c.* 80 BC, that is, from the reign of Ptolemy
II Philadelphos to the death of Ptolemy XII Soter II. Important periods of
economic change during the early period of Ptolemaic rule under Ptolemy I
Soter and the very end of this rule under Kleopatra VII are not represented
in these data. Not all information, moreover, is equally useful for economic
analysis, and several prices just duplicate each other. Moreover, despite the
relative wealth of information, we have to bear in mind some fundamental
problems.

The first problem addresses the question of generalization: Is our material representative of prices in Egypt as a whole? The largest proportion
of Greek papyri containing price information comes from areas of Greek
occupation in the Fayum and the adjacent areas of the Oxyrhynchite
and Herakleopolite *nomes* in Lower and Middle Egypt. Although markets and coinage were not totally absent from the less Hellenized areas
of Upper Egypt, levels of urbanization, population density and economic
organization – in short, the conditions of price formation – varied considerably. Especially the southern regions of the Nile valley continued to
be dominated by a land tenure regime where the distribution of surplus
was likely to have been different from the practices we know from the

---

[1] Wheat prices in Roman Egypt have been explored above all by Duncan-Jones (1976); see also Mrozek
(1975); Rickman (1980); Corbier (1985); Rathbone (1997); Drexhage (1991); and, most recently, Kessler
and Temin (2008).

Greek papyri.[2] Even within the areas of Greek occupation our evidence tends to concentrate on the activities of a fairly limited range of social groups. These include military immigrants endowed with a piece of land (*cleruchs*), their agents, local administrative officers, civil immigrants of the Ptolemaic and pre-Ptolemaic period, and the military. They formed a social in-group and provide a partial picture of a more complex social reality.

We have to ask, secondly, what differing prices in our sample represent. The information we have spreads over several generations and belongs to different locations within the *nomes* we mentioned. Rarely can we tell whether a cluster of high or low prices is the result of short- or long-term variation. Accidents of the evidence that we are unaware of, or some monetary change that is not known, add further uncertainties to the analysis of change. Prices, moreover, were subject to individual negotiation, conditions of sale and its location. Market prices were higher than farm-gate rates where the buyer carried the costs of transport and risk of the journey. So-called penalty prices (for which further below) were fixed by the government in compensation for unfulfilled rental obligations in kind and thus are likely to reflect prices conceived of as normal or typical. Yet their variation over time in private contracts may not reflect directly changing levels of market prices, but varying degrees of state control over private contracts. Contractors at different times might not have felt equally compelled to follow government regulations.

A third factor that affects the interpretation of our data is the question of the money supply. We know that Egypt was heavily dependent on foreign resources for the minting of bronze and silver coinage, which strongly influenced its monetary and mint policy from the early years of Ptolemaic rule onwards (see above, chapter 3). By the late third century BC, very few transactions in silver are attested in the countryside, while the state made internal and external payments in bronze coinage. The fact that the Romans continued to use Ptolemaic coins in Egypt until the reign of Trajan further suggests that the Egyptian coin supply remained precarious. How the supply of coinage and monetary metal influenced prices and monetary behaviour is open to question, as we just saw. Yet rather than abandoning quantitative projects altogether, it is more helpful to pursue them in the light of a range of uncertainties and include these in the discussion.

---

[2] Manning (2003); Muhs (2006), for monetary taxes in Upper Egypt.

THE NATURE OF THE DATA

The range of prices that we will consider can be divided into three categories.[3]

1. Wheat prices recorded in accounts, or letters relating to market transactions.
2. Conversion rates of cash into wheat and wheat into cash, recorded in contracts or accounts.
3. Monetary penalty prices payable in lieu of grain for un-fulfilled rental obligations in kind.

Conversion rates are grain prices adopted for the conversion of an obligation in kind into cash or *vice versa* (*adaeratio*). There were standard conversion rates which may even have been fixed officially in order to regulate the payment of obligations towards the government. In the mid-third century, such a standard or official rate of conversion was two drachmas per artaba of wheat. Yet individuals could agree other rates, depending on whether the grain payment was to be collected from the threshing floor, or elsewhere, and whether prices were converted in the market, or within a labour contract where payer and payee belonged to the same household or estate; employees on large agricultural units could usually convert their cash wages into grain at very favourable rates.

The penalty prices (*epitima*) of category (3) also provide a special kind of price information. Penalty prices were standardized or iconic prices, believed to be the normal price and taken by the administration to give a monetary value to a payment in kind. They come from lease contracts, and occasionally from loan- or sales-contracts in kind. If a debtor failed to discharge the obligation on time, the creditor could ask for a penalty payment to be stipulated in the penalty clause of the contract. Parties could agree either that the obligation in kind be increased by 50 per cent, or that a cash equivalent be paid instead. In the case of the latter, there were two options. Either the debtor agreed to pay the price for the grain that was current in the market at the time when the obligation was due; or he agreed to pay a penalty price, which was generally an official rate

---

[3] Heichelheim (1930) derived wheat prices from two further categories of evidence: wheat prices derived from sales and penalty prices of barley and olyra (Egyptian emmer); and wheat prices derived from the conversion of taxes that were paid sometimes in cash and sometimes in wheat. But both are unreliable, indirect sets of data. An exception is the price series in table 6, No 23, which gives the wheat equivalent of the median price of olyra of that year at the conversion rate of 2:5. Because this is based on an average of several prices over a period of time, it is more likely to be linked to the general price level of wheat in that year.

fixed by the government for contracts with the state. In the third century BC, it seems to have been twice the amount of the official conversion rate of wheat into cash, that is four drachmas per *artaba* (*P. Col.* I 54 (250 BC)). It is important to emphasize, however, that the official penalty price was not twice the current market price, and that contracting parties were free to agree other penalty prices as well. Only in those contracts where the parties had agreed that execution should be 'according to the rules of the king' (*praxis kata to diagramma*, or *hōs pros basilika*), can we be sure that the official rate was applied. As we see from table 7 in Appendix 1, penalty prices could vary. This is likely to reflect an adaptation of the official penalty price to a change of general price levels, but there is no reason to exclude the possibility that some of these variations represent an individual rate adopted just by the contracting partners. Because penalty prices only indirectly reflect market prices of grain, they must be treated separately from them.

Sales prices, penalty prices and conversion rates represent three different kinds of price that have a different relationship to the market. Although they were anchored in notions of current market prices, they are likely to have responded differently to short-, mid- or long-term change.

DIFFERENTIATING THE DATA

Sale prices

The category of sales prices at first seems to be the most relevant for the question of market integration. Of the entire sample of price information (tables 6 and 7 in Appendix 1), they form just one quarter of our total of prices, or 23 data (figure 6).

Unfortunately we lack sufficient information to differentiate the data within this group. In particular we would like to know some surrounding factors in order to eliminate variations that have other than economic origins. Grain prices of category (1) varied according to season, location, and conditions of sale, that is, variables that need to be corrected for before comparison over time. Six categories can be distinguished within this group:

1. pre-harvest prices
2. post-harvest prices
3. prices paid by the administration
4. market prices
5. prices paid on the threshing-floor ('farm-gate prices')
6. prices paid outside the Fayum.

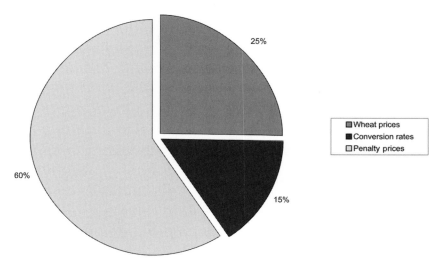

Figure 6: Relative proportion of attested price information from third- to
first-century Egpyt

Different market conditions and transport costs determined prices, for
example, in the capital Alexandria as opposed to the *chora* (Nile valley);
and possibly different degrees of monetization and market development
affected price formation in Upper as opposed to Lower Egypt, especially the
Fayum. The Fayum was monetized to an exceptional degree, as well as being
closely connected to markets in the Delta, Alexandria and the Mediterranean coast. This means that prices in the Fayum can be treated in the
same way as those that we happen to have from other areas in the Aegean.

Seasonal variation

There are two examples of seasonally specific sales prices in our sample
(nos (4) and (27) in table 6 Appendix 1). The harvest in Egypt started
in late March/early April; thus the prices (in March and on 16 March
respectively) are likely to represent higher than average prices within the
agrarian year. However, the same document ((27) = *P. Tebt.* I 112, (113) and
112, (118)) mentions payment for 'this year's grain' which suggests that new
grain already was, or would soon become, available. In Egypt, moreover,
seasonal variation of cereal prices seems to have been relatively slight. If
similar rules applied to wheat as to olyra prices, the degree of seasonal price
variation in Egypt within one year can be taken from the graph (figure 7).

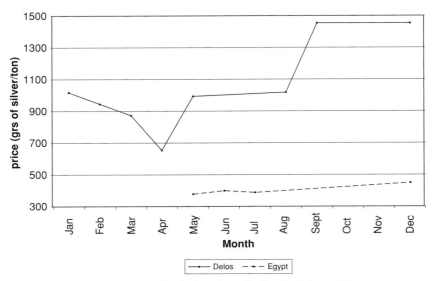

Figure 7: Interannual variation of cereal prices in Delos and Egypt

In comparison with the seasonal variation of cereal prices on Delos, it was moderate.

Regional variation

We have two documents relating to Alexandria (table 6, (2) and (12)), which indicate, unsurprisingly, significantly higher wheat prices in the capital than in the *chora*. We have also one price from Thebes in Upper Egypt (table 6, (29)), showing no particular difference from price levels in the Fayum and adjacent areas. This is somewhat surprising, since, in Duncan-Jones's analysis of wheat prices in Roman Egypt, the median average in Lower Egypt is twice the median average of wheat prices in Upper Egypt.[4] Such price discrepancy might be reflected in the lower penalty prices from Thebes in 109 and 108 BC (table 7, (39) and table 7, (40)), but yet lower penalty prices are attested in the Arsinoite, Herakleopolite and Hermopolite nomes ((22) and (24)–(26) in table 7). There is thus no positive evidence for regional price variation between Upper and Lower Egypt in our sample, although it is quite possible that it may have existed.

[4] Duncan-Jones (1976): 243.

Official grain prices?

We have two figures for official grain purchases by a local tax office ((25) and (27) in table 6). But both belong to the same dossier representing the activities of Menches, a village clerk in Kerkeosiris in the Arsinoite *nome*. It may be significant that the price of 2 drachmas per *artaba* comes from a time when official penalty prices oscillated around 3 to 5 drachmas (table 7 (22)–(31)). So 2 drachmas might reflect the 'normal' price which the government set for the conversion of debts in kind into cash. But the documents reveal nothing about special conditions under which grain was purchased by public officials.

Location of sale

How can we distinguish between market and farm-gate prices? In very few cases is it clear from the context that it is market prices that are being mentioned. Table 6 (2) and (12) explicitly refer to current prices in Alexandria, while (4), (13) and (34–6) relate quite unequivocally to market prices in the *chora*. For the rest, however, the distinction is difficult. Can we infer that if a named individual (that is, not an anonymous marketer) occurs in an account as recipient of money for grain that this grain was not exchanged in the market? This would be a quite untenable assumption. Do sales prices entered in accounts belonging to the Zenon archive, which as a large agricultural unit had a large amount of surplus production to distribute, normally refer to farm-gate prices? This would be an equally untenable assumption, because we know that surplus was sold in a variety of ways both on the estate and in markets. To take, furthermore, exceptionally low prices as farm-gate prices would lead us into tautologies. We are bound to conclude that there is often no way of identifying precisely the conditions of sale among the sample of prices we have.

Conversion rates

A fair number of our prices are not real prices at all but conversion rates of wheat into cash, or cash into wheat (15 per cent, or 14 in total). Documents (6) to (8) and (15) in table 6, all belonging to the Zenon archive, represent the practice of private employees converting their monetary salary into payments in kind at an 'internal' rate (see also (14), (33) and (34)). Documents (5) and (9), belonging to the same archive, represent the rate at which the manager of the estate himself converted a cash sum into wheat equivalent.

Documents (26) and (28) represent the practice of converting cash salaries into wheat by a local tax office. It is notable that these conversion rates were very similar to those on a semi-private estate. Moreover, conversion rates remained remarkably stable over a period of 150 years, which is an important observation to be kept in mind. No distinction, furthermore, seems to have been made whether a landlord, employee or tenant commuted cash into kind: there were apparently no 'privileged' rates. It should be noted, however, that interpersonal conversion rates negotiated between individuals, tended to be lower than the official rates applying to wages and contracts. They were also below the rate of current market prices.

Penalty prices

Penalty prices (*epitima*) form the largest category of attested prices (60 per cent, or 54 in total). During most of the third century BC *epitima* remained stable at 4 drachmas per *artaba*, representing the official conversion rate of wheat into cash of 2 drachmas per *artaba* of wheat. In about 220 BC, however, the penalty rate that had been applied for at least eighty years climbed to 5 drachmas, representing a conversion rate of grain into cash of 2½ drachmas. Soon afterwards penalty prices were raised further to 10 drachmas. However, the increase is likely not to reflect a real price increase, but was a nominal increase related to a monetary reform (see next section).

The fluctuation of the official penalty prices is variously suggestive in relation to market prices. First, penalty prices were related roughly to current market prices and responded, if slowly, to changes of this price (in 220 BC and possibly in the middle of the second century). Secondly, there was a great stability of wheat prices over a period of two and a half centuries. One might perceive a slightly increased volatility in the mid- to late-second century. However, this might be an accident of our evidence, or a reflection of temporary currency changes that we do not know of. It may also be the result of a lesser degree of state control over *epitima* in private contracts. There is not sufficient ground to regard these variations as indicative of changing market conditions. Thirdly, there may have been an increase of market prices by the late third century BC.

CREATING A TIME SERIES OF PRICES

In order to compare prices over time and place, local weight and currency systems must be translated into comparable units. One method for translating ancient units into a cross-cultural system is to use modern metrological units of weight. In the case of cereals this means that measures of capacity must be translated into measures of weight. However, different varieties of cereals, as well as the same variety grown in different regions, have a different weight per volume, and we need to rely on modern experiments to get an idea of the difference.[5] Cereals also have a different weight/volume relationship depending on whether they are sold before or after sifting and winnowing. In Egypt, cereals could be sold in either condition. In a Ptolemaic grain account, for example, $2\frac{1}{2}$ per cent is added to the price when the grain was sifted before sale.[6] There were also different measures in use in different parts of Egypt and its imperial possessions. The *artaba* used most commonly in the Arsinoite *nome* measured 40 *choinikes* (1 *choinix* c. 1.08 l), but *artabas* of different capacity are attested in other texts.[7] Contracting partners sometimes distinguished as to whether a payment was made in the 'receiving' (*dochikon*) or in the 'paying' (*anelotikon*) measure, the former containing 42 as opposed to 40 *choinikes* of grain (e.g. *P. Tebt.* I, 11 and *P. Lond.* VII 1996, 40). Rents in kind were usually raised in the paying measure, but when grain was purchased and sold, it was done so in the receiving measure. Any 'difference in measure' (*metrou diaphoron*) was accounted for in terms of a 5 per cent surcharge on the price.[8] In order not to complicate things further, and since the majority of our prices come from the Arsinoite *nome*, I shall assume for all prices an *artaba* of 40 *choinikes* representing roughly 40 litres or 30 kilograms of Egyptian wheat (note, however, the exceptions table 6 (10); and table 7 (1) and (25)).

According to conventional understanding, the Egyptian *artaba* was c. 20 per cent smaller than the Attic/Delian *medimnos* containing 48 *choinikes* of the same size as the Egyptian *choinix*. Foxhall and Forbes (1982), following the metrological system proposed by Hultsch (1862), calculated the *medimnos* of wheat at 40 kilograms with a *choinix* of 1.08 litres equivalent to c. 840 grams of wheat. An inscription from the Athenian agora has called this calculation into question, however. According to this inscription, the Attic *choinix* was equivalent to just 623 grams of wheat, rendering the weight of grain contained in an Attic *medimnos* quite similar to that of the Egyptian *artaba*, that is just over 30 kg.[9] Since, however, Egyptian wheat was bulkier than the variety grown in Attica and the Aegean, Attic and Egyptian measures which were equivalent in volume were not the same weight. As the difference, on current understanding, was within the range of 25 per cent, this might explain the difference in weight, but not in volume of the Attic *choinix* of grain on the one hand and that of the Egyptian on the other.

[5] Foxhall and Forbes (1982).   [6] *P. Lond.* VII 1996, with editorial comments.
[7] E.g. in *P. Cair. Zen.* I 59004, 16; *P. Loeb. dem.* 3, 11.
[8] Best examples come from the Roman period; see Rowlandson (1996): 242–3.
[9] *Agora* inv. I 7557; no. 26/*RO* 26; and Rosivach (1998).

Table 2: *Ptolemaic and Attic currency standards in the third century* BC

Ptolemaic currency standard

1 stater (4 drachmas)	14.3 g	(multiplied by 1.25 => Attic silver stater)
1 drachma (6 obols)	3.6 g	(multiplied by 1.15 => Attic silver drachma)
1 obol (8 chalkoi)	(0.6 g)	(bronze coin)
1 mina (100 drachmas)	(357 g containing 27.8 g gold)	(gold and silver coin; silver:gold = 13:1)
1 talent (6,000 drachmas)	(22.42 kg)	(unit of account)

Attic/Delian currency standard

1 stater (4 drachmas)	17.4 g	(= 5 drachmas of Ptolemaic currency)
1 drachma (6 obols)	4.36 g	(= 1 drachma 1 obol of Ptolemaic currency)
1 obol (8 chalkoi)	0.728 g	(bronze coin)
1 mina (100 drachmas)	(436 g)	(unit of account)
1 talent (6,000 drachmas)	(26.196 kg)	(unit of account)

Translating different currency systems into comparable units is even more problematic, as Egypt was affected by several fundamental monetary changes during the late third and first centuries BC. In order to create some comparability, the monetary unit of a drachma must be converted into the amount of silver (measured in grams) contained in the stater of the coinages.[10] This conversion can serve as a heuristic tool only, since the real value of silver coins depended in Egypt for some time during the period under consideration on a fluctuating market price of silver. By conversion into grams of silver we simply create a common denominator for comparing prices across currency systems.

During the late third to late second century BC, moreover, no silver currency was used in Egypt for the payment of grain at all. While some prices were reckoned in silver, all were paid in bronze coinage (if paid in coinage at all), while the bronze coinage had a flexible relationship of value to monetary units reckoned in silver as well as to the value of actual silver coins. There is much debate over the interpretation of the currency changes in Egypt. Here we will apply the model, developed by Maresch (1996), with the qualifications I made in von Reden (2007a). The relationship between the third-century Ptolemaic currency and the more widespread Athenian standard is summarized in table 2. The changes within the Ptolemaic currency during the second century are summarized in table 3.

---

[10] This does not include the considerations of different degrees of fineness, nor of different silver prices, but as silver coinage in the classical Greek and Hellenistic period seem to have been evaluated by its weight standard, rather than fineness and the price of silver, these aspects do not seem to be relevant here.

Table 3 *Currency changes in Egypt from the late third to first century* BC

Period 1: (*c.* 220–*c.* 200; Ptolemy IV)
→ *1 silver drachma = 2 bronze drachmas*

Period 2: (*c.* 200–*c.* 180 or later; Ptolemy V)
Bronze currency is tariffed at the conventional relationship of value between bronze and
silver metal of 1:60:
→ *1 bronze drachma = 1/60 of former silver drachma*

Period 3: (*c.* 180–164/3; Ptolemy VI)
Value relationship between bronze and silver metal increased, or value of bronze coins
retariffed at 50 per cent of their former value:
→ *1 bronze drachma = 1/120 of former silver drachma*

Period 4: (164/3–*c.* 130; Ptolemy VIII):
Value of bronze coins further decreased by 50 per cent
→ *1 bronze drachma = 1/240 of former silver drachma*

Period 5: (*c.* 130–30; Ptolemy VIII–Kleopatra VII)
Bronze currency linked to silver currency again, but in a new relationship of value:
→ *1 bronze drachma = 1/120 of silver drachma (but also 1/60 of silver drachma)*
→ *1 drachma (bronze or silver) no longer a quarter of the stater ('tetradrachma') but 20 silver
drachmas are counted to the stater*

Using the metrological scheme and the model of currency changes proposed, the graphs of figures 8 to 10 can be drawn. They reveal that wheat
prices remained fairly stable over a period of 200 years. Where there are
sufficient data about wages for us to glean some understanding of their
development over time, the data suggest that their relationship to grain
prices remained equally stable: in 257 BC, for example, an *ergates* (worker)
earned 1 obol a day, buying 2 *choinikes* of wheat at 2 drachmas 2 obols
per *artaba*. In 182 BC an *ergates* earned 20 drachmas daily, again buying 2
choinikes of wheat at 160 drachmas per *artaba*. In 94 or 61 BC an *ergates*
earned 120 drachmas as a daily wage, buying 2½ *choinikes* of wheat at 2,000
drachmas per *artaba*.[11]

ECONOMIC CONCLUSIONS

Heichelheim argued that there was an increase in the purchasing power
of the Greek drachma during the first half of the third century, causing
prices all over the Mediterranean to fall. Towards the end of the century
purchasing power decreased, either because of an increase in production,
or a decrease of liquid capital caused in turn by the movements of capital

[11] Maresch (1996): 191–4, for a list of extant data.

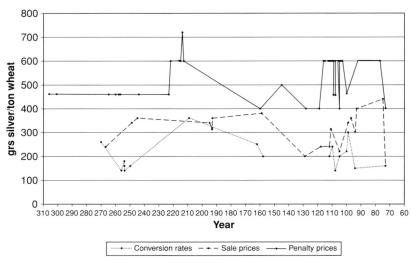

Figure 8: Egyptian wheat prices differentiated by category

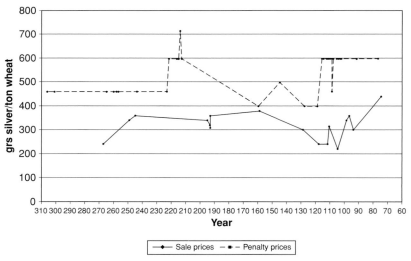

Figure 9: Sale prices in comparison to penalty prices

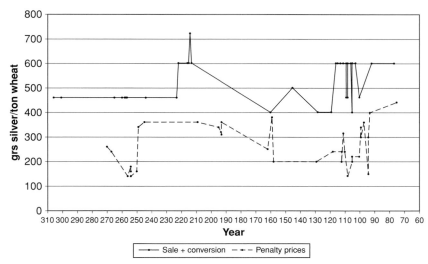

Figure 10: Sale prices plus conversion rates in comparison to penalty prices

beyond Egypt, or substantial hoarding of money within the country (for which, incidentally, there is no numismatic evidence). The dynastic crises and local revolts in the second century, moreover, destabilized prices further.

In light of the foregoing discussion, and the qualification of the material produced in tables 6 and 7 one must be more moderate in drawing conclusions for economic history. There are simply too few *comparable* data for creating a generalizing model. If, however, between the third and first centuries BC there was some population increase, as is arguable in light of the growth of the capital Alexandria, Greek immigration, agricultural improvement and increase of the cultivated area, price stability over two centuries can be regarded as indicative of an increase in economic performance. Increasing aggregate consumption was met by an increase of aggregate production that filtered through to the population relying on grain purchased in the markets of the *chora*. Price stability can also be taken as an indication of a high degree of internal market integration. But the data from Egypt are too few to distinguish market forces from what might have been just a strong notion of normal price, which did exist throughout the Ptolemaic period and made prices settle and resettle at a certain level. The stability of governmental conversion rates and penalty prices over long periods of time presupposes that grain prices might have been similar throughout the country and that they should have remained similar over longer periods of time. Conversely, state conversion rates and fixed penalty prices stabilized perceptions of what the price of wheat should be.

One might further observe that there was a slight but general increase in real and iconic prices of about 25 per cent by the end of the third century, as is reflected in the long-term increase of the penalty price from 4 to 5 drachmas from that time onwards. The most significant change, however, might be a more intense fluctuation of prices in the second as compared to the third century BC. This might be a reflection of the troubled currency, or of our lack of understanding of what really happened from one year to another. But it is also possible that the greater variation of wheat prices is a reflection of increased monetization that predictably leads to a greater volatility of prices, as these are affected increasingly by market forces rather than custom and perceptions of normal price. The problems of the silver currency, and the corresponding increase of bronze coinage (in terms of aggregate value) that seems to characterize the currency development from the end of the 220s BC onwards, need not be the fatal consequence of the enormous (or excessive) expenditure of Ptolemy III – as our moralizing literary sources would have it. But they may well be equally, and more plausibly, the result of an increasing demand for coinage in face of increasing monetization and limited silver resources.

EGYPTIAN PRICES IN THE LIGHT OF MEDITERRANEAN PRICE INFORMATION

The price series from Hellenistic Egypt may be compared with the prices of wheat from classical Athens and Hellenistic Delos (tables 4 and 5 in the Appendix 1). As very few data have survived under very different circumstances, only the most general observations can be made. In Athens, both price data and explicit statements convey that there was a firm notion of the 'normal' price which governments and benefactors aimed to maintain, or re-establish, at times of crisis. Both honorary decrees and the orator Demosthenes praise individuals who imported grain at times of crisis in order to achieve a return to the normal price of grain. Such normal price seems to have ranged between 5 and 6 drachmas per *medimnos* of wheat, and 3 to 5 drachmas per *medimnos* of barley. These prices lie significantly above those attested in the Egyptian *chora* during the Hellenistic period, but only about 15 to 20 per cent above those attested for Alexandria (e.g. (2) and (12) in table 6). The prices are comparable to Delian summer prices, but the inter-annual variation of the Delian price material also puts into perspective the Athenian emergency price of 335 BC (which is just over 50 per cent above the Delian winter price of wheat). Still, it is noteworthy that in Athens substantial deviation from the normal price occurred, reaching up to three times the normal level. In the Egyptian papyri, price variation of no more than 20 to 30 per cent is represented in the extant material. This may be due to the general agrarian wealth of the region, and the ability to compensate for crop failure and poor harvests by means of import (above all from nearby Syria) more effectively than in either Athens or Delos. Comparison with Athens, however, renders it more plausible that Kleomenes of Naucrates, governing Egypt during the 320s BC, tampered with a grain price which had climbed up to three to five times the normal price in the *chora* (see table 6, no (0)). Equally noteworthy is the fact that the normal price of wheat in Athens and other Greek cities remained as stable as the normal price level in Egypt between the third and first centuries BC.

The data from Delos reveal above all the extent of inter-annual variation of wheat prices in the market of, most probably, imported grain (see above). An increase by as much as 60 per cent of the summer price during the winter months may have been considered quite normal. In Egypt, no more than 20 per cent price difference between summer and winter prices is attested (figure 7). The difference can easily be accounted for by the fact that a market of imported goods is generally more volatile than local markets. Incidentally, the great inter-annual range of wheat prices on Delos may also explain why a benefactor could be praised for selling imported grain at just 50 per cent above the normal price (*IG* II/III² 408). But beyond the observation that prices in Athens, Delos and Alexandria were fairly comparable, there is no indication that prices in the Greek cities of the Mediterranean were dependent on each other, let alone that Mediterranean markets were integrated during the Hellenistic period.

CHAPTER 7

Sacred finance

INTRODUCTION

In post-war scholarship money has been approached almost exclusively within a secular framework of understanding. Religious meanings of money have not received any serious attention, not least because Aristotle, the most influential ancient authority on monetary history and theory, does not proclaim a particularly close connection between money, cult and ritual (see above, introduction and chapter 2). Temple finance tends to be dealt with in accounts of individual temples or ancient religion more generally, but is not well integrated into ancient economic history.[1] However, the consecration of property, fines and tithes, and the thesauration of some or all of a collective's wealth in temples and shrines, suggest a strong interpenetration of political economics and sacred finance. In the classical city, moreover, a city's patron god had the important function of creating identity and trust in coinage, as well as adding force to commercial contracts backed up by oaths. Temples performed the function of guarding public and private contracts recorded on stone a role which before the Hellenistic period secular institutions were unable to fulfil.

It has been argued, furthermore, that, if not coinage itself, at any rate important conceptual preconditions for the emergence of money in the form of metal tokens developed in the context of cult practice. Bernhard Laum at the beginning of the twentieth century argued that the most important aspect of money was its function as a substitute.[2] The idea of substitution was typical of ancient cult. The sacrificial animal was a substitute for the sacrificer, and so the idea of money, understood as a general standard of value measuring the value of all other goods, was ultimately grounded in the sacrifice of cattle as the substitute for the sacrifice of human life. At the most tangible level, iron spits which were used for roasting

---

[1] An exception is Davies (2001).   [2] Laum (1924).

sacrificial animals became a pre-monetary form of money in archaic Greece.[3] Louis Gernet, too, regarded 'substitution' and the reification of ideas in precious objects (*agalmata*) as an important conceptual step towards the notion of coined money. The mythical Golden Fleece, for example, a symbol of agrarian wealth and royal entitlement, is in Pindar represented as a garment with golden tassels (Pind. *Pyth.* 4.231). *Agalmata* at first embodied aristocratic wealth. They were characteristically mobile goods used as objects of exchange, and their possession by individual humans was transitory. *Agalmata*, moreover, were a particular class of goods produced by human labour: metalwork, statues, textiles and so on. Typically, *agalmata* were acquired by a particular class of people in particular contexts: as booty in war, prizes in games, marital gifts or in other situations of ritualized gift exchange; they were never purchased from outsiders. Thus they circulated in exclusive networks of exchange, were used as offerings and dedications to gods, and did not function as commodities in trade.[4] However, once mass-produced, *anathemata* (dedications) of cheaper material could replace *agalmata* as offerings, and once mythical images played with the interchangeability of image and object, there was only a small step towards the invention of coinage. Immediately before the invention of coinage, *agalmata* were regarded as valuable because they represented things endowed with magical properties. The magical quality of, and gradual abstraction of value from, figurative substitutes were the harbingers of the invention of coinage and its value.[5]

The religious origins of coinage are likely to have been overstated during early twentieth-century scholarship as part of the wider project of constructing an evolution from religious to political meanings of Greek institutions. Yet while religion continued to permeate, rather than precede Greek political life, mythical associations remained present in money and coinage.[6] The close connection between religion and politics, as well as divine and civic *nomos* (law) gave the concept of *nomisma* (coinage) an arguable background in either of these contexts.[7] The need to come to terms with the abstract value of civic silver coins vis-à-vis golden *agalmata* is one of the major concerns of archaic poetry.[8] Conversely, the economic role of the gods, receiving property from individuals and cities to finance

---

[3] Strøm (1992): 41–51; cf. *ThesCRA* V, 2.b: p. 329 f.
[4] Gernet (1981): esp. 113 f.; cf. von Reden (1999): 53 f.   [5] Gernet (1981): 139–46.
[6] See below, epilogue. The image of metals as the earth's *viscera* (organs; Plin. *NH* 33.1) may have conjured up images of links between coins and sacrificial offerings.
[7] Will (1954); (1955); Murray (1990) for a valuable account of the interpenetration of myth, ritual and politics in the Greek *polis*.
[8] Kurke (1999): 65–101; Seaford (2004): 147–72.

cult and sacrifice had symbolic meanings. Tithes, dedications and fees are likely to have resolved at a ritual level tensions between private and supra-individual wealth.[9] The interdependence of public and sacred property shows up the neglected link between the politics, economics and religion of a Greek *polis*.

This interaction will provide the focus of this chapter. In the first section I shall look at the monetization of cult in the course of the introduction of coinages during the sixth and fifth centuries BC. The monetization of dedications and payments transformed the nature of the property of sanctuaries and temples, while gradually creating a new relationship between cities and their gods. In the second part I shall look at temple economics and the mechanisms of creating public control over it. In the final section, I shall explore the contribution of private and public benefactors to the foundation of new and to the growth of existing cults. Some of the contracts drafted in order to regulate benefactions and endowments represent the most innovative forms of transaction known from the Greek world.

THE MONETIZATION OF CULT

The rise of sacred finance is closely linked to the rise of the *polis* and the emergence of coined money. In the pre-monetary world of Homer, cult and collective worship are represented above all by sacrifice and the sharing of common meals, but rarely by dedications.[10] In three of the five detailed Homeric descriptions of sacrificial meals, the (financial) question of how the victims are acquired receives little attention. Nestor 'sends' to the plain for an ox (*Od.* 3.321), the swineherd Eumaios provides his own swine (*Od.* 14.421) and the Greeks contribute their own animals for the worship of particular gods (*Il.* 2.397–417). The personal provision of the sacrificial animal by the host and sacrificers goes along with the distribution of equal shares to an egalitarian group of participants. It is possible, for example, that the two words for food distribution at the occasion of a sacrifice within the epics – *nemein* and *daiesthai* – express an historical development from food distribution among a group of equals (*daiesthai*) to the sharing out of pieces by a leading warrior (*nemein*). Yet in both cases the economics of the sacrificial meal are organized by the group itself, expressing an emphasis on worship as a collective enterprise for which a social in-group is economically responsible. A similar attitude is expressed in the nature of dedications which seems to represent a relatively late layer of the composition of

---

[9] *ThesCRA* I, 2 d II F 12. s.v. 'Money', pp. 314 f.   [10] Seaford (2004): 76 f.

the epics. Dedications in Homer are representations of aristocratic gift exchange. The objects used as gifts or dedications are the same: textiles, armour and *agalmata* comprising tripods, drinking and mixing cups. Also the guiding principles are the same: they create community, obligations and loyalty, they are understood as memorials or signs (*semata*), and the return exchange is delayed as well as qualitative in value rather than immediate and calculated in quantitative terms.[11] They also evoke the same kind of delight (the root meaning of the word *agalma*).[12] Dedications in Homeric epic bear great similarity to the contents of splendid heroic storerooms and point forward to the massive accumulation of *agalmata* attested archaeologically in eighth-century sanctuaries.

Comparison between the Homeric representation of sacrifice and dedications and Near Eastern temple economics helps to elicit the cultural frame of Greek religious economics.[13] The temple in Mesopotamia was the place for housing the divine image and the collection, storage and distribution of food. Vast amounts of perishable foods were supplied to the temples by their subjects, to be consumed by the temple personnel or traded against other needs. Humans participated in the meal of the gods, to whom real food was presented as to a living king. Even as late as the Seleucid period, we have a text that enumerates daily contributions of 500 kilograms of bread, 40 sheep, 2 bulls, 70 birds and ducks, 4 wild boars, as well as beer and wine, to a temple in Uruk.[14] Offerings, moreover, were generally enforced and combined a redistributive social function with the function of sustaining a political elite of priests. As Seaford suggests, because of the divine demand for food, there was considerable similarity of religious and economic form.[15] In Greek religion, human tributes to the gods were less closely identified with human needs. In Homer the gods are not recipients of food, nor do they normally participate in person in the sacrificial meal which takes place in the open. The food for the gods that ascends in the form of incense-laden smoke to the heaven is a *substitute* for real food. Dedications, too, can be regarded as substitutes for perishable offerings. There is, moreover, no external provisioning for cult activities, but the heroes contribute their own property. This 'egalitarian inclusiveness', as Seaford has put it, remained a major parameter for Greek religious finance, even when the Near Eastern model of temples as housing for the gods was adopted. When the Greek sanctuaries became treasuries, they combined storage with communal ritual outside the temple.

[11] von Reden (1995): 13–27.   [12] Compare *Od.* 4.602; 18.300 with 3.274, 438; 8.509; 12.347.
[13] Seaford (2004): 68–87.   [14] Lambert (1993): 194 for this text.   [15] Seaford (2004): 74.

When coined money was introduced, there was a great cross-over between payments and dedications in 'cash' and in kind. The earliest coin hoard found was in the foundations of the Artemis temple at Ephesus (see chapter 1). A silver plaque recovered from the foundations of the same temple recorded in detail the payments towards the reconstruction of the new temple:

Side A: – 40 minai were first weighed out from the ?gifts of gold: they were brought from the *polis*. 5 and 10 minai of silver were brought in with the first gold. From the wood six minai were weighed. Ten minai of gold were weighed out from here. 33 minai of silver were weighed out from here. Silver fr(om the) ship(s –) 70 minai. – 10 from the salt

Side B: – in addition to the half-mina (from the w)ood ?of silver 20 minai lacking a (half)-mina. 30 minai were ?weighed ?to the stater and a sixth from the salt – 14 minai. There resulted from this – a half-mina of the cup and five half-sixths. [2 lines missing]. From what we worked 40 minai – and 8 stat(ers were weighed. From the gar)den 30 minai of silver were brought (*IEph*. 1 (550) with *SEG³* 34.1079).

The inscription lists the contributions from the *polis*, the temple and from regular or dedicated taxes (wood, salt, maritime and garden taxes). The quantities of silver and gold are reckoned according to weight, but the reference to staters suggests that coins were also involved. Later temple treasurers continued to inventory their precious metal and coin income in units of precious-metal weight. But archaic coin hoards show that in the early days of coinage the boundary between precious metal and coins as payments to temples was even more fluid.

Precious-metal containers counted by number, bullion measured by weight and coined money were comparable media in which payments to temples were rendered. Moreover, such kinds of deposits became liquid money in as much as they were no longer just stored and preserved but spent for further purposes. It may not be accidental that by the sixth century BC we hear for the first time about contributions applied specifically to material costs of temple building, in particular construction work and communal sacrifice (Hdt. 2.180). The introduction of coinage and its function as a medium of religious payments went hand in hand.

At the same time, reasons for dedications show a correlation between the growth of the wealth of temples and the growth of the power of political institutions. Not all *poleis* experienced the formation of political institutions and growth of temple treasuries at the same time, but many seem to have gone through the same stages of gradual transformation. In the seventh-century constitution of Tiryns, for example, the *platiwoinarchontes* (probably presiding over the participants in common meals) had to impose a penalty of thirty *medimnoi* (of grain) for any offence the *platiwoinoi* committed, and the penalty was to be paid to the temple of Zeus and Athene. The *hieromnamon* (the main religious administrator) was in charge of this treasury as had been decided by the demos (Koerner (1993) no. 31). In an early fifth-century *rhetra* of Elis, the highest magistrate and the king *basileus* of the city incurred a penalty of 10 minai (1,000 drachmas) each, payable to Olympian Zeus, if they did not attribute certain rights to Patrias the scribe (*IvOl* 2; Koerner (1993) no. 37). A sixth-century law from Gortyn prescribes penalties if a *kosmos* (chief official) repeats office within three years, a *gnomōn* within ten years, and a *xenios* within five years (*ICret* IV 14g–p; Koerner (1993) no. 121). Penalties for these offences were assessed in a certain number of *lebetes* (sacrificial cauldrons). The same fragment contains a penalty of 50 *lebetes* for an unknown offence. Better preserved is a law from fifth-century Erythrai. It stipulates that the offices of scribe (*grammateus*) and treasurer (*tamias*) are not to be iterated nor to be held at once by the same person. Breach of the law is punished with a curse, *atimia*, and a penalty of 100 staters (*IvEr* I.1; Koerner (1993) no. 74 and 75). Not all penalties were payable to a god or temple; but the interdependence of political legislation (normally recorded on documents fixed to a temple wall), the nature of payment and the function of the treasuries collecting penalties show that the authority of political institutions was linked to the ritual of monetary dedication.

Other illustrations of the interdependence of monetization and cult finance are the transformation of dedications into monetary fees, or the transformation of cult utensils into monetary means of payment. The *pelanos* (or *pelanor*), originally referring to a round cake burnt on an altar, came to denote (though not always) a monetary fee.[16] *Obeloi* (iron spits) were transformed from cooking utensils into a medium of payment that was valued by the handful of six making one drachma.[17] Rhodopis, the Thracian courtesan, famously made a dedication of spits at Delphi as a tithe of her notoriously monetary profits made in the *emporion* (harbourtown) of Naucratis.[18] Iron *obeloi* dedicated in sanctuaries, or left as remnants of animal sacrifices nearby, are found all over Greece. The most famous find is from the Argive Heraion, probably dedicated in the sixth century BC. Considerable numbers of spits were also found in or nearby the Hestitorion

---

[16] Sokolowski (1954): 153–64; Davies (2001).   [17] Schaps (2004): 83–8; Strøm (1992).
[18] Hdt. 2.153.

at Perachora (probably sixth century BC), the Apollo temple at Delphi, the sanctuary of Hera and Zeus at Olympia, the shrine of Artemis Orthia in Sparta, the Heraion of Samos (600 BC), and those of Zeus at Dodone and Nemea (late sixth century BC).[19] Whether *obeloi* served a monetary function outside temple economies is hard to tell. It is striking, however, that their dedication clusters around the time immediately before the use of coinage in many parts of Greece, and that they were used in multiples and fractions of six. In the Herodotus story about Rhodopis, moreover, there is certainly an allusion to the comparability between spits and coins. Written for an audience living in largely monetized *poleis*, the story of the dedication of spits by a non-Greek prostitute in the most prestigious Greek temple must have carried considerable irony.

THE PROPERTY OF GODS AND TEMPLES

The monetary property of gods and temples increased through the *aparchai* (tithes) from spoils and harvests, voluntary dedications of cash and other precious-metal items, proceeds from the sale of confiscated property, penalty payments for breach of secular or sacred law, fees for cult services, public taxes, revenue from interest-bearing loans, rents of land and houses, and the sale of sacred property such as hides of victims and revenues in kind.[20] The temple inventories of Athens, Delphi and Delos attest to the vast monetary resources some temples amassed in their treasuries. At the same time, outlay for the rituals in their care was equally vast. In addition there were regular expenses for construction, maintenance and repair of temple buildings, wages and the feeding of personnel and animals. The accounts from the Apollo temple of Delos reveal that the *hieropoioi* bought regularly not only olive oil, wine and (occasionally) wheat for human consumption, but also barley for the geese in their care, pigs, firewood, charcoal, pitch and garlands for sacrifices, natron and sponges for cleaning the temple, and much more. Besides those there were numerous purchases on a less regular, though not infrequent basis, such as of lead, ivory, papyrus, perfume, frankincense and other spices.[21] There were also regular and irregular workers employed, such as builders and flute-players.

---

[19] Strøm (1992); Schaps (2004): 84.
[20] For these various types of revenue and their relative proportion in the balance sheet of temple income, see Horster (2004): 80–91; 190–208.
[21] Linders (1992): 2–9; Reger (1997).

Temples were households, not just in the physical but in the economic sense.

In large public sanctuaries the expenses for festivals and sacrifice were by far the largest regular financial commitment. Construction work was the largest irregular expense. Cities contributed public tax income to running costs and thereby created some collective ownership of the city's temples and rituals. Private and public benefactors increasingly provided resources for temple construction and cult in order to enhance their standing and prestige in the cities. In cases where the temple treasury was under the control of a state, public officials were placed in charge of it.[22] The public financial responsibility for major festivals and sacrifices continued into the Hellenistic period when ruler cult and dynastic festivals, too, had to be financed by taxation unless there was a benefactor. Given the collective responsibility of citizens, kings and subjects for the cult of their common gods, it seems to have been felt justified to apply funds in temple treasuries, by public authority, to other than religious purposes. The most famous example is the use in Athens of Athena's money for campaigns in the Peloponnesian War (*IG* I³ 370 a–e = *GHI* 77 (418–414 BC); cf. Thuc. 2.1).[23]

During the Hellenistic period when ruler cult and dynastic festivals were added to the financial responsibilities of cities and temples, kings and royal personnel joined the circle of financial contributors. Other examples are known, and the boundary between public use and embezzlement of sacred funds was fluid.[24]

Given the particularly close relationship between public and divine ownership of sacred property, there has been some debate over the relationship between civic and temple finance. The discussion has been particularly intense in the case of temples in Hellenistic Asia Minor which had a heterogeneous religious tradition oriented towards Greek religious culture in the Western coastal areas, on the one hand, and towards Eastern religious practices in central Anatolia, on the other.[25] Classical Greek texts distinguish between public resources and those 'set aside for the gods'.[26] Treasurers in charge of public and sacred funds carried different designations.[27] At the

---

[22] This, however, is not to be taken as an indication of a 'secularization of sacred property', which has often been misleadingly attributed to the Kallias Decrees (*IG* I³ 52 (=*GHI* 58, 433/4 BC)).

[23] Harris (1995): 28–36.   [24] *Ibid.*   [25] Debord (1982); Dignas (2002).

[26] Arist. *Rhet.* 1425b; cf. Solon fr. 4, 12–14; Arist. *Pol.* 1267b; 1329b–1330a; Plat. *Nom.* 745d–747e; see also *IG* I³ 253 13 and 17; and Dignas (2002): 13–15.

[27] Dignas (2002): 16.

same time, those in charge of sacred funds (*hieropoioi, tamiai, prostatai,* and *epistatai*) belonged to the secular personnel of a temple and were often, though not always, elected by civic governments or councils. Yet in most respects, temples were autonomous economic units despite the fact that they were accountable to the public.[28] In the non-Greek Eastern tradition, politics and social power were more closely intertwined with religious roles. Yet there is no conclusive evidence that different 'types' of temples were treated differently in Asia Minor, nor that there was a notable transformation of the relationship between cities and temples in the Hellenistic period.[29]

The degree of civic control over urban or rural sanctuaries did not follow a single pattern. The relationship depended on the nature of the cult, the nature of the circle of worshippers, the tradition of the sanctuary, and individual negotiation. In the Hellenistic period, kings constituted a third party in the relationship between public and divine ownership of temple property, and it is noteworthy that they made their benefactions to the temples directly, rather than via civic governments.[30] In some cases they even guarded sacred funds against civic interference.[31] An inscription regulating the disposal of the contents of the treasure boxes (*thesauroi*) in the Asklepieion of Kos illustrates the differentiated treatment of temple property, and the interaction of autonomy and civic control, particularly clearly:[32]

The *prostatai* shall be in charge of the keys of the *thesauroi* and open them together with the priestess each year in the month Dalios. Half (of the sum) belongs to the priestess, the other half they shall send to the public bank where it is put into the account which the goddess has, and they shall record the transaction in the public archive. This money shall be available for construction work as the assembly decides and for repair of the sanctuary.[33]

THE MANAGEMENT OF SACRIFICE

The Athenian orator known familiarly as the *Old Oligarch* commented in the late fifth century BC on the *raison d'être* of public contributions to large civic sacrifices:

---

[28] Debord (1982): 92; Dignas (2002): 17, by contrast, suggests that the city of Athens controlled the finances of Athena exceptionally closely.
[29] Thus Dignas (2002): *passim.*   [30] Dignas (2002): 59–106.
[31] Dignas (2002): 106, with several examples.   [32] For such treasure boxes, see Kaminski (1991).
[33] Kaminski (1991): 89; Dignas (2002): 21–3 with further examples.

For sacrifices and sacrificial victims and festivals and sacred lands, the *demos*, knowing that it is not possible for each one of the poor to sacrifice and feast and banquet and live in a great and beautiful city, has found a way for these things to happen. And so the *polis* sacrifices many victims at public expense, but it is the *demos* who feast and share the victims among themselves ([Xen]. *Ath. Pol.* 2.9).

Not all sacrifices taking place in a city were financed with public money. There were private sacrifices financed and celebrated in greater or lesser splendour by the individuals who organized them, and who invited a closer or broader circle of friends into their house. There were the sacrifices of cult associations (*orgeones* or *thiasoi*) who financed their rites by the voluntary contributions and compulsory fees of their members. There were sacrifices at the level of sub-units of the *polis* (demes, tribes, trittyes and phratries), the costs of which were borne either by local temples, or by the local treasury of the community involved. Indeed, it has been argued that the reason for keeping local deme (village) treasuries was the maintenance of local cults for the demesmen.[34] Some large temples with considerable revenue, especially the inter-regional temples at Delphi, Olympia and Delos, paid for their sacrifices out of their own regular income derived from sacred land and financial assets, donations of public and private benefactors, or the compulsory contributions of participating cities and individuals.[35] The greatest sacrifices and festivals of individual cities, however, were paid for by public contributions, or by a combination of civic and temple funds.

From the sixth century onwards many cities and demes established sacrificial calendars publicly inscribed and erected in the agora.[36] These calendars, which are particularly well-known from Athens and its constituent demes, recorded the name of the deity and the victim to be allocated for the sacrifice. Some entries specified a group of people responsible for the organization of the sacrifice. It has been suggested that the prime function of the calendars, rather than establishing and co-ordinating their sequence during one year, was to define the amount of money the citizens were to spend on each god.[37] When the old law code of Athens was revised between 409 and 399 BC, there was some controversy over what monies had been allocated to what purpose, and whether Nicomachus, the official in charge, had done so in the most honourable way (Lys. 30). In 363 BC two branches

[34] Whitehead (1986b): 164.
[35] Linders (1992): 9 f.; Horster (2004): 208–10; the Athenians purchased a large number of oxen for the quadrennial festival at Delos (in 375/4 it was 109: *IG* II²1635, 35–6); *CID* I 13 (early fourth century BC) exempts the citizens of Skiathos from the fees and contributions payable for sacrifice at Delphi.
[36] Rosivach (1994): 14–67.　　[37] Parker (1996): 53.

of the *genos* (lineage) of the Salaminioi erected a stele bearing the agreement they had reached about their mutual property and the continuation of their cults. They appended a cult calendar of the joint sacrifices to be funded from the rents they now collected separately, 'so that the *archontes* (officials) on both sides may know what money is to be contributed by each party for all the sacrifices'.[38] Religion in the Greek city meant that ritual was paid for by the people who benefited from it.

Rosivach (1994) has calculated that an Athenian could celebrate a sacrifice in his local deme about twenty times a year, together with an additional ten at supra-deme level. To these could be added about fifteen sacrifices that the whole *polis* celebrated per year. Some were not part of the regular calendar, but *ad hoc* celebrations on the occasion of a victory or the inauguration of a new cult. In total, an Athenian could expect to participate in around fifty such occasions per year, or one on average every week.

Several officials were in charge of the financial administration of religious cults. At Athens, Isocrates contrasts *patrioi thusiai* (traditional animal blood sacrifices) which were funded by the rental income from sacred property in Attica with *epithetoi heortai* benefiting from a different source (*Areop.* 29).[39] The same categories are used by the author of the Aristotelian *Constitution of Athens* when mentioning that the *archon basileus* (head of religious affairs) and the *polemarch* (concerned with war matters) were in charge of *patrioi thusiai*, wheras the eponymous *archon* (the civil head of state) was in charge of the others (*Ath. Pol.* 3.3). The passage suggests in addition that *epithetoi heortai* were a category of newer ('supplementary') sacrifices. There is also some possibility that the 'supplementary' sacrifices were considerably larger and more costly. Isocrates suggests, furthermore, that the raising of monetary funds for the newer sacrifices was contracted out to individuals by auction.[40]

The so-called *dermatikon* (hide) accounts of the years 334–330 BC detail the proceeds from the sale of the hides of victims sacrificed at the major 'supplementary' sacrifices (*IG* II[2] 1496). It is possible that the sale of the hides was one of the innovations introduced by Lycurgus, who reformed Athenian finances in the 330s when they were in somewhat dire straits.[41] Moreover, it is most likely that the *dermatikon* accounts give us a comprehensive list of the annual sacrifices celebrated in Athens during these years. On the assumption that the sale price of an ox-hide was in the range of 4 to 10 drachmas, and on the further assumption that the hides on sale

---

[38] *Hesp.* 7 (1938): 3–5; esp. ll. 85–94.   [39] For this and the following, Rosivach (1994): 55 f.
[40] *Areop.* 30.   [41] Rosivach (1994): 48, n. 99; for Lycurgus, Parker (1996): 242–53.

were all ox-hides, the costs of the oxen required for the annual Athenian sacrifices (excluding the penteteric (quadrennial) and irregular sacrifices) can be calculated at around 87,300 drachmas (*c.* 14.5 talents).[42] On a less careful count, it has been calculated that the total costs for public sacrifices were in the range of as much as 40 talents per year.[43]

There are few sources that tell us how this enormous sum was raised. There is no evidence that the *polis* owned its own animals, but public officials were responsible for the purchase of sacrificial victims.[44] During the time when the Athenians could use allied tributes, of which a sixtieth was dedicated to the treasury of Athena, the financial side of the sumptuous festival culture was fairly secure. But from the late fifth century onwards, the sacrifice industry had to be budgeted more carefully. The pressure to which finances had been subjected surfaces in the prosecution of Nicomachus who allegedly had included new sacrifices in the Athenian calendar, costing the city 6 talents and thereby making impossible payments for older ones at the level of 3 talents (Lys. 30.19–20, see above).

It is likely that regular sacrifices were paid for from designated resources. When the Asklepieion in Zea in the Piraeus harbour of Athens received the status of a public sanctuary, the Athenians resolved that the preliminary sacrifices were to be funded from money derived from the mines (*IG* II² 47.23–31). In the same century the Athenians also levied a new annual tax, in support of the cult of Apollo, on citizens active in military service. Cavalrymen had to pay 2 drachmas, hoplites 1 drachma and foot soldiers 3 obols from their stipends (*IG* I³ 138 (before 434 BC)). A new 5-drachma tax (*pentedrachmia*) was introduced to pay for the sacrifices of the new cult of Theseus.[45] An embarkation tax (*embatikon*) on ships passing through the Piraeus was allocated shortly before the outbreak of the Peloponnesian War to the cult of the Spartan Anakes (= the Dioscuri Castor and Pollux), protectors of sailors. Their accounts henceforth were subjected to public scrutiny by examiners and assessors (*IG* I³ 133). In Anaktorion, moreover, when a sanctuary had been badly damaged by war in the third century BC, the re-construction work, sacrifices and games of that year were decreed

---

[42] Rosivach (1994): 169. The figure for the Panathenaia is not preserved in the *dermatikon* accounts. The amount must be the composite figure of the *hekatombaion* (100 oxen) sacrificed traditionally at the Panathenaia plus nine additional oxen distributed as gifts to the Pyrrhic dancers. There were further 41 oxen paid for by the 41 minai which since the early 330s were allocated to the purchase of sacrificial oxen for the Lesser Panathenaia from the proceeds of the land of Oropos received as a gift from Philip II in 338/7 BC (*IG* II² 334 [335/4 BC]).

[43] Healey (1990): 313.   [44] Rosivach (1994): 108–14.

[45] Parker (1996): 169 and 318 with *Agora* XIX P26.479 and Plut. *Thes.* 23.5.; see also, Dem. 24.96 f.

to be paid out of the harbour tax raised during the festival.[46] The few indications we have hint at a complex system of sacred finance based on regular and irregular taxes, and rental and other income allocated to cults by public decision. Sometimes *ad hoc* solutions had to be found. An Oropian decree of 329/8 BC orders the *tamiai tou demou* (treasurers of the demos) to provide the funds for the sacrifice at the newly established festival in honour of Amphiareus for that year, but to direct the matter of permanent funding to the *nomothetai* at their next meeting (*IG* VII 4254.37–45).

THE MANAGEMENT OF MONETARY ASSETS

Evidence for temple credit dates back to the fifth century BC. Thucydides tells us that at the beginning of the Peloponnesian War the Corinthians suggested borrowing money from the inter-regional sanctuaries of Delphi and Olympia in order to pay foreign sailors for their navy (Thuc. 1.121, 3).[47] The Athenians put a similar plan into practice when over a period of seven years they borrowed money from Athenian temple treasuries to a total sum of over 4,750 talents (some 28.5 million drachmas). The loans were related to the military efforts at the beginning of the Archidamian War and continued, albeit at a lower level, until 423 BC. Some interest was charged on the principal. In the first period, it seems to have been an annual rate of about 7 per cent. In the subsequent period the rate dropped to 1 drachma per day on the talent, which meant 1.2 per cent per year. In total, the Athenians borrowed 5,600 talents (33.6 million drachmas) over eleven years from their treasuries, earning the temple, in theory, a total of 2,500 talents (15 million drachmas) of interest.[48] Yet there is little evidence that the treasuries of Athena made a profit on these loans. By the end of the war all Athenian funds were exhausted. Whether the treasurers had expected repayment at interest is a moot point.

Similar in date but different in context are the loans of 200- and 300-drachma lots granted by the people of the deme of Rhamnous over a period of four years to their fellow citizens from the treasury of Nemesis (*IG* I³ 248 = *GHI* 53 (*c.* 440 BC)).[49] The treasury was under the control of *hieropoioi*, that is, civic officials in control of both cult and finances of the sanctuary. The inscription lists from one year to the next the amount of money lent and the sum total of the money belonging to the treasury

---

[46] *IG* IX 1.2, 383 with Linders (1992); see also below.
[47] Migeotte (1984): no 22; for an earlier, but probably not historical example, see Horster (2004): 197.
[48] *GHI* 72 (426/5 and 423/2 BC) with editorial comments pp. 214–17.
[49] Davies (2001); Millett (1991): 175 f; Horster (2004): 198 f.

at the end of the year. Within five years the total increased from 39,728 drachmas in year one (of which 37,000 had been lent) to 56,606 drachmas in year five (of which 51,400 drachmas were lent). If there were no other revenues increasing the stock, the growth of the total represents 7 per cent per year, which is the same rate as charged on the loans from the Athenian treasuries during the Archidamian War.[50]

In the late fifth century the people of the deme of Plotheia allocated sums to specific purposes: to the two treasurers of the sacred objects 5,000 drachmas, for the Herakleion 7,000 drachmas, for the Aphrodisia 1,200 drachmas, and so on.[51] Subsequently it was moved that *epimeletai* should keep them safe for the Plotheians, but extract interest from loans already made. They should also contract new loans on a competitive basis to those borrowers who would offer the highest interest (ll. 11–22). From the money thus earned, and possibly from the rents of landed property into which the surplus money was invested, the *epimeletai* should finance 'the holy acts, both those which are common to the Plotheieis and those made to the Athenians on behalf of the commonwealth of the Plotheieis, and those of the quadrennial festivals; and also for the other holy acts, whenever it is necessary for all the Plotheieis to contribute money for holy acts' (ll. 22–33). In the final section, the quantities of sweet wine to be expended on the holy acts are specified as well as the fees payable to the various attendants of the rituals (33–40). The volume of the sums raised and the economic scheme deployed to raise them by a relatively small rural deme are remarkable: lent at interest to the highest bidder, the surplus of monetary assets was re-invested into landed property from which rents were derived. The schemes anticipate what is attested more regularly by the accounts of large and small sanctuaries from the Hellenistic period onwards.

The temple accounts of the Apollo temple at Delos from the fifth through to the second century BC contain abundant evidence for monetary assets lent to neighbouring islands.[52] Throughout the classical and Hellenistic period, loans were extended for 4-year periods, but periods could be accumulated and loans become quite long-term. The island of Paros, for example, was continuously indebted to Apollo from the beginning of the fourth century to 341 BC. Interest was charged at a fixed sum of an annual 10 per cent on the principal payable in 4-year intervals. In the period 377–374 BC the total interest received amounted to 26,060 drachmas (some interest payments were in arrears), suggesting more than

---

[50] Davies (2001): 118.
[51] *IG* I³ 258, ll 1–10 (420 BC); with Davies (2001): 124; Millett (1991): 173–5.
[52] Migeotte (1984): no 45 I–VI; see above, chapter 5; and Reger (1994).

260,600 drachmas or 43.5 talents were being lent to collective citizen bodies, and an additional 53,250 drachmas to private individuals (5,325 drachmas interest).[53] This was lending on a grand scale. Another example is provided by the temple of Zeus Olympios at Locri Epizephyrii which, from the proceeds of the sacred rents, lent to the Locrians 747 talents and at another time 1,247 talents. From the income of two other tenancies the Locrians borrowed each year fixed sums of 20 talents and 56 talents respectively for three consecutive years. The explicit purpose of the latter is said to have been a (?subsidy) payment to a king.[54] There is also the small city of Dryma which between 162 and 157 BC appears as borrower of 90 minai (1.5 talents) from sacred funds (*IG* IX 1). Priene also appears, honouring Moschion for having assisted the city in paying the interest on a loan made from the sacred funds of the Panionion (*IPriene* 108, late second century BC).[55]

Within the total corpus of public and private loans known from the classical and Hellenistic period temple loans are rare.[56] No Greek sanctuary functioned as a bank, although some temples in the Eastern Aegean, probably under the influence of their eastern neighbours, took the money of individuals on deposit.[57] Lending money, though potentially more lucrative than renting out estate, was a capital-intensive, high-risk enterprise subject to the availability of surplus money as well as reliable creditors.[58]

John Davies has raised the interesting possibility that sacred funds were conceived as monetary reserves rather than circulating capital. Sea powers especially, with their permanent threat of having to raise massive amounts of money in moments of need, were reluctant to lend out temple funds. Instead they were eager to know the monetary value of the temple treasuries. Thus all precious metal possessions including coinage were assessed in standard units of weight for inventory purposes. Thus also the Athenians decided to turn the proceeds from the confiscated properties of the Thirty Tyrants into *pompeia* (precious-metal containers) of roughly standard weight. It is possible that it was for the same reason that the Athenians required uniform weights for honorific crowns voted by the demos to Athena, and uniform weights of 100 and 500 drachmas for the *phialai* dedicated by manumitted slaves in the 330s and 320s, and some liturgists in 331/0 BC. All this may suggest that the measure proposed by Androtion in

---

[53] *ID* 98, 1–56 + *IG* II² 1635; *Syll.*³ 153.
[54] Costabile (1992): 229–307 with tab. 10, 29, 23, 30, 31 (probably third century BC).
[55] Migeotte (1984) nos. 29 and 94.
[56] Migeotte (1984) has only four examples of public borrowing from temples.
[57] Bogaert (1968): 279–304.
[58] There may have been religious prohibitions against doing so; Davies (2001): 122, quoting *SDGI* 1557.

c. 360 BC to melt down temple treasures in order to monetize them was an idea inherent in the way temple treasures were maintained in the classical period.[59]

THE FINANCIAL MANAGEMENT OF LANDED PROPERTY

The consecration of parcels of land (*temene*) was part of the foundation of cults and temples from the early archaic period onwards. Later authors such as Hippodamos and Aristotle, who mapped out in theory the territory of ideal *poleis*, suggested that one third of *polis* land should be sacred in order for *poleis* to be able to perform the required duties towards the gods (Arist. *Pol.* 1267b; 1329b–1330a). Alongside private citizens and the public, it was believed that the gods should be landowners within a *polis* (Plat. *Nom.* 745d–747e). Thus Isocrates seems to imply that the *patrioi thusiai* of old were financed from agricultural surplus rather than money (*Areop.* 30, see above). But just as in the case of credit activities, permission for using land productively might require oracular authorization. Exemplary is the story of the dispute in the fourth century BC between Athens and Megara over the sacred *Orgas* that lay in their joint borderland. The oracle of Delphi was consulted as to whether the area should remain fallow or whether it should be cultivated and the money used for the construction of the sanctuary in Eleusis. After a positive response, the land was marked off as fallow with boundary stones. Unfortunately, the stones were gradually removed, and private farmers took over Demeter's land and cultivated it for their own benefit.[60]

It is noteworthy that, with some notable exceptions, leases of sacred land were based on fixed-term rental payments in cash. Exceptions are the properties of Dionysos and Athena in Herakleia in Southern Italy which were let for life.[61] The rents, which were payable to public officials, were assessed in grain. It is important to note, however, that only one third of the sacred property was agricultural land, while the other two thirds were forests. Moreover, special clauses of the contracts suggest that the land was to be planted with vines, olives, figs and other fruit (II, 11.169–78). Thus the payment of grain was not a payment in kind, but a special arrangement for the purpose of raising an income in grain. The other exception is the short-term tenancy of one part of the land belonging to Demeter and Kore

---

[59] Davies (2001) with Dem. 22.69 ff and 24.176 ff.
[60] *IG* II² 204; Horster (2004): 139–91, also for the following.
[61] The land of Athena may not have been leased for life, since rents are accounted for in five-year intervals; *IG* XIV645 II, l. 35 with Horster (2004): 166.

in Attica. On that part, the income was 619 *medimnoi* of grain (*IG* II²1672, ll. 252 f.). It is likely that the grain rent, payable to the sanctuary directly, once again was devoted to the particular ritual purposes related to the agrarian cult of Demeter and Kore.

Temple leases were normally mid- to long-term. The leases of the land from Kodros, Neleus and Basile in Attica were for 20-year periods. Some temples, such as that of Dionysus in Herakleia, rented their land 'for ever', that is, the tenant was permitted to bequeath it to his heirs. More market-oriented was the Apollo of Delos who leased his land for 10-year periods, renewable for the same period if the tenant agreed to increase the rent by 10 per cent.[62] Cult associations leased their land for shorter periods. On the whole, however, treasurers were interested in a regular income rather than the price-driving effects of competitive bids at short intervals.

Sacred land could be let by a variety of bodies, depending on who was entitled to its profits. In the case of the lands of the city gods in Athens, the council decided about the leases, while the *archon basileus*, the civil official in charge of religious affairs, acted as lessor in the actual contracts.[63] Correspondingly, the income from land belonging to the gods of local demes was under the control of the *demarch*. The collection of rents was probably farmed out to private contractors, as in others cases of sacred income, but was finally received by the *apodektai* ('receivers') who paid over the rents to the treasury entitled to it.[64] Not all rental income went to the treasury of the god to whom the land belonged. In the case of the land of Kodros, Neleus and Basile, the rent was paid into the treasuries of the Other Gods. But the income from land on Samos, which the Athenians had confiscated or received from the Samians in the fifth century and consecrated to Athena, Ion and the Eponymous Gods, is likely to have been paid to the treasury of Athena in Athens, rather than benefiting local cults.[65]

Only cult associations, organized and endowed by private individuals who were often foreigners, cultivated their land themselves. Both landlords and tenants seem to have been members of the cult association. In the six lease contracts extant from the fourth to the first centuries BC the tenants are always members of the association. They were obliged to pay a rent in

---

[62] For which see Reger (1994): 216 ff.
[63] Similar mechanisms are known from Delphi and temples in Southern Italy, Horster (2004): 186–9.
[64] *IG* I³84 (= *LSCG* 14) regulating the lease of the land of Kodros, Neleus and Basile in Attica (418/7 BC).
[65] Parker (1996): 144 f., and Horster (2004): 30 f. for discussion.

cash, to contribute in kind to the cult festivals, and look after the property adequately. In a tenancy contract related to the *temenos* of the hero Egretes, the tenant was obliged to pay a rent of 200 drachmas per year, payable in two half-year instalments.[66] The lease extended over 10 years. The tenant had to look after the walls, buildings and the trees of the property, replacing each tree if it died. He was also obliged to give access to the house and prepare the sanctuary for the annual festival. He was permitted to erect further buildings, which he was required to remove at the end of the rental period. There were no penalty clauses in the contract. In case of breaches of the contract, the tenant simply lost the lease, having to leave behind the land and any constructions and building materials that he had added.

The management of the land of Delian Apollo was somewhat different. The god owned about twenty properties located on Delos itself, on the neighbouring islet of Rheneia and, after 237 BC, on Mykonos. Most of these lands were used as farms producing grain, figs, wine and livestock. In line with many other extant sacred and civil rental agreements, tenants had to provide sureties for the rent. The properties had to be cultivated according to certain conditions aimed at maintaining the quality of the assets. Rents were regularly paid in cash.[67] During the time of Delian dependence on Athens and Delphi, the accounts were recorded by the amphictyons (sacred commissions) in Athens or Delphi; during the time of independence the *hieropoioi* of Delos were in charge (see chapter 5). But in both periods the revenue was applied directly to the temple's treasury from which expenditure for sacrifices, festivals, prizes for victors, animals and so on was paid. In the third and second century BC, the total income from all estates was considerably larger than in the previous centuries, most likely due to more land being submitted to cultivation and tenancy. The level of rents also fluctuated from period to period. There was a sharp increase of individual rents between 310 and 304 BC in the aftermath of the liberation of the island from Athens and Athenian tenants, followed by a collapse in 290 BC; there was another drop, though less marked, between 249 and 219 BC. Reger suggests that the *hiera sungraphe* (sacred contract) laid down in 299 BC made leases less attractive to high bidders, who after the liberation from Athens had fiercely competed for the prestigious tenancies. The *sungraphe* described in detail forms of execution of unfulfilled contractual obligations. So, for example, the *hieropoioi* had the

---

[66] *IG* II² 2499 (= *Syll.*³ 1097), 306/5 BC.

[67] The most detailed economic analysis of the development of rents on Delos is that by Reger (1994): 189–247, with lists in Appendix IV: 304–49.

right of seizing all the belongings of both renters and their sureties if they failed to pay the full rent (*ID* 503). Many instances in the subsequent years attest that the *hieropoioi* made use of the new regime.[68] The effect was that more land fell back into the possession of the temple because of confiscations from defaulting tenants and a lack of attractiveness of the new contracts. The relatively short rental periods, shortened yet further during the early years of Delian independence, the increasing rental income over time, and the attempt to increase the efficiency of collecting rental obligations suggest that the Delian *hieropoioi* were by comparison more profit-oriented than other temple authorities in the management of their sacred assets.

TAXES AND FEES

Temples and cults associations extracted taxes and fees for the provision of their services which in turn helped to finance the provision of these services and additional ritual practices. The huge discrepancy in the income of different sanctuaries, and the discrepancy in their expenditure become particularly apparent when their different incomes from fees and taxes are considered.

Fees could be exacted in connection with medical treatment, consultation of an oracle, initiation into mysteries, purification, performance of sacrifice, and so on. According to the regulations of the cult of Asolepius at Erythrai, a fee of 1 or 2 obols was prescribed in addition to a sacrifice before and after the incubation.[69] It was, however, up to the sanctuary whether the fee was payable in cash or kind, or in the form of a sacrifice, or a combination of them. The consultation of an oracle was usually preceded or followed by a sacrifice, and a portion of the offering could then be treated as the consultation charge. The agreement between Delphi and Skiathos, for example, mentions the offering of a goat as a fee for the consultation of the oracle (*BCH* (1939): 184). The statutes of the Labyadae of Delphi mention a charge for priority of treatment (*prothyon, promanteuomenos, LSCG* 77 D 40 f.). This charge was composed of skins and entire victims, payable at first to the treasury of Bouzyges and Lykeios, but later collected by the Labyadae themselves. Some fees in kind were also monetized, the case of the *pelanos* being just the most famous example. In the regulations for the envoys from Andros at Delphi it still had the tangible sense of

---

[68] Reger (1994): 221–30.
[69] For this and the following Sokolowski (1954), Horster (2004): 206 f.

being a cake (*CID* 1, 8). Yet in a slightly later document it is a monetary fee:

It seems good to the Delphians that Phaselitai are to give the *pelanos*: the public one, 7 Delphian drachmas, 2 obols; the private one, 4 obols. [Decreed] when Timodikos and Histiaios were *thearoi*; Herylos was *archon* (*CID* I, 9).[70]

Initiation into mysteries required a fee, too. The list of fees paid to various cult officials performing the rites give us an idea of their scale:

Priest of Demeter	1 obol
Hierophants	1 obol
Hierokeryx	1 obol
Priest at altar's service	½-obol
Phaidyntes	½-obol
Priest of the purification	½-obol

The right to initiate postulants into the mysteries at Eleusis had been traditionally that of the Kerykes and Eumolpidae, priestly families who for their service had received five portions from the sacrifices. By the sixth century BC, however, there was some re-organization of local religious finance, and by the fifth century the treasury of Eleusis was stored as part of the treasury of the Other Gods on the Acropolis of Athens in the Opisthodomos 'in a box on the fourth shelf' (*IG* I³ 386). In 408/7 the total income from the Great Mysteries amounted to the considerable sum of 4,299 drachmas 4 obols in addition to 46 drachmas from the Little Mysteries. This income stood against the revenue of a mere 500 drachmas from the lease of land (*ibid.*). Private cult associations raised funds through entry fees, contributions in kind and monetary contributions. Thus the *orgeones* of Bendis in the Piraeus paid 2 drachmas per year for sacrifices (*IG* II² 1361 = *LSCG* 45 (fourth century BC)); and in the third century BC the Iobacchi had to deliver a quantity of wine each month for the cult (*LSCG* 46).

In addition to the fees raised by the deities and cult associations themselves, demes and states could direct part or all of a particular tax to a sanctuary, as we saw above. Notable here is the exceptional effort made by the Hellenistic kings to finance ruler cult and public ritual. References to irregular *stephanoi* (taxes for crowns), *trichalkia* (3-*chalkoi* tax) or

---

[70] Already in an inscription of *c.* 500 BC, shortly after Delphi had begun to coin, the *pelanus* occurs as a monetary fee; *CID* I, 1; see further Davies (2001): 119 f.

dodekachalkia (12-*chalkoi* tax) designated for festivals and sacrifices suggest that, if money was necessary for certain celebrations, a tax could be raised.[71] The most famous, and probably also the most extensive, regular tax designated for a cult was the Ptolemaic *apomoira* levied from the 260s BC onwards on all vineyards and orchards in Egypt and its imperial possessions. It was destined for the cult of Arsinoe, the divinized second wife and full sister of Ptolemy II, which after her death was to be celebrated in all Egyptian temples.[72] The tax, which was levied as a sixth of the produce of vineyards and orchards, was a harvest tax and could also be understood as a tithe.[73] In the case of wine, it was collected in kind; in the case of fruit, it was a monetary tax. The *apomoira* both on fruit and on wine was collected under the tax-farming scheme according to which contractors guaranteed a pre-determined amount of tax delivered to the local tax offices in the course of the year. The administration then appointed licensed retailers who sold most of the produce in the market, and the monetary proceeds, together with some wine for libation, were forwarded to the temples.[74]

The collection of the *apomoira* was subject to an extensive administrative procedure beginning with the surveying of the taxable land, and the self-declaration of yields by the tax-liables, and continuing through to the appointment of tax-farmers and their sureties, the drawing up of contracts, the collection and accounting process, the appointment of retail sellers, the transfer of the money to the temples, and the execution of tax-farming contracts in case of un-fulfilment, involving the confiscation of the tax-farmers' or their sureties' property and its sale. The costs of the collection were outweighed by the considerable revenue gained from the tax. It was by far the largest source of individual tax income in Egypt. The total amount of wine collected in 190 BC under the *apomoira* scheme in the Arsinoite nome was 37,965 $\frac{1}{2}$ *metretai*, equivalent to a monetary value of between about 190,000 and 228,000 drachmas (31–8 talents).[75] If we consider that the Arsinoite district was just one, albeit large, wine-producing area, and that there was the *apomoira* derived from fruits in addition, the collection and administration of tax income for ruler cult were big business.

---

[71] E.g. von Reden (2007a): 86, 93–4.

[72] Koenen (1994): 25–115; and Clarysse and Vandorpe (1998): 5–42 for this much-discussed tax.

[73] Privileged tax payers paid the tenth (*dekate*) rather than the sixth (*hekte*) of the produce; *P. Rev.* 24–37.

[74] Most scholars believe that the *apomoira* of wine was delivered in that form to the temples, until the tax was fully monetized at the beginning of the second century; I have argued against this view in von Reden (2007a): 95–102.

[75] *P. Köln* V 221 (190 BC) with Clarysse and Vandorpe (1997): 67–73: 68 f. The price per *metretes* of wine is set in *P. Rev.* 35 at 5 or 6 drachmas.

THE LONG-TERM MANAGEMENT OF ASSETS: BENEFACTIONS AND ENDOWMENTS

Alongside public taxes and temple income, sanctuaries and cults were funded by private and public benefactions. In the Hellenistic period evidence for public benefactions massively increases, but the phenomenon goes back to the aristocratic ideal of *megaloprepeia* (conspicuous financial generosity) that at least from the late archaic period onwards belonged to the public duties of aristocrats and was regarded as a sign of social and economic standing (Arist. *EN* 1119b19–1122a17).[76] As it was a way of showing off and maintaining social superiority, it ran certainly contrary to democratic principles. But *megaloprepeia* could also have egalitarian ends, as for example when an athletic victor from his lofty heights of heroic achievement re-integrated himself into his civic community by acts of munificence to fellow citizens and city gods.[77] In the Hellenistic period a particular culture of *euergetism* (from *euergetes* meaning benefactor) emerged, in which a wealthy citizen or king for the purpose of prestige and power supported public projects, cult activities and ruler cult. In the following I shall distinguish between one-off monetary benefactions, on the one hand, and complex forms of endowment, on the other.[78] Yet all transactions were part of a culture which created a triangular relationship between elite self-presentation, monetary dedications and collective piety.

A famous starting point for the long history of conspicuous payments of individuals to temples in order to demonstrate piety and generosity is provided by the aristocratic Athenian family of the Alcmaeonids who took over the contract of rebuilding the temple of Apollo in Delphi in the sixth century BC after the sanctuary had been destroyed by fire (Hdt. 2.180; see chapter 2). Similar acts of generosity continued in the classical and Hellenistic periods when sanctuaries increasingly became the sites of political displays. A democratic counterpart to the example of the Alcmaeonids are the donations by Greek cities towards the rebuilding of the temple in Delphi after the earthquake of 373 BC. They were raised by a 1-obol tax levied upon all citizens of the *amphictiony* (the religious commission administering the shrine) and paid – most notably from a symbolic point of view – in the home currency of each contributing state (*FD* III 5, 3).

---

[76] Kurke (1991): 167 ff.   [77] *Ibid.* 163–224.

[78] Bringmann and von Steuben (1995) treat both together, also including *aparchai* from spoils in their collection of 'donations' (e.g. no. 288–90 (*aparchai* dedicated by Prusias II)); Laum (1914) contains the most complete (though not up-to-date) collection of both private and public documents.

A typical example of royal *euergetism* in the Hellenistic period is also represented in a second-century BC inscription, again from Delphi. The Delphians erected a stele honouring Eumenes II, king of Pergamon, for having provided money for the grain fund, as well as for having 'made dispositions concerning the equipment and construction of the theatre and the other *anathemata*'. It is not entirely clear whether the *anathemata* were part of the building of the theatre or a separate gift, but in any case the term *anathema* rendered the donation an act of religious consecration.[79] Philokles, son of Apollodoros, moreover, dedicated to the gods of Thebes 100 talents when the town was rebuilt in 304 BC, and many Hellenistic rulers collectively supported the project. Demetrios Poliorketes dedicated the tithe of the spoils from the sack of Rhodes so that oil could be purchased for the worship of the gods (*IG* VII 2419 = *Syll*[3] 337). Hieron and Gelon from Syracuse gave several precious-metal containers together with 10 talents of money to the Rhodians after the devastating earthquake that had ruined the city in 227/6 BC. But the gifts helping to re-establish their cults were part of a more comprehensive package of payments in aid of rebuilding the city. And 'as if it was they who owed thanks to the Rhodians they erected a group of statues showing the Rhodians being crowned by the people of Syracuse' (Polyb. 5.88.5–8). In 219 BC Philip V of Macedonia may have financed or part-financed the rebuilding of the temple of Zeus at Dodona. This has been inferred from a series of Macedonian bronze coins showing Zeus of Dodona in celebration of the victory over the Aitolians who had destroyed the temple. The connection is inconclusive, but an inscription found in the sanctuary of Dodona is noteworthy: it gives an account of payments made by the citizens of Epirus; and it is likely that these were civic contributions to the rebuilding of the temple.[80]

Alexander the Great, of course, epitomized and provided a link between religious benefaction and self-representation. He was credited in Priene with having endowed the temple of Athena Polias. Yet he is likely not to have financed the whole project, but, if at all, just to have contributed to the costs. For the building of the temple was well under way, or even completed, when he adopted the title of *basileus* in which capacity he was praised by the Prieneans.[81] In Ephesus he is said to have intended to spend all tributes paid by the Ephesian citizens on the reconstruction of the Artemision that had been damaged by fire in 356 BC (Arr. *An.* 1.17.10). Timaios picks up on the tension between Alexander's self-representation and his piety towards

---

[79] *FD* III 3.237; see also *Syll*[3] 671; Bringmann and von Steuben (1995), no. 93 and 94 with comm.
[80] Bringmann and von Steuben (1995) *ad* no. 402.
[81] *IPriene* I 56 with commentary by Bringmann and von Steuben (1995) *ad* no. 268.

city gods when reporting the Ephesians' rejection of the offer: it was not appropriate for a god to make gifts to the god (Timaios, *FrGrHist.* 566 F 150 b).[82] The Alexander historians describe Alexander's generosity towards the gods in exuberant terms. In the memorandum that Perdikkas is said to have read out to the army after Alexander's death in 323 BC, the king is said to have ordered temples to be built at Delos, Delphi and Dodona; and in Macedonia to Zeus at Dium, to Artemis Tauropolus in Amphipolis, and to Athena in Cyrnus (Diod. 18.4.5). The memorandum cannot be regarded as historical, but it shows the role that religious benefactions played in the symbolic construction of monarchy in the wake of Alexander's empire.[83]

Smaller sanctuaries were addressees of royal benefactions as well. Thus, for example, Philip Arrhidaeus (357–317 BC) and Alexander the Great consecrated land to the Cabeiroi on Samothrace; Ptolemy II and Arsinoe II (275–270 BC) endowed land for the Muses at Thespiai; Ptolemy IV (223–204 BC) vowed a *phiale*, weighing 100 Ptolemaic drachmas, and Eumenes a statue, to the temple of Amphiaraos in Oropos, and king Hieron II of Syracuse (*c.* 271–216) vowed armour to the sanctuary of Lindian Athena.[84]

Religious donations frequently, though not always, had an explicit reason and purpose. In 189/8 BC a benefactor of the citizens of Chios was honoured for having contributed both in cash and in kind to a festival in honour of Roma celebrated after the festival of the Chian *theophania*. He had given each citizen an amphora of wine and financed the procession, sacrifices and games in honour of the goddess. He had also hosted and paid the travel expenses of the Romans who had attended the festival. Although the generosity was aimed not just at pleasing Roma, the splendour of the festival in her honour seems to have been the most appropriate way for a Hellenistic city to show its submission to Roman influence.[85]

Another form of benefactions to temples were endowments, which are the most noteworthy transactions in ancient economic history. The term had no ancient equivalent, but the arrangements outlined in extant contracts correspond very closely to the modern legal institution. According to Laum, who published the still authoritative collection and commentary of the evidence available at his time, the constitutive elements of an endowment were that the donation had (a) a long-term purpose and (b) the principal of the endowment remained untouched throughout the period

[82] Bringmann (2000): 61.
[83] See also Plut. *Mor.* 343 D with implicit comparison with Pericles' building programme.
[84] Bringmann (2000): 54, for these and further examples. [85] *SEG* 30.1073.

of its use (often 'for ever').[86] The earliest example is that of the Athenian general Nicias (*c.* 470–413 BC) who consecrated to the Delians a *temenos* worth 10,000 drachmas. From the income of the land they should make sacrifice, pay for festivals and other prayers. Plutarch tells us that 'Nicias erected a stele as guardian of the gift which he left behind in Delos' (Plut. *Nic.* 3.5). Although brief and unelaborated, Plutarch's report suggests that by the fifth century BC the institution was well established. Another early example is the endowment Xenophon made on behalf of Artemis shortly after 400 BC in gratitude for his fortunate return from the Persian expedition. In his own report of the event he quotes from the text engraved upon the stele he had erected on the plot:

Holy be this land (*chora*)! Whoever holds this land and cultivates it shall give a tithe to the goddess, and from the surplus her temple shall be maintained. But if he fails to do so, may the goddess avenge it (Xen. *Anab.* 5.3.13).

There is in these early examples no hint that public officials supervised the correct use of the endowment or that there were civic regulations dealing with offences against the property. The sacred stelai were the only 'guardians' of the sacred property.[87] By the Hellenistic period endowment contracts were closely controlled by civic law without the stele losing its function as proof of the contract. Contracts contained detailed contractual arrangements following a regular pattern. Each contract contained the name of the donor, the nature of the transaction, its purpose, the nature and size of the asset, the beneficiary, the administration of the asset, as well as prohibitions and penalties.[88]

Endowments could be made to charitable institutions and other secular addressees just as to cult associations and temples. Among the recipients of religious endowments are gods, heroes, mysteries and cult associations both for the celebration of traditional ritual and the performance of ruler cult. The purpose of religious endowments was the financing of sacrifice and other ritual activities, sacred equipment and its maintenance as well as the foundation of new cults. The endowment was administered by public officials in the case of endowments to public cults, but by representatives of the cult association in the case of private cult associations. Because of the public control over endowments to public temples, it is certain that

---

[86] For this and the following, see still above all Laum (1914); more recent discussions of particular endowments in Roman Asia Minor are Wörrle (1988): 151–82; and Rogers (2001).

[87] Some priority of sacred law over public execution may be implied in the prohibition of members of the Athenian *boule* to consecrate their property, or make a dedication, before they have completed their audit; Aesch. 3.21.

[88] Laum (1914): 2.

the endowment became the property of the city, rather than of the deity or priests to whom it was consecrated.[89] Endowments could be made by any persons, both men and women, who had some property to dispose of; they could be part of a will or the disposition of a living person, and their motivations could be manifold. In fact, a systematic historical analysis of the institution is overdue.

Hellenistic rulers acted as donors just as their predecessors in the fifth and fourth centuries BC. According to an inscription from the time of Ptolemy III, Ptolemy II and Arsinoe II had endowed some property to the *technitai* of Dionysus in Thespiai. The Ptolemaic dynasty had some interest in these associations as their own self-representation intersected with cults of Dionysus. The annual payment received from the endowment (which may have been land or a tax) was 25,000 drachmas in year 220 BC. The Thespians decreed that with this money sacred land was to be purchased and appointed a board of officials entrusted with the purchase of the land. The inscription specified the pieces of land to be purchased and the costs of each parcel.[90] Similarly, Philetairos, son of Attalos III of Pergamon (158–138 BC) consecrated to the Muses and the cult association of the Philetairoi land so 'that they may have oil forever'.[91]

The complexity of endowment contracts is best illustrated by two transactions made by private benefactors of the Delphian Apollo in 182 BC, on the one hand, and to Poseidon in third-century Calauria in the Saronic gulf, on the other. In the first document, which is a witnessed *sungraphe*, a certain Alkesippos, son of Butheras, from Calydon bequeaths 130 staters of gold and 22 minai of silver to the city of Delphi. From the interest earned on this money, the city was annually to celebrate a sacrifice, a meal and a procession in honour of Apollo; and the celebration was to be named after the donor. The *archontes* were to write the contract on a stele and erect it in the sanctuary so as it should serve as witness for the endowment having been made. Alkesippos also bequeathed his other property and his female slave to the temple, although not in the form of an endowment.[92]

In the other example, the Calaurians disposed of the piece of land that Agasikles and Nikagora had consecrated to Poseidon. Two *epimeletai* were to be appointed to mortgage the land against 30 drachmas, each backed up by sureties that were deemed appropriate by the *epimeletai*. Each mortgage

[89] Lippert (1967): 77–95.
[90] *BCH* 19 (1895): 379; Laum (1914): no. 24; Bringmann and von Steuben (1995), no. 85.
[91] *BCH* 26 (1902): 156; Bringmann and von Steuben (1995), no. 88; cf. nos 86 and 87 relating to the same transaction.
[92] Laum (1914): no. 28.

in addition was to be subject to the approval of the assembly, as had been laid down in the foundation decree. And after the *epimeletai* had collected the interest payments, they were to sacrifice to Poseidon and to Zeus Soter a full-grown victim, and erect an altar in front of the *bouleuterion* (council house) where statues of the benefactor were erected. On the day after the sacrifice, they were to appoint officials to whom they should render account; and on the same day the *epimeletai* for the next financial year should be appointed.[93]

Endowments served specific ritual and political purposes. The financial management was subject to public administration, and the procedures of public audit to which all political officials were subjected at the end of their period of office applied. The endowments were made productive by lending them out on a competitive basis. The endowment contracts, moreover, followed the rules of public and private contracts subject to the civic law of execution. All of which combines to suggest that endowments for cultic purposes were conceived as transactions between donors and the city, rather than between donors and deities. Yet they should not therefore be interpreted as purely secular economic enterprise. Their function was a religious one within the symbolic power structure of a city through which the donors gained public recognition 'for ever'.

FINANCING NEW TEMPLES AND CULTS

Throughout this chapter we have seen that cult finance was a highly dynamic process which demanded public resources to be allocated and re-allocated, new taxes and tithes to be created, and new transactions to be invented in order to accommodate the changing needs of public and private ritual. Although Greek religion was conservative and faithful to its own traditions, it was not bounded off against innovation in the economic management of its property. There were, moreover, recognized civic procedures for the introduction of new cults, the election of new priesthoods, the erection of new temples, and the allocation of resources.[94] Land had to be consecrated, resources assigned and temples built, all being accompanied by sacrifice and ritual. One of these rituals was that coins were consecrated in the foundations of a new temple, although the evidence for this being a regular practice is limited.[95]

Founding and funding new cults could be the responsibility of either a cult association or of the state. In the former case it was the responsibility

[93] *IG* IV 841; Laum (1914), no. 58.   [94] For the following, Garland (1992); Weikart (1986).
[95] Weikart (1986): 181–84.

of a private individual or group of worshippers to consecrate property to the god, in the latter that of the state to create resources for funding. When a cult changed its status from private to public, its mode of funding also changed. This can be clearly observed in the case of the cult of Asclepius in the fifth and fourth centuries BC.[96] The cult seems to have been started on the initiative of a certain Telemachos, son of Theangelos, of the deme Acharnai in Attica (*IG* II² 4691). In the Asklepieion in the city of Athens an inscription was found which identified Telemachos as 'the first to erect the shrine and altar to Asklepios'. The priesthood of Asclepius was presumably transmitted through his family line, for three generations later, under the priesthood of a certain Theangelos, the sanctuary was enhanced by a wall and an offering table (*IG* II² 4963, first half of the fourth century BC). Later in the century, however, the priesthood was transferred to a certain Demon by appointment of the Athenian *demos*. At that time, and probably as a condition for receiving the priesthood, Demon endowed his house and garden to the god as a source of income to be managed by Athenian officials. The allocation of these resources was subject to the approval of Apollo at Delphi (*IG* II² 4969).

In the case of the introduction of the cult of the Thracian goddess Bendis into the Piraeus, we know only the moment when it became an official Athenian cult. The cult may either have been introduced in Athens at that time, or transferred to the state's responsibility. In any case, the Athenians decreed that a priesthood be elected by the Athenian assembly and first-fruits be voted to the goddess from an unknown source (*IG* I³ 136 = *LSCG* I 6). If the cult of Bendis in Piraeus had been private at first, the cult association would have had to have the right of owning land (*enktesis*) in Attica. The Athenians did grant that privilege to foreign cult associations on occasion. An example are the Phoenician merchants from Kition on Cyprus who in 332/1 BC received the right to own a plot of land on which to establish a sanctuary to Aphrodite 'just as the Egyptians have built the temple to Isis' (*IG* I³ 337 = *Syll.*³ 280). In *c.* 432 BC when a cult of probably Delian Apollo which up to then had been supported by voluntary contributions only, was designated to receive public support, a tax (*eparche*) was levied on all ship owners (*naukleroi*) on completion of each journey of their ships. The Athenians also voted to provide up to 500 drachmas towards the building of a shrine to Apollo, the remaining costs to be borne by voluntary subscriptions (*IG* I³ 130). We also mentioned above that when a new festival in honour of Amphiaraios was founded in

[96] Garland (1992): 128 f.

329/8 BC, the *tamiai tou demou* were ordered to provide the funds for the sacrifice of that year, but to direct the matter of permanent funding to the *nomothetai* at their next meeting (*IG* VII 4254.37–45). For the new cult of Asdepius, finally, the Athenians assigned money 'from the quarries', and what was left over from that money for the building of the temple (*IG* II² 47, 23 ff., early fourth century BC).

Detailed provisions for the permanent establishment of a new cult association have also survived from Teos at around 200 BC.[97] Dionysian *technitai* who had shown their goodwill to the *polis* were granted the right of theatrical performances and religious rituals for the benefit of the *polis*, and given a piece of land by the city. It was decreed that the land should have the value of 6,000 drachmas and that the *technitai* should own it free of taxes (*ateles*). In addition they were granted a suspension of payment for five years of any debts they still owed to the city. There follow specifications about the procedures for the transactions: two officials were to be appointed to purchase the land with money of which half was to be taken from the surplus of the grain-purchasing account to which excess money had been transferred from the account for the construction of fortifications. The other half should be taken from the first instalment paid into some royal account belonging to the city. The officials in charge were to be accountable for the transaction, and a stele erected near the temple of Dionysus; and the text was to be inscribed a second time on the wall of the theatre in which the *technitai* were to make their performances. Finally, an envoy should be appointed to inform the association about the decisions.

CONCLUSION

Temple economics cut across the notions of 'primitivism' and 'modernism' which have been applied to ancient economic history. Temples and cult associations did not just practise a traditional agrarian economy but used their property profitably, especially in lending their financial assets and leasing their land. There was some need for divine approval and civic control of the financial management of resources, but this was aimed at preventing embezzlement and fraud, rather than any kind of inappropriate economic behaviour. However, despite some profit-orientation in the use of financial and landed resources, temples in the Greek Mediterranean were by no means commercial centres. Evidence for cash-crop production or manufacture for markets, as we have it for Near Eastern and Egyptian

---

[97] *BCH* 46 (1922): 312 ff.; Bringmann and von Steuben (1995): no. 262.

temples and their vast estates, is lacking. Greek temples established markets on the occasion of games and festivals, but they served to supply visitors and participants with food and foreign luxuries rather than to sell the products of the sanctuary.[98]

Civic governments could decide to use temple treasuries for non-sacred purposes, especially in times of war. This may have put some limits on the freedom of sacred economic enterprise. Yet the active participation of temples in the process of monetization, and some notably innovative ideas in the use of temple property, show the dynamic role that temple households filled in the ancient monetary economy.

[98] Migeotte (2004): 109–10.

Epilogue: monetary culture

In this book I have concentrated on the economic consequences of money and coinage in classical antiquity. But it is well known that money does not just affect economies but is a collective signifier through which individuals and societies construe their identities and lives. Surprisingly, very little positive has ever been said about the social impact of money. Texts from Greco-Roman antiquity, too, express their anxieties about money. Already before the first coins were minted, Solon compared virtue with false (monetary) wealth. 'Many bad men are rich, good men poor; but we will not exchange virtue for these men's wealth. For the one lasts, whereas the other belongs now to this man and now to that' (Solon frg. 4 (Bergk)). Kreon proclaimed in Sophocles' *Antigone* that money was a force that destroyed cities, uprooted men from their homes, twisted good minds and set them to the most atrocious schemes (*Ant.* 295 ff.), while Plato associated contact with money with lying and deceit:

It is pleasant enough for a country to have the sea nearby for the pleasures of everyday life, but in fact it is a 'briny and bitter neighbour' in more than one sense. It fills the city with trade, and moneymaking because of the retail breeds shifty and deceitful habits in a man's soul, and so makes a community distrustful and unfriendly within itself as well as towards the world outside (*Nom.* 705a).

Attitudes to money tend to be extreme. 'We are sinking in the Devil's excrement' writes *OPEC* founder Perez Alfonso, engaging with the drastic imagery associated with the usurer in Western thought and literature.[1] Conversely, money has been associated with spirits, magic and divine power. Seaford suggests that such symbolic associations arise from the general effectiveness of money. 'Whatever the associations of modern money (conscious or unconscious, universal or specific), its central and predominant

---

[1] Coronil (1997): 321, for the quotation; Le Goff (1986) for the medieval imagery of usury; further, Shell (1982): 196; Seaford (2004): 3; Hörisch (1996): 57–63. Villard (1994): 88, suggests that Aristophanes in *Plut.* 1184 alludes to money being associated with excrement.

function – requiring precisely its identity in all contexts, unaffected by any incidental associations – is to embody abstract value as a general means of payment, of exchange, of the measurement and storage of value.'[2]

Yet the discrepancy between the economic convenience and the social impact of money can also be related to the duality on which the value of coinage rests in the Western tradition. Since Aristotle, coinage has been described both as a commodity with intrinsic (and often aesthetic) metal value, desired as a store of value and medium of exchange, and as a mere token having value only by social agreement in order to achieve intra-communal justice. Actually, on the one hand, Aristotle deliberately suppressed the intrinsic value of coinage in his argument about money being a token for achieving social justice. Whereas, on the other, when suggesting that coinage had its origin in inter-community trade he played down the fact that coinage carried a political stamp of local identity. This double evaluation of the phenomenon of coinage enabled him to castigate those members of a *polis* who took a medium of exchange to be worth accumulating as a store of value, despite acknowledging elsewhere that coined money had value outside the frame of communal conventions in inter-communal trade.[3]

The duality of the value of coinage has given rise to a host of debates over the past centuries.[4] Among classical scholars, it has led above all to the separation of the social symbolism and the economic function of both coinage and money. Thus Leslie Kurke writes:

Scholarship on Greek coinage has tended to polarize into what we might call symbolist and materialist readings of the phenomenon [of coinage]. Thus the former category (mainly literary scholars and some historians) see coinage only as a symbolic token, while the latter group (mainly ancient historians and numismatists) focus on the matter of coinage, framed almost exclusively in a positivist, economistic account of cause and effect. It is my contention that we cannot properly understand Greek coinage until we see the two sides together, and the dialectic of symbol and matter that takes place between them.[5]

In particular, she argues that silver coinage in classical Athens seems to have operated:

in a variety of contexts, symbolically and discursively, as a boundary phenomenon, articulating the border between the citizen community and its others. Insofar as a citizen is like a coin, he is not a slave, a metic or barbarian, or the victim of a tyrant; nor is he overwealthy or divine. Implicated in these various systems

---

[2] Seaford (2004): 2.   [3] Arist. *Pol.* 1257a31–8; *EN* 1132 a 20–34; see above introduction and chapter 1.
[4] Hart (1986) for a brief historical summary.   [5] Kurke (1999): 320.

of difference, the coin's reassuring materiality reifies and guarantees a category defined by exclusions. We know what citizens are made of – what they are – partly because of the analogy with coin. And the power of that guarantee derives in large measure from the naturalizing symbolism of precious metal ('our autochthonous silver') imprinted with the stamp.[6]

The dialectics of the substance of money and its symbolic meanings may help us to understand why coined money creates such unease among many of its users. Yet although some anxieties seem perennial, the phenomenon of money also provides a space within which culturally specific issues can be expressed.

In what follows, I shall give some illustration of what I mean by the latter. The text I shall discuss purports to convey knowledge about the nature of minerals, mining and metallurgy. Woven into its descriptive account is an invective against money. Yet the invective has little to do with the power of money itself, but rather censures the 'politics of immorality', as Catharine Edwards has termed the combination of power, excess and luxury that was typical of first-century AD Rome.[7]

The *Natural History* of the elder Pliny in book 33 deals with metals and metallurgy. This includes, as he explains, the matter 'which forms wealth itself and the prices of things' (*ipsaeque opes et rerum pretia* 33.1). In the ensuing discussion Pliny drifts between an encyclopedic collection of knowledge on mining and precious-metal artefacts towards a personal diatribe against luxury and moral decline caused by coined money. Historians have frequently pointed out that the book contains a rather 'standard ethical diatribe against luxury and aristocratic excess.'[8] Numismatists, on the other hand, take the book as an historical account of Roman coinage, soon to be qualified and dismissed. 'Italic peoples of the early Iron Age (*c.* 900–500 BC) employed as their media of exchange iron spits and cast bars of bronze. Pliny the Elder in the first century AD, recalling a popular etymology, relates that the clumsy first forms of money (*pecunia*) substituted for cattle (*pecus*), and he cite(s) a much later cast oblong ingot of bronze bearing a bull as testimony to this association.'[9] And Andrew Burnett writes:

Pliny's date for the first silver coins is, according to all three methods he uses, 269 BC; he is drawing at least in part on an earlier source (Timaeus), and his date has the support of the main tradition of other ancient authors. Leaving aside Timaeus, who wrote in the third century BC, since we do not know exactly what he said, but have only Pliny's interpretation, the earliest occurrence of the date 269 seems

---

[6] Kurke (1999): 316.   [7] Edwards (1991).
[8] Thus Purcell *OCD*[3]: 1197 f. *s.v. Pliny the Elder;* also Beagon (1992).   [9] Harl (1996): 21.

to be from the reign of Augustus, since the historian Livy apparently included the story of the beginning of coinage in his work . . . Nowadays, it is widely accepted that neither the inception of the early silver nor the denarius can be dated to 269/8, since the numismatic and archaeological evidence simply cannot be made compatible with either hypothesis, and various attempts have therefore been made to accommodate what Pliny says. Whether these attempts are really worth the effort is doubtful, as Pliny's remarks contain an astonishing number of mistakes and misdatings.[10]

While Pliny's discourse thus seems to be useful for discussing numismatics in a dialogue with ancient representations, both literary historians and numismatists have ignored the link that Pliny posits between the origins of coinage and Rome's political development. Pliny's enquiry into the nature of metal objects and his vision of Roman history are related, as metal itself was not just a natural resource but a substance loaded with symbolic significance. More precisely, Pliny's representation of the relationship between money and its metallic substance engaged with the political meaning of the Julio-Claudian myth of the Golden Age, which had climaxed under the emperor Nero but was deliberately rejected by Vespasian to whom the *Historia Naturalis* was dedicated.

Pliny opens his comprehensive account of gold and silver artefacts, money use and mining in the following way:

> Our topic now will be metals, and the substance of wealth itself and the prices of things (*rerum pretia*) – resources diligently sought for in the bowels of the earth in a variety of ways.[11]

Rerum pretia is a key concept in the *Natural History* and represents the discrepancy which Pliny observed between the human propensity to follow or to pervert nature. It may be translated literally as the 'price of things', but it contains a deliberate ambiguity between the true material value of objects (and coins) and the value people bestowed by convention on objects. Pliny uses the term in the usual sense of the price of things developing quite arbitrarily through human demand and desires that can be and are mistaken (9.137). In the final section of book 1, however, Pliny gives a list of what he regards as the true hierarchy of the value of things, which he too calls *comparatio rerum per pretia* (comparison of things by means of value). Gold ranks here no higher than tenth. It seems as if Pliny wishes to leave open the question whether precious metal, deployed to

---

[10] Burnett (1989): 10 f.
[11] Metalla nunc ipsaeque opes et rerum pretia dicentur, tellurem intus exquirente cura multiplici modo.

assess *rerum pretia*, is a measure of true, or of socially determined value (which makes it more liable to collective abuse).

He continues:

> For in some places the earth is dug into for riches, when life demands gold, silver, electrum and copper, and in other places for luxury, when gems and colours for tinting walls and beams are demanded, and in other places for rash valour, when the demand is for iron, which amid warfare and slaughter is prized even more than gold. We trace out all the fibres of the earth, and live above the hollows we have made in her, marvelling that occasionally she gapes open or begins to tremble – as if it were not possible that this may be an expression of the indignation of our holy parent. We penetrate her entrails (*viscera*) and seek for riches in the abode of the spirits of the departed, as though the part we tread upon were not sufficiently bounteous and fertile... Earth bestows upon us on her surface fruits, bountiful and generous as she is in all things for our benefit. The things that she has concealed and hidden underground, those that do not quickly come to birth, are the things that destroy us and drive us to the depth below; so that suddenly the mind soars aloft into the void and ponders what finally will be the end of draining her dry in all the ages, what will be the point to which avarice will penetrate. How innocent, how blissful, indeed how luxurious life might be, if it coveted nothing from any source but the surface of the earth, and, to speak briefly, nothing but what lies ready to hand (33.1–3).[12]

The particular direction of this 'standard' Roman linkage of money, luxury, moral decline and social self-destruction lies in its significant omissions. There are telling silences and gaps in Pliny's opening of book 33. First, he does not call money by its common name (*pecunia* or *nummus*), but circumscribes it as the substance of wealth itself and the prices of things (*ipsaeque opes et pretia rerum*). He then elides various issues by relating them to the same activity of mining. Proposing, on the one hand, to talk about metals, minerals and money, he causally connects (*quippe alibi... alibi*) the importance of the search for gold (representing wealth, luxury and monetary metal) with the search for the iron tools of warfare. The link was made, because iron was equally ambivalent. 'Iron is an excellent or

---

[12] Quippe alibi divitiis foditur quaerente vita aurum, argentum, electrum, aes, alibi deliciis gemmas et parietum lignorumque pigmenta, alibi temeritati ferrum, auro etiam gratius inter bella caedesque. Persequimur omnes eius fibras vivimusque super excavatam, mirantes dehiscere aliquando aut intremescere illam, ceu vero non hoc indignatione sacrae parentis exprimi possit. imus in viscera et in sede manium opes quaerimus, tamquam parum benigna fertilique, qua calcatur; ... Quamquam et hoc summa sui parte tribuit ut fruges, larga facilisque in omnibus, quaecumque prosunt. illa nos peremunt, illa nos ad inferos agunt, quae occultavit atque demersit, illa, quae non nascuntur repente, ut mens ad inane evolans reputet. quae deinde futura sit finis omnibus saeculis exhauriendi eam, quo usque penetratura avaritia. quam innocens, quam beata, immo vero etiam delicata esset vita, si nihil aliunde quam supra terras concupisceret, breviterque, nisi quod secum est.

detrimental instrument for human life depending on the use to which we put it', he writes in the following book (34.138). Yet the causal connection of gold and iron had a tradition in Roman literature and may be related to the anxiety caused by the conflation, which both money and weapons represent, of the elementary dichotomy between natural and artificial.[13] Both had been considered principal and related sources of mutual destruction in the civil wars of the late republic. In *Elegy* I.10, Tibullus cursed whoever invented the art of making iron weapons as well as gold which perverted this invention into a cause for all human unhappiness. To Ovid, mining of iron and gold was the ultimate violation of the earth, one of the evil findings of Iron Mankind (*nocens ferrum ferroque nocentius aurum*: 'baneful iron, and gold more baneful than iron, *Met.* 1.138). While in Virgil's *Eclogue* 4 sheep that are red, yellow and purple by nature (*sua sponte*) are a sign that nature acknowledges mankind's need for symbolic luxury and naturally produces these goods herself – in order to prevent humans from trespassing on her rights.[14] Pliny has set the stage for a more comprehensive culture critique which plays on the transgressive nature of coined money embodying both social and divine power.

The following remarks about human violation of natural integrity in search for gold and minerals engage conspicuously, albeit tacitly, with the memory of the Golden Age. This myth, first entering the Mediterranean world with Hesiod, tells the story of an age under the reign of Kronos in which a Golden Race of men inhabited a fertile earth which brought forth its fruits unasked, without human labour and without the use of the plough (cf. *nascuntur repente* in Pliny's version). In this age, men lived a blissful life, supplied by the abundance of Nature and therefore innocent (Hes. *W&D* 119–22; cf. *innocens. . . beata. . . delicata*). Lucretius used the myth to describe the origins of human civilization where there were no ploughs, no commerce and no money (*De rer.* 5. 925–38). By the time of Augustus, the idea of a Golden Race had turned into a timeless age in the past, an inversion of the present, in which the absence of labour was imagined as a form of peaceful and pastoral well-being.[15] For Virgil, the age before Jupiter was one of vigorous physical and mental exertion, but without the need for productive labour (*Georg.* 1.121–8). In the *Metamorphoses* Ovid depicts the Golden Age as lacking both virtues and vices; no greed and warfare were known, but neither were skill and sophistication (I.89–112). Seneca associates the Golden Age with agrarian fertility and the natural right to

---

[13] Graf (1999): 322–6.   [14] Virg. *Ec.* 4. 5–10; Graf (1999): 322.
[15] Barker (1996); cf. Galinsky (1996): 90–128; Gatz (1962).

rule: wool is precious yarn that weaves the age of its own accord, without labour (*sua sponte . . . nulloque labore, Apocol.* 4.6–13). Pliny stays neutral on these matters, but his praise of natural plenty and growth alludes to the Golden Age without naming it.

It was a key part of Julio-Claudian propaganda to hail the reign of the emperor as a return of the Golden Age.[16] Yet the Golden Age was not a fixed symbol but a mobile discourse. It was, as Duncan Barker writes:

a composite of different positions taken by different Romans at different times around the idea of a returning golden age. We can no longer say that in the Augustan Age 'the myth of the Golden Age stopped developing and became a fixed poetic, political and philosophical symbol', rather we must agree that the concept had become a complex and variegated one, and so remained. The very range of interrelated discourses incorporated into that of the golden age – discourses on peace and militarism, virtue and happiness, the earth and agriculture – was such that no Roman can have assented to the whole nexus of ideas simultaneously. Insofar as the myth continued to be re-presented, so the discourse of the golden race became more rather than less complex, and, as it did so, the idea of a returning golden race is likely to have become morally more and more ambiguous.[17]

Yet only a few proclamations of the return of the Golden Age were unequivocally enthusiastic. In the famous fourth *Eclogue* Virgil anounces the birth of a boy who will end the iron race at last and raise a golden one through the world:

> Now the last age of Cumae's prophecy has come;
> The great succession of centuries is born afresh.
> Now, too, returns the Virgin; Saturn's rule returns;
> A new begetting now descends from heaven's height,
> O chaste Lucina, look with blessing on the boy
> Whose birth will end the iron race at last and raise
> A golden one through the world: now your Apollo rules!
>
> (Virg. *Ecl.* 4.9–10).

Horace linked the return of a Golden Age (*tempus/saecula aurea*) more closely to the ending of civil discord and the return of justice: 'Jupiter set apart these shores for a righteous people, ever since with bronze he dimmed the lustre of the Golden Age. With bronze and then with iron did he harden the ages, from which a happy escape is offered to the righteous, if my prophecy is heeded' (Hor. *Epod.* XVI. 63). To these may be added an

---

[16] See Zanker (1988) and Galinsky (1996): 106–20 for visual representations of the Golden Age.
[17] Barker (1996): 436, against Reckford (1958).

example from the *Georgics* where the designation of Italy as *Saturnia tellus* (the land of Saturn/Kronos), alongside the repeated play on Hesiodic imagery, implies a special connection between Italy, the Augustan present, and the Golden Race.

The traditional discourse of luxury and moral decline, climaxing at the end of the republic and epitomized by the golden splendour of its most corrupt politicians, rendered gold an ambivalent signifier. Moreover, the issue of a regular gold coinage under Caesar introduced in totally un-Roman fashion the portrait of a ruler on the republican coinage and created an uneasy link between gold, money and dictatorship. Ovid exposed the ambivalence between money and political symbolism in the *Ars Amatoria*: 'Golden is truly our Age: with gold comes the most honour, gold is what buys you love' (*Aurea sunt vere nunc saecula: plurimus auro/venit honos: auro conciliatur amor; AA* 2.277–8). In the *Metamorphoses* he brings the interdependence of the symbolism and materialism of precious metal more subtly into play. Pygmalion prays to Venus that she may turn his ivory statue, to which he feels sexually attracted and which is the most valued object in his life, into his wife. Venus, explicitly referred to as 'the golden', is said to have turned the ivory statue into a real person, ivory into flesh, and made her Pygmalion's lover (*Met.* 10.262–90). The combination of different materials and desire (ivory/statue; flesh/lover; gold/Venus) brings the hierarchical value of different materials into focus, but at the same time questions the symbolic hierarchy with which these different materials are endowed.

Throughout antiquity, the relationship between gold, money and agrarian wealth was problematic, as only the latter guaranteed secure political, and in some cases, civic status. Yet in Rome, the monetary censuses for the senatorial and equestrian orders, as well as the reality of the activities of urban elites, had increasingly undermined the hierarchy of monetary and agrarian property. Horace's *Epistle* I.12 is highly instructive for the way a comparison of them could be deployed to expose the ambivalent meaning of Roman power and human wealth.[18] The central theme of the letter is the relationship between crops, vegetation, and the necessities of life, on the one hand, and monetary profit, on the other. Both could be referred to by the term *frux/fruges* (fruit/fruits), a semantic field which Horace fully exploits in his poem. The Latin text begins with the very word *fruges*, and Horace assures Iccius that he could ask for no greater riches only if he uses them properly (*si recte frueris*):

[18] Again Barker (1996) for the following.

If, Iccius, you are enjoying as you should the Sicilian products which you collect for Agrippa, Jupiter himself could not give you greater abundance (*copia maior*). Away with complaints; for he is not poor who has enough of things to use. If stomach, lungs, and feet are all in health, the wealth of kings can give you nothing more. If you hold aloof from what is within your reach, and live on nettles and other greens, you will go on living in the same way, though Fortune's stream suddenly flood you with gold: either because money cannot change your nature, or because you count all else below the one thing, virtue (*Ep.* I.12.1–11).[19]

While the opening lines create a clear hierarchy between wealth and virtue, gold (money) and agrarian sufficiency, the end of the epistle complicates the meaning of *fruges*. Here 'fruits' become the exploits of the army – money, spoils and slaves – which were the true origins of contemporary plenty:

Yet, that you may not be ignorant how the world goes in Rome, the Cantabrian has fallen before the valour of Agrippa, the Armenian before that of Claudius Nero. Phraates, on humbled knees, has accepted Caesar's imperial sway. Golden plenty (*aurea Copia*) from full horn has poured her fruits (*fruges*) upon Italy (25–9).[20]

The fruits which golden *Copia* pours upon Italy from her full horn may be as ambiguous as the fruits of the earlier part of the poem. They could be read either literally as the agricultural fruits of Italy itself (or the empire), or metaphorically as the luxurious spoils of imperial monetary exploitation, which in turn is reflected in the golden nature of Plenty who pours them.

---

[19]   Fructibus Agrippae Siculis, quos colligis, Icci,
          si recte frueris, non est copia maior
          ab Iove donari possit tibi. tolle querellas;
          pauper enim non est cui rerum suppetit usus.
          si ventri bene, si lateri est pedibus tuis, nil
          divitiae poterunt regales addere maius.
          si forte in medio positorum abstemius herbis
          vivis et urtica, sic vives protinus, ut te
          confestim liquidus Fortuna rivus inauret,
          vel quia naturam mutare pecunia nescit,
          vel quia cuncta putas una virtute minora.

[20]   ne tamen ignores, quo sit Romana loco res:
          Cantaber Agrippae, Claudi virtute Neronis
          Armenius cecidit; ius imperiumque Phraates
          Caesaris accepit genibus minor; aurea fruges
          Italiae pleno defudit Copia cornu.

In the light of the epistle, and Horace's wider discourse on luxury and gold, the goldenness of *Copia* may be taken to imply danger just like money.[21]

It becomes apparent, then, why Pliny phrases his opening paragraph so carefully. Wishing to align himself with the pre-Augustan tradition of imagining primeval plenty without money (e.g. Lucr. *De rer.* 5.1281 ff.), he deliberately suppresses the notion of the Golden Age associated with the political symbolism of the Julio-Claudian dynasty and its perversion under Nero. Pliny wrote under the powerful patronage of the first Flavian emperor Vespasian to whom, as we already noted, the *Historia Naturalis* was dedicated. Tacitus fashioned the transition from the Julio-Claudian period to the Flavians as a turn from extreme luxury to deliberate moderation, a configuration of change which must probably be read with a pinch of salt in both directions. Yet in line with this political affiliation Pliny castigates the last emperor of the Julio-Claudian dynasty Nero as the incarnation of luxury, degeneration and disorder. Not only is his work replete with scathing remarks about Nero and his horrific life style, but this emperor in book 7 is explicitly named an enemy of mankind (*hostis generis humani*, 7.45). In fact, he is the very antithesis of the humanitarian ideals set out in the work. Mary Beagon has observed that for Pliny Nero not only is luxurious, but shows a perverted ingenuity for innovations and refinements in luxury. His use of medicine is not connected with health (*humana salus*), but with his immoral lusts and pleasures (13.126; 28.238). His interest in magic shows cruelty (*saevitas*) against mankind (30.14–15). His private use of splendour stands in stark contrast to the traditional Roman idea that art and culture should serve public rather than private adornment (36.12). There is an implicit contrast between the building schemes with which Augustus and Vespasian adorned the city of Rome, and the private luxury of Nero's Golden House.[22] The Golden House is called the 'prison' of the works of Famulus (Nero's court painter), while Vespasian dedicated productions of similar quality to the Temples of Honour and Virtue (35.120). The omens which foreshadow his death are particularly spectacular examples of the perversions which Nero has brought about, and are predicated on an ironic analogy between the emperor's golden reign and his monetary nature: meadows and trees move over to the other side of the road and rivers begin to flow in the opposite direction (2.199, 232). The man who has

---

[21] Barker (1996): 443–4. In the *Odes* Horace is more explicit about the ambivalence of gold; cf. *Od.* 2.10; 2.18; 1.31 In *Odes* 3.3 Juno advises the Romans that gold is better left underground, and in *Odes* 3.24 Horace recommends people either to dedicate their gold on the Capitol or to throw it into the sea. Gems and useless gold have become the 'stuff of our greatest ill' (*summi materies mali*, 3.24.49).

[22] Beagon (1992): 18.

shown that everything is exchangeable now makes Nature exchange itself. Nero's perversion of values and his monetary nature are not just coincidence. They place the emperor in opposition to the harmony of the natural order, to explain which lies at the heart of Pliny's project in the *Historia Naturalis*. Read within this context, Pliny's condemnation of luxury and precious metal is a political rather than moral statement.

Pliny's political agenda becomes the frame for his explanation for the development of coinage and money. We saw that gold was easily associated with money, despite the fact that the majority of Roman coins were minted in silver and bronze (see above, chapter 2). Pliny follows this tradition by constructing a continuous decline from the first use of gold in rings for self-adornment to the invention of a gold coinage. After identifying the introduction of golden rings and necklaces as the first and 'worst crime which humans committed against life' (*pessimum vitae scelus*, 33.8), the issue of a gold denarius is made the second:

Next in degree was the crime committed by the person who first coined a gold denarius, a crime which itself also is hidden and its author unknown. The Roman nation did not even use a stamped silver coinage before the conquest of King Pyrrhus [279BC]. King Servius [regal period] was the first to stamp a design on bronze; previously, according to Timaeus, at Rome they used raw metal. The design stamped on the metal was an ox or sheep, *pecus*, which is the origin of the term *pecunia* . . . Silver was first coined in the 485th year of the city [269–268 BC], in the consulship of Quintus Ogulnius and Gaius Fabius, five years before the first Punic war . . . The first gold coin was struck 51 years later than the silver coinage [217 BC], a scruple of gold having the value of 20 sesterces; this was done at 400 to the pound of silver, at the then rating of the sestertius. It was afterwards decided to coin denarii at the rate of 40 from a pound of gold [i.e. the aureus first minted under Caesar], and the emperors gradually reduced the weight of the gold denarius; and most recently Nero brought it down to 45 denarii to the pound . . . But from the invention of money came the original source of avarice when usury was devised, and a profitable life of idleness; by rapid stages what was no longer mere avarice but a positive hunger for gold flared up . . . (33.42–8)

Although Pliny asserts that the Romans did not at first use gold for making coinage, he places the invention of bronze for money at the beginning of the dynamics of decline, which he ties in with his model of degeneration caused by the social use of gold. Instead of describing gold coinage as the relatively late invention which it was, it becomes the manifestation of the beginning of Roman degeneration which had begun, quite independently of the use of gold, with the stamping of metals as money. Before the introduction of a regular gold coinage under Caesar, gold had been coined temporarily only. Yet Pliny had particular reasons for putting such emphasis on gold coinage. It did not embody only the combination of human greed for gold and money, but also a particular kind of un-Roman self-aggrandizement.

Although Caesar is usually associated with the first gold portrait coinage in Rome, the first extant aureus dated to the lifetime of its issuer bears the head of Antony. There had been some reluctance under the republic to represent individuals in gold, a practice which had been common in the Eastern Hellenistic kingdoms where gold statues and coinages presented kings and queens as religious figures and recipients of cultic veneration. In Rome, it created an uneasy link between republican rule and Hellenistic monarchy, as well as Alexandria and Rome as the centres of power. By the close political and personal affiliations which Antony and Caesar had spun with the Ptolemaic queen Cleopatra, they had transgressed Roman interests and republican values at the level of both politics and propriety. Pliny is careful not to attribute the introduction of gold coinage to the Roman people. Its inventor was 'hidden and unknown', while the Romans, allegedly, never imposed tribute in the form of gold (33.15). Yet the unduly Hellenizing Antony had shown himself to be enough of an enemy to the Roman people to be associated in memory with the most perverted use of gold. Pliny tells a tale according to which Antony used gold for his chamber pot, rendering him more extravagant even than women and Eastern kings:

The triumvir Antony used vessels of gold to satisfy all his indecent needs, an enormity that even Cleopatra would have been ashamed of. Till then the record in extravagance had lain with foreigners – King Philip sleeping with a gold goblet under his pillows, and Alexander the Great's prefect Hagnon of Teos having his sandals soled with gold nails; but Antony alone cheapened gold by this contumely of nature (33.50).

Pliny emphasizes the enormity of Antony's behaviour by linking his prover-bial extravagance to women and Eastern tyrants.[23] Within the context of the previous discussion, the reference to Cleopatra's, Philip's and Alexan-der's use of gold alludes to their, and implicitly Antony's, gold coinage. Not accidentally, it was Nero, the last emperor of the Julio-Claudian dynasty, who in the eyes of Pliny was degenerate enough to debase the gold coinage which carried his own portrait (33.47 quoted above).

Pliny's history of mining, metals and coinage occupied a place within the contested space of money, authority, power and Roman identity. It not only situated its author in an anti-Neronian and pro-Vespasianic value system, but was embedded in a wider symbolic system in which gold, agrarian

---

[23] Edwards (1991) *passim* for this topical link.

plenty and monetary wealth had been cast into a problematic relationship. Set within the natural history of minerals and metals, on the one hand, but linked with the symbolism of the Golden Age and primordial plenty, on the other, the discussion of metals became an arena in which a range of symbolic tensions were negotiated: those between past and present, natural history and mythical origins, and agrarian wealth and human avarice for money. In the preface to the *Natural History* Pliny states, 'my subject is nature which is to say life' (*natura hoc est vita narratur*). Pliny's quest for a rational account of the purposes of a nature that comprised both natural resources and human life led him into an exploration of the relationship between natural values and human evaluation, and the ambivalent meaning of gold as both a natural store of wealth and a symbol of human monetary extravagance. He resolves that tension by describing metals as a possession of the earth not made for human consumption, and by rejecting the political symbolism that the Julio-Claudians had bestowed on the Golden Age. The abuse of gold as a means of human adornment and monetary metal was a crime. But it had been committed anonymously, by outsiders or enemies of the Roman people. True *romanitas* was alien to the false use of gold and money.

Table 4: *Wheat prices on Delos, third to first centuries* BC [1]

Date/month	Price/medimnos	Grs silver/ton	Reference
282/1	7 dr	1017.9	*ID* 158 A 37–8
282/2	6 dr 3 ob	945.2	*ID* 158 A 39–40
282/3	6 dr	872.5	*ID* 158 A 41–2
282/4	4 dr 3 ob	654.4	*ID* 158 A 42–3
282/5	6 dr 5 ob	993.6	*ID* 158 A43–4
282/8	7 dr	1017.9	*ID* 158 A45–6
282/9	10 dr	1454.2	*ID* 158 A46–7
190/12	10 dr	1454.2	*ID* 401, 22
178/12	10 dr	1454.2	*ID* 445, 13
174/12	11 dr	1599.6	*ID* 440A69
169/12	10 dr	1454.2	*ID* 461B b53

[1] Reger (1994): 306.

Table 5: *Wheat prices in Athens, fifth to fourth centuries* BC

Date	Price/medimnos	Grs silver/ton	Reference	Comments
415	6 dr 3 ob	945.2	*IG* I³ 421, 137	Grain sale by auction
415	6 dr	872.5	*IG* I³ 421, 138	Grain sale by auction
415	6 dr 2 ob	920.48	*IG* I³ 421, 139	Grain sale by auction
392	3 dr	436.25	Aristoph. *Ecc.* 545; cf. Suidas *s.v. hekteus*	?Comic distortion

(*cont.*)

Table 5: (*cont.*)

Date	Price/medimnos	Grs silver/ton	Reference	Comments
Early 4th c.	6 dr	872.5	*IG* II/III² 1356, 17	Grain purchase
335	16 dr	2326.66	Dem. 34.39	Emergency price
334	5 dr	727.1	Dem. 34.39	Normal price
c. 330	9 dr	1308.75	*IG* II/III² 408	Special price for imported grain; reading of measure uncertain
330	5 dr	727.1	*SIG*³ 304	Special price for imported grain
329/8	5 dr	727.1	*IG* II/III² 1672, 282ff.	Grain purchase
329/8	6 dr	872.5	*IG* II/III² 1672, 282ff.	Grain purchase
324	5 dr	727.1	*IG* II/III² 360	Special price for imported grain
300	6 dr	872.5	*SIG*³ 354	Normal price

Table 6: *Wheat prices in Egypt, third to first centuries* BC

	Date	Price/artaba	Silver Price/art	Grs of silver/ton	Reference	Comments
0	c. 330	10 dr	10 dr	1200	Ps-Arist. *Oik.* 1352 b	Emergency price in the *chora*; possibly distorted
1	270	2 dr 1 ob	2 dr 1 ob	260	*P. Hib.* I 99, 14	*Adaeratio* of wheat rent
2	270	4 dr 5 ob	4 dr 5 ob	580	*P. Hib.* I 110, 11	Market price in Alexandria
3	267	2 dr	2 dr	240	*P. Hib.* I 100, 6	Payment for grain
4	256/Mar.	2 dr 5 ob	2 dr 5 ob	340	*P. Mich. Zen.* 28	Bulk sale in harbour (March)
5	256?	1 dr 1 ob	1 dr 1 ob	140	*SB* XIV 11659, 4	Tenancy contract. Conversion of monetary loans into wheat rent
6	254/Jan. and Feb.	1 dr 3 ob	1 dr 3 ob	180	*P. Cair. Zen.* III 59499, 3 and 5	Conversion of monetary payment into wheat

Table 6: (*cont.*)

	Date	Price/artaba	Silver Price/art	Grs of silver/ton	Reference	Comments
7	254/Mar.	1 dr 2 ob	1 dr 2 ob	160	*P. Cair. Zen.* III 59499, 7	Conversion of monetary payment into wheat
8	254	1 dr 1 ob	1 dr 1 ob	140	*P. Lond.* VII 1974, 38	Payment for *sitometria* grain
9	250	1 dr 2 ob	1 dr 2 ob	160	*P. Col. Zen.* I 54, 16	Tenancy contract. Conversion of monetary loans into wheat rent.
10	*c.* 250?	3 dr	3 dr	360	*P. Lond.* VII 1996, 41	Sales price of grain in '*dochikon*' measure
11	*c.* 249?	2 dr 5 ob	2 dr 5 ob	340	*P. Lond.* VII 2002, 28	Price of grain
12	249	5 dr 2 ob	5 dr 2 ob	640	*P. Cair. Zen.* III 59320	Price in Alexandria
13	Mid 3rd c.	3 dr	3 dr	360	*P. Sorb.* 33, 15 f.	Market price
14	Mid 3rd c.	1 dr 3 ob	1 dr 3 ob	180	*P. Petr.* III, 47 (a), 3	Payment for *sitometria* grain
15	Mid 3rd c.	1 dr 3 ob	1 dr 3 ob	180	*P. Cair. Zen.* IV 59698, 5	Payment for *sitometria* grain
16	3rd c.	2 dr	2 dr	240	*P. Petr.* III 80 (a), ii 16; 22	Payment for grain
17	209	6 dr	3 dr	360	*P. Heid.* VI 383, 20	Prodomatic tenancy agreement. Repayment of monetary loan as rent in kind
18	195?	170	2 dr 5 ob	340	*P. Köln* V 217, 6 ff.	Sales price of grain
19	193/87	160	2 dr 4 ob	320	*BGU* VII 1536, 3	Sales price of grain
20	193/87	155	2 dr 3.5 ob	310	*BGU* VII 1532, 12	Sales price of grain
21	193/87	180	3 dr	360	*BGU* VII 1532, 13	Sales price of grain
22	158	400	1 dr 5 ob	200	*SB* V 7617, 98	Account. Payment for *sitos* in Serapeium; farm gate price?

(*cont.*)

Table 6: (*cont.*)

	Date	Price/artaba	Silver Price/art	Grs of silver/ton	Reference	Comments
23	159	750 [300 olyra]	3 dr 1 ob	379, 6	*UPZ* I 91–3	Median price of *olyra* in that year. Converted into wheat price at the rate of 2:5
24	*c.* 129	(400) 600	(1 dr 5 ob) 2 dr 5.5 ob	(200) 300	*SB* VI 9420, 6	Price of wheat in 'sale with deferred delivery'. Loan repayable in kind with 50 per cent interest
25	118	1200	2 dr	240	*P. Grenf.* I 22, 11	Purchase price of grain bought by local tax office
26	112/Mar.	1000	1 dr 4 ob	200	*P. Tebt.* I 112, 58	Conversion of wage in kind paid by local tax office (12 March)
27	112/Mar.	1200	2 dr	240	*P. Tebt.* I 112, 113	Purchase price of grain bought by local tax office (16 March)
28	112/Mar.	800	1 dr 2 ob	160	*P. Tebt.* I 112, 118	Conversion of wage in kind paid by local tax office (16 March)
29	111	1560	2 dr 4 ob	315	Botti, *Test. dem.* 4 *recto*	Price for grain (Thebes)
30	110/Sept.	1200	2 dr	240	*P. L. Bat* XIX 6, 33	Purchase price of land converted into payment in grain (Pathyris)
31	108	720	1 dr 1 ob	140	*P. Tebt.* I 224 *verso*	Conversion of wage in kind
32	100?	1080	1 dr 4 ob	220	*SB* XVI 12675, 16	Account. Payment for grain
33	Late 2nd c.	1000	1 dr 4 ob	200	*P. Tebt.* I 116, 2	Payment to individual. Conversion rate of wage in kind?
34	Late 2nd c.	1100	1 dr 5 ob	220	*P. Tebt.* I 116, 32	Payment to named individual. Conversion rate of wage in kind?

Table 6: (*cont.*)

	Date	Price/artaba	Silver Price/art	Grs of silver/ton	Reference	Comments
35	99	1680	2 dr 5 ob	340	*P. Tebt.* I 117, 10	Purchase of grain
36	99	1500	2 dr 3 ob	300	*P. Tebt.* I 117, 18 n.	Purchase of grain
37	99	1680	2 dr 5 ob	340	*P. Tebt.* I 117, 47	Purchase of grain
38	97/64	1800	3 dr	360	*P. Tebt.* I 120, 72	Account. Payment for grain
39	94/61	840	1 dr 1.5 ob	150	*P. Tebt.* I 208 descr.	Account. Payment for grain
40	94/61	1500	2 dr 3 ob	300	*P. Tebt.* I 121, 140	Account. Payment for grain
41	93	2000	3 dr 2 ob	400	*P. Tebt.* I 109, 15	Prodomatic tenancy agreement. Prepayment of rent in kind as loan of money
42	1st c.	?800	?1 dr 2 ob	?160	*PSI* VIII 968, 3	Price of grain. Reading uncertain.
43	1st c.	2200	3 dr 4 ob	440	*P. Oxy.* IV 784 *descr.*	Price of grain

Table 7: *Penalty prices for wheat in Egypt, third to first centuries* BC

	Date	Penalty Price	Penalty Price/Silver	Grs of silver/ton	Reference
1	306	4 dr	4 dr	460	*P. Loeb dem.* 3, 18 (Tenis, Hermopolite)[2]
2	301/300	4 dr	4 dr	460	*P. Hib.* I 84a, 8–9
3	*c.* 265	4 dr	4 dr	460	*P. Hib.* I 65, 24
4	260/59	4 dr	4 dr	460	*BGU* VI 1226, 13
5	258/7	4 dr	4 dr	460	*BGU* 1228, 13
6	257	4 dr	4 dr	460	*P. Sorb.* 17 a, 15; b, 16
7	244/3 or 218/7	?4 dr	?4 dr	460	*P. Hib.* I 91, 11
8	3rd c.	4 dr	4 dr	460	*BGU* VI 1267, 13

(*cont.*)

Table 7: (*cont.*)

	Date	Penalty Price	Penalty Price/Silver	Grs of silver/ton	Reference
9	223/2	4 dr (silver)	4 dr	460	*P. Tebt.* III. 1 815 fr. 3 ii, 14
10	222	5 dr (? silver)	5 dr	600	*P. Hib.* I 90, 15
11	216/5	10 dr (bronze)	5 dr	600	*BGU* VI 1262, 13
12	215/4	10 dr	5 dr	600	*BGU* VI 1264, 22 f.
13	215/4	10 dr	5 dr	600	*BGU* X 1969, 8
14	215/4	10 dr	5 dr	600	*BGU* XIV 2383, 12
15	215/4	10 dr	5 dr	600	*BGU* X 1943, 12–14
16	214/3	10 dr	5 dr	600	*BGU* VI 1265, 20
17	214/3	10 dr	5 dr	600	*BGU* X 1944, 12
18	214/3	10 dr	5 dr	600	*P. Frankf.* I, 23
19	214/3	12 dr	6 dr	720	*BGU* XIV 2397, 10–11; 29
20	213/2	10 dr	5 dr	600	*BGU* X 1946, 12
21	173	500 dr	4 dr 1 ob	500	*P. Amh.* II 43, 12
22	160/59	400 dr	3 dr 2 ob (1:120)	400	*BGU* XIV 2390, 34 (Herakleopolite nome)
23	Before 145	1000 dr	4 dr 1 ob	500	*BGU* VI 1271, 8
24	128/7	2000 dr	3 dr 2 ob	400	*P. Loeb dem.* 55, 13 (?Tenis, Hermopolite nome)
25	119	2000 dr	3 dr 2 ob	400	*P. Tebt.* I 11, 17 (Kerkeosiris, Arsinoite nome)[3]
26	116	2000 dr	3 dr 2 ob	400	*P. L. Bat.* XXII 34, 11 (Tenis, Hermopolite nome)
27	116	3000 dr	5dr	600	*P. L. Bat.* XXII 26, 18
28	c. 115	3000 dr	5 dr	600	*P. Fay.* 11, 17
29	113	3000 dr	5 dr	600	*P. L. Bat.* XXII 21, 22
30	113/2	3000 dr	5 dr	600	*P. L. Bat.* XXII 27, 19
31	112	3000 dr	5 dr	600	*P. L. Bat.* XXII 13, 24
32	111	3000 dr	5 dr	600	*P. L. Bat.* XXII 22, 21
33	110	3000 dr	5 dr	600	*P. L. Bat.* XXII 14, 25
34	110	3000 dr	5 dr	600	*P. L. Bat.* XXII 1, 16
35	110?	3000 dr	5 dr	600	*P. L. Bat.* XXII 28, 27
36	109	3000 dr	5 dr	600	*P. L. Bat.* XXII 2 dem, 11
37	109	3000 dr	5 dr	600	*P. L. Bat.* XXII 15, 23
38	109	3000 dr	5 dr	600	*P. L. Bat.* XXII 16, 28
39	109	1200 dr	4 dr (1:300)	460	*P. Chicago Field Mus. dem.* 31323, 14 (Thebes)
40	108	1200 dr	4 dr (1:300)	460	*P. Turin dem. Suppl.* 6086, 16 (Thebes)
41	108	3000 dr	5 dr	600	*P. L. Bat.* XXII 3, 15

Table 7: (*cont.*)

	Date	Penalty Price	Penalty Price/Silver	Grs of silver/ton	Reference
42	108	3000 dr	5 dr	600	*P. L. Bat.* XXII 4, 16
43	108	3000 dr	5 dr	600	*P. L. Bat.* XXII 23, 22
44	Late 2nd c.	2000 dr	3dr 2 ob	400	*P. L. Bat.* XXII 32, 17
45	106	1500 dr	5 dr (1: 300)	600	*P. L. Bat.* XXII 5 dem, 20
46	105	3000 dr	5 dr	600	*P. L. Bat.* XXII 19, 21
47	104	3000 dr	5 dr	600	*P. L. Bat.* XXII 25, 28
48	104/3 or 102/1	3000 dr	5 dr	600	*P. Köln* VI 275, 11
49	103	2000 dr	3 dr 2 ob	400	*P. Louv. dem.* 2436 b
50	100	2400 dr	4 dr	460	*P. Adler* 15, 9
51	92 or 59	3000 dr	5 dr	600	*P. Tebt.* I 110, 9
52	73 or 44	4000 dr	3 dr 2 ob (1:300)	400	*P. Oxy.* XIV 1639, 13
53	77	3000 dr	5 dr	600	*P. Merton* I 6, 24 f.
54	51	3000 dr	5 dr	600	*PSI* X 1098, 28

[2] The rent in kind is specified as payable in an *artaba* of 28 *choinikes*. This does not seem to have affected the penalty price.

[3] The *dochikon* measure is used for the calculation of the wheat rent, but this may not have affected the penalty price; see previous note.

Table 8: Archaic mints and their weight standard[1]

Name of city	Material of coin	Comment
Milesian (14.1 g/tetradrachm)		
Ephesus	electrum then silver	
Karpathos	silver	
Chersonesos (Thrace)	silver	
Chios	silver	later Chian
Klazomenai	silver	
Miletos	electrum then silver	
Knidos	electrum then silver	later Aiginetan
Lindos	electrum then silver	later Aiginetan
Teos	electrum then silver	later own standard
Termera	silver	
Phokaian (16. 1 g/tetradrachm)		
Phokaia	electrum	
Erythrai	electrum	later Persian then Chian
Kyzikos	electrum	silver from *c.* 450 BC
Lampsakos	electrum	later Persian then Chian
Mytilene	electrum	
Aiginetan (12.2 g/didrachm)		
Aigina	silver	
Andros	silver	
Akraiphnion/Boiotia	silver	
Haliartos/Boiotia	silver	
Mykalessos/Boiotia	silver	
Orchomenos/Boiotia	silver	
Pharai/Boiotia	silver	
Tanagra/Boiotia	silver	
Thebes/Boiotia	silver	
Delphi	silver	
Karthaia	silver	
Mantineia	silver	
Naxos	silver	
Paros	silver	

Name of city	Material of coin	Comment
Sikyon	silver	
Siphnos	silver	
Tegea	silver	
Tenos	silver	
Thera	silver	
Kameios	silver	
Sinope	silver	
Attic (17.2 g/tetradrachm)		
Athens	silver	
Delos	silver	
Barke	silver	
Cyrene	silver	
Euhesperides	silver	
Akanthos	silver	
Peparethos	silver	
Sermyle	silver	
Akragas	silver	
Gela	silver	
Samians in Zankle	silver	
Selinous	silver	?Attic
Syracuse	silver	
Euboian (17.2 g/tridrachm)		
Chalcis	silver	
Eretria	silver	
Kalymna	silver	
Samos	silver	later Milesian
Aeneia	silver	
Mende	silver	
Olynthos	silver	
Poteidaia	silver	
Stageira	silver	
Torone	silver	later own standard
Mende	silver	
Olynthos	silver	
Skione	silver	
Himera	silver	
Messana	silver	
Naxos (Sicily)	silver	
Zankle	silver	
Rhegion	silver	
Corinthian (8.6 g/tridrachm)		
Corinth	silver	
Leukas	silver	
Corcyra	silver	compatible with Corinthian

(*cont.*)

Name of city	Material of coin	Comment
Italic (8 g/tridrachm)		
Kaulonia	silver	
Kroton	silver	
Metapontium	silver	
Serdaioi	silver	
Sybaris	silver	
Taras	silver	
Campanian (7.5 g/didrachm)		
Poseidonia	silver	
Velia	silver	
Thraco-Macedonian (various weight standards)		
Oreskioi	silver	
Laiai	silver	
Derrones	silver	
Ichanioi	silver	
Bisaltai	silver	
Lete	silver	
Dikaia	silver	
Edonoi	silver	
Aigai	silver	
Neapolis	silver	
Samothrake	silver	
Thasos	silver	
Therma	silver	
Tenedos	silver	
Persian (5.35 g/*siglos*)		
Kolophon	silver	
Kos	silver	
Golgoi	silver	
Kition	silver	
Paphos	silver	
Idalion	silver	
Lapethos	silver	
Salamis (Cyprus)	silver	
Unknown		
Methymna (Lesbos)	elektron[2]	
Selge	silver	
Idyma	silver	
Caria	silver	
Dardanos	silver	

[1] Based on Kraay (1976); Osborne (1996): 253–5; and Figueira (1998): 563–98.

[2] Figueira (1998): 96 f.

Glossary

See also Greek and Roman monetary system and coin denominations p. xv

agora Greek market

agoranomos Greek magistrate in charge of market control; in Egypt an official who kept safe public and private contracts

annona public grain supply in Rome

antoninianus numismatic term for Roman silver coin minted from the time of the emperor Caracalla (Marcus Aurelius Antoninus, AD 211–17) onwards

archaic period period of Greek history referring to the time between the late ninth century BC to the end of the Persian Wars in 479 BC

aroura square measure in Greco-Roman Egypt of *c.* 2,760 square metres

artaba corn measure in Greco-Roman Egypt of *c.* 40 l.

choinix Greek grain measure of *c.* 1.08 l.

choregia Athenian liturgy involving paying for the production of a chorus at the musical or dramatic festival

cura annonae see *annona* and *frumentatio*

daric/dareikos Persian gold coin equivalent to 20 *sigloi*

deme/demos local district or village in Greece

denarius Roman silver coin

didrachm numismatic term for a two-drachma piece

drachma Greek silver coin

dupondius Roman coin denomination

eisphora tax on capital levied especially when a (Greek) city was at war

electrum natural alloy of gold and silver, used for some coinages in archaic Asia Minor and the Hellespontine region

epigraphy the study of inscriptions

eranos friendly, interest-free loan to a member of a Greek *polis* by a group
  of fellow-citizens
euergetism (from Greek *euergetes* 'benefactor') Modern term for the system
  of benefactions by which citizens and kings supported public purposes
  and cult with their own money
forum Roman market
frumentatio grain handouts to entitled citizens of the city of Rome
horos boundary stone marking debt on land
HS = *sestertius*
iugerum Roman square measure of *c.* 2,500 square metres
kapithe Persian corn measure equivalent to 2 Attic *choinikes*
kistophoros Greek silver tetradrachm minted in Pergamon from the time of
  Eumenes II (197–159 BC) and equivalent to 3 Attic-weight silver drachmas
libra Roman unit of weight equivalent to 12 *unciae* or *c.* 329 g.
liturgy in Athens a form of taxation which required wealthy men to undertake certain work for the state at their own expense; in Egypt a system of
  corvée which all inhabitants had to perform unless they paid financial
  compensation
medimnos Attic grain measure of *c.* 54.5 l.
metretes Greek liquid measure of *c.* 30.4 l.
mina Greek and Persian monetary unit
modius Roman corn measure of *c.* 8. 62 l.
nome/nomos administrative subdivision or local district in Greco-Roman
  Egypt
numismatics the study of coins
obol/obolos Greek fractional coin
obverse the front of a coin
oikos ancient (Greek) household
ostraka/ostrakon small potsherd(s) used in antiquity for everyday notes, in
  particular receipts (Egypt) and voting (classical Athens)
panegyris temporary market
papyrology the study of papyri, surviving mostly from the deserts of Egypt
patrimonium (Roman) inheritable property
polis Greek city state usually comprising an urban centre and its hinterland
prodoma prepayment of rents and wages, known from Greek papyri
reverse the back of a coin
sestertius Roman coin
shekel = *siglos*
siglos = *shekel*. Persian monetary unit and silver coin equivalent to 1/60 or
  1/50 of a mina

solidus Roman monetary gold unit introduced by the emperor Constantine (AD 306–37)

sungraphe Greek formal written contract. In Egypt it was typically witnessed by six witnesses named at the end of the document

tetradrachm numismatic term for a four-drachma silver coin

talent Greek monetary unit equivalent to 6,000 drachmas

Bibliographical essay

ECONOMIC CONTEXT

Access to the economic context of ancient money is now much facilitated by *The Cambridge Economic History of the Greco-Roman World* (Morris, Scheidel and Saller (2007)). Other new approaches are explored in Cartledge, Cohen and Foxhall (2001), Manning and Morris (2005), and Bowman and Wilson (2009), *Introduction*. Many aspects of the ancient economy are described from a new perspective in Horden and Purcell (2000) who also offer a wealth of information from places outside the centres of Greece and Rome. The development of research in ancient economic history during the years after Moses Finley is sampled in Scheidel and von Reden (2002), which includes useful synoptic essays by Cartledge and Andreau; see also W. Harris (1993). Finley's *The Ancient Economy* (1985) and the collection of some of his most important articles in Finley (1981) remain essential reading for understanding the Greek, but less so the Roman, economy. For a new approach to the Roman imperial economy, Bang (2008); more conventionally, Garnsey and Saller (1987): chapters 3–5. For the nature of ancient supply and demand, the most helpful comments can be found in Erdkamp (2005) and Morley (2007).

INTRODUCTORY WORKS

Several books offer valuable introductions to Greek and Roman money and coinage. Howgego (1995) covers the broadest period of time (*c.* 600 BC – *c.* AD 400) and is not just on coinage. Schaps (2004) is the best introduction to money in ancient Greece (sixth to fourth century BC) and contains a discussion of Near Eastern monetization as well. His argument that monetization began with the introduction of coinage, however, may not be shared by all readers. Harl (1996) contains many valuable chapters on the Roman monetary economy, but unfortunately is not always reliable. Crawford (1985) and Hollander (2007) are thus better alternatives for the republican period. Burnett (1987) and Carradice and Price (1988) are introductions for numismatists, and unfortunately lack footnotes, but contain very good chapters on coinage in use. In von Reden (2002) I have provided a synopsis of the most important international work on monetary history published between *c.* 1975–2001.

NUMISMATIC INTRODUCTIONS

Recommended introductions to Greco-Roman coinages in English are still the volumes in the Methuen series: Kraay (1976); Crawford (1985); Mørkholm (1991). Here references to the standard catalogues of coins can be found. However, the series does not cover the late Hellenistic and Roman imperial period, and is in need of updating in light of new material and research.

FURTHER READING

In recent years some attempt has been made to create closer co-operation and more intense discussion between economic historians and numismatists. The collection of articles in Carradice (1987a), Meadows and Shipton (2001) and Harris (2008) shows the fruits of such co-operation. Those in Harris (2008) provide an excellent overview of issues currently under discussion. A combination of numismatic and economic approaches is also synthesized in the volumes by Crawford (1974) (1985), and Duncan-Jones (1982), (1990) and (1994). Although their statistical analyses are not for the beginner, they provide a starting point for any quantitative study on Roman money and coinage.

MONETIZATION

The transition from pre-monetary to monetary exchange and the use of coinage in the Greek world are well explored by Kim (2001b); Kroll (1998) (2001) and (2008). Schaps (2004) (2008) offers an alternative approach (see 'Introductory works'). An instructive comparison between monetization in Greco-Roman antiquity and that in ancient China has been made available by Scheidel (2008). Roman monetization has been investigated by Burnett (1982) (1985) as well as Crawford (1985). I have studied monetization in Ptolemaic Egypt (von Reden (2007a)), while Katsari (2005) (2008) has looked at the monetization of several Roman provinces in late antiquity. The fascinating topic of the monetization of the Celtic world has been explored above all by Haselgrove (e.g. (1987a), (1987b) (2006a and b)) and Nash (1978) (1981) and (1987). See also the volume edited by Cunliffe (1981). For an update in the light of rapidly changing quantities of evidence, see de Jersey (2006a) (2006b).

MONETARY NETWORKS

The economic implications of shared coinages and weight standards in the ancient monetary system have not been much investigated. See, however, Figueira (1998) who pays close attention to the Athenian/Euboian weight standard and its capacity to create a currency network in the fifth century BC. Modern treatments of currency connections, which can offer a theoretical starting point, are the books by B. Cohen (1998) (2004). Information about Greek weight standards can be obtained from Kraay (1976) and Mørkholm (1991). The spread of the Chian weight standard is discussed by Meadows in *Coin Hoards* IX. Burnett, Amandry and Ripollès (1991) offer an overview of the gradual spread of the Roman denarius in the Julio-Claudian period.

CREDIT

Introductions to the ancient culture of credit are Millett (1984) (1991) and Verboven (1997). The function of Greek credit and banking has been the subject of an important debate between Millett (1991) and E. E. Cohen (1992), the former following a Finleyan, the latter a modern banking, perspective. Roman credit and banking has been approached rather differently. See above all Andreau (1999), Rathbone and Temin (2008), and the collection of articles in Lo Cascio (2003), many of which are in English. The rich material from Greco-Roman Egypt forms the basis of Bogaert (1994) and (1998/9). The use of money beyond cash has been explored above all by E. E. Cohen (1992), von Reden (2007a), Harris (2006) and Hollander (2007); while Howgego (1992) has made a good case for the interdependence of coin circulation and credit in the first centuries BC/AD.

PRICES AND PRICE FORMATION

A collection of ancient price data can now be accessed under nomisma.geschichte.uni-bremen.de (from the archaic to classical Greek period); and www.stanford.edu/~scheidel/NumIntro.htm (Roman). The main printed collections of wages, rents and prices are Loomis (1998) (excluding prices); Drexhage (1991); and Szeivert and Wolters (2005). The nature of ancient price formation has been the subject of a conference the papers of which are published by Andreau *et al.* (1997). The best case study is that by Reger (1994), based on the rich price material from Hellenistic Delos, which is conveniently listed in the appendices. Ancient price inflation and deflation have been discussed by Burnett (1987) and Howgego (1995), while detailed discussions of individual cases can be found in Cadell and Le Rider (1997), von Reden (2007a) (both third-century BC Egypt), Rathbone (1996) and Corbier (1985) (both third-century AD). A good analysis of the alleged price deflation in the late Roman republic is Verboven (1997).

SACRED FINANCE

The economics of temple finance are unfortunately not well integrated into the study of ancient economic history so far; see however Reger (1994) and Davies (2001). Rosivach (1994) has studied the finances of Athenian sacrifice, while the collected essays in Linders and Alroth (1992) offer a good introduction to Greek temple economics. The accounts of Greek temple treasuries have been analysed by D. Harris (1995) and Linders (1972), but are in need of comprehensive treatment in connection with the finances of Greek cities; see some comments by Kallet-Marx (1994). Temples, cults and their relation to the Near Eastern, Roman and Greek monetary economy will be the subject of an article by Giovanangelo, Scheid and von Reden in the forthcoming supplementary volumes to the *Thesaurus Cultus et Rituum Antiquorum* (*ThesCRA*).

MONETARY CULTURE

During the 1990s, there has been a particular interest in the cultures of money and the cultural consequences of its use. As all studies make abundantly clear, there was not one single monetary culture in antiquity, but individuals and collectives negotiated the problematic relationship between identity, power, wealth and money in their own ways. Seaford (1998) and (2004) has concentrated on the conceptual impact of money on philosophy and tragedy in late archaic and early classical Greece. Kurke (1995) (1999) (2002) has looked from different perspectives at the tension between metals and money in the construction of self in late archaic Athens. In von Reden

(1995) I have explored the tension between economic function and social symbolism of coinage in late archaic and classical Athens. Kraus (1999) has investigated monetary imagery in relation to one of Rome's most anti-Roman politicians, Jugurtha. Harl (1987), and, more recently, Howgego, Heuchert and Burnett (2005) have looked from a numismatic point of view at provincial identities and forms of Romanization constructed through, and expressed by, Roman provincial coinages.

References

Aleshire, S. B. (1989) *The Athenian Asklepieion: The People, their Inventories, and their Dedications*. Amsterdam.

Allam, S. (ed.) (1994) *Grund und Boden in Altägypten*. Akten des internationalen Symposiums in Tübingen 18–20 Juni 1990. Tübingen.

Allen, D. F. (1980) *The Coins of the Ancient Celts*. Edinburgh.

Amemiya, T. (2007) *Economy and Economics of Ancient Greece*. London.

Ampolo, C. (1992) 'The economics of the sanctuaries in southern Italy and Sicily' in T. Linders and B. Alroth (eds.) *The Economics of Cult*. Uppsala: 25–8.

Andreau, J. (1987) *La vie financière dans le monde romain, les métiers de manieurs d'argent (IVe siècle av. J.-C. – IIIe siècle ap. J.C.)*. Rome.

(1999) *Banking and Business in the Roman World*. Cambridge.

(2008) 'The use and survival of coins and of gold and silver in the Vesuvian cities' in W. Harris (2008): 208–25.

Andreau, J., P. Briant, R. Descat (eds.) (1997) *Prix et formation des prix dans les économies antiques*. Entretiens d'archéologie et d'histoire, Saint-Bertrand-de-Comminges 3. Saint-Bertrand-de-Comminges.

Appadurai, A. (ed.) (1986) *The Social Life of Things*. Cambridge.

Ashton, R. (2001) 'The coinage of Rhodes 408 – *c.* 190 BC' in Meadows and Shipton (2001): 79–117.

Austin, M. (2006) *The Hellenistic World from Alexander to the Roman Conquest. A Selection of Ancient Sources in Translation*, 2nd edn. Cambridge.

Badian, E. (1972) *Publicans and Sinners*. Oxford.

Bagnall, R. (1977) 'Prices in sales with deferred delivery', *Greek, Roman and Byzantine Studies* 18: 85–96.

(1999) Review of Cadell and Le Rider (1997) in *Schweizerische Numismatische Rundschau* 78: 197–203.

Bagnall, R. and R. Bogaert (1975) 'Orders of payment from a banker's archive: papyri in the collection of Florida State University', *AncSoc* 6: 79–108 (repr. in Bogaert (1994): 219–44).

Bang, P. (2008) *The Roman Bazaar: A Comparative Study of Trade and Markets in a Tributary Empire*. Cambridge.

Barker, D. (1996) '"The Golden Age is proclaimed"? The Carmen Saeculare and the renascence of the Golden Race' *CQ* 46: 435–46.

Beagon, M. (1992) *Roman Nature. The Thought of Pliny the Elder*. Oxford.

Beyer, F. (1995) *Geldpolitik in der römischen Kaiserzeit. Von der Währungsreform des Augustus bis Septimius Severus*. Wiesbaden.

Bingen, J. (1978a) 'Économie grecque et société égyptienne au IIIe siècle' in H. Maehler and V. M. Strocka (eds.) *Das Ptolemäische Ägypten*. Mainz: 211–19 [Engl. trans. in *Hellenistic Egypt* (ed. R. Bagnall). Edinburgh 2007: 215–28].

   (1978b) 'The land leases at Tholthis', *ICS* 3: 74–80.

Bivar, A. D. H. (1999) 'Symbolon, a noteworthy use for a Persian gold phiale' in G. R. Tsetskhladze (ed.) *Ancient Greeks West and East*. Leiden: 379–84.

Bloch, M. (1967) 'Natural economy and money economy: a pseudo-dilemma' in *Land and Work in Medieval Europe*. London: 230–47 [trans. from French orig. 1966].

Bogaert, R. (1968) *Banques et Banquiers dans les Cités Grecques*. Leiden.

   (1988) 'Les opérations en nature des banques en Égypte gréco-romaine', *AncSoc* 19: 213–24 (repr. in Bogaert (1994): 397–406).

   (1994) Trapezitika Aegyptiaka. *Recueil de recherches sur la banque en Égypte gréco-romain*. Papyrologica Florentina 25. Leiden.

   (1998/9) 'Les opérations des banques de l'Égypte Ptolémaïque', *AncSoc* 29: 49–149.

Bowman, A. and A. Wilson (eds.) (2009) *Quantifying the Roman Economy*. Oxford.

Bresson, A. (2005) 'Coinage and money supply in the Hellenistic Age' In Z. Archibald *et al.* (eds.) *Making, Moving and Managing. The New World of Ancient Economies*. Oxford: 323–31.

Bringmann, K. (ed.) (2000) *Geben und Nehmen. Monarchische Wohltätigkeit und Selbstdarstellung im Zeitalter des Hellenismus*, 2 vols. Berlin.

Bringmann, K. and H. von Steuben (1995) *Schenkungen hellenistischer Herrscher an griechische Städte und Heiligtümer. I. Zeugnisse und Kommentare*. Berlin.

Brunaux, J. L. (1988) *The Celtic Gauls. Gods, Rites and Sanctuaries*. London [trans. from French 1987].

Burford, A. M. (1969) *The Greek Temple Builders at Epidaurus*. Liverpool.

Bürge, A. (1987) 'Fiktion und Wirklichkeit: Soziale und rechtliche Strukturen des römischen Bankwesens', *ZRG* Röm. Abteilung 104: 465–558.

Burnett, A. (1982) 'The currency of Italy from the Hannibalic War to the reign of Augustus', *AIIN* 29: 125–37.

   (1987) *Coinage in the Roman World*. London.

   (1989) 'The beginnings of Roman coinage', *AIIN* 36: 33–64.

   (2005) 'The Roman West and the Roman East' in Howgego *et al.* (2005): 171–80.

Burnett, A., M. Amandry, and P. P. Ripollès (1991) *Roman Provincial Coinage I: From the Death of Caesar to the Death of Vitellius (44* BC *–* AD *69)*. London.

Buttrey, T. V. (1982) 'Pharaonic imitations of Athenian tetradrachms' in Hackens, T. and Weiller, R. (eds.) *Proceedings of the 9th International Congress of Numismatics. Berne 1979*. Luxemburg: 137–40.

Cadell, H. (1994) 'Le prix de vente des terres dans l'Égypte ptolémaïque d'après les papyrus grecs' in Allam (1994): 289–305.

Cadell, H. and G. Le Rider (1997) *Prix du Blé et Numéraire dans l'Égypte Lagide de 305–173 av. J-C.* Brussels.

Carey, S. (2004) *Pliny's Catalogue of Culture. Art and Empire in the* Natural History. Oxford.

Carradice, I. (ed.) (1987a) *Coinage and Administration in the Athenian and Persian Empires.* BAR International Series 343. Oxford.

(1987b) 'The regal coinage of the Persian empire' in (1987a): 73–107.

Carradice, I. and M. J. Price (1988) *Coinage in the Greek World.* London.

Cartledge, P. (2002) 'The economy (economies) of ancient Greece' in Scheidel and von Reden (2002): 11–32.

Cartledge, P., E. E. Cohen, and L. Foxhall (eds.) (2001) *Money, Labour and Land. Approaches to the Economics of Ancient Greece.* London.

Christiansen, E. (1984) 'On denarii and other coin-terms in the papyri', *ZPE:* 54: 271–99.

Clarysse, W. and D. J. Thompson (1995) 'The salt-tax-rate once again', *CdÉ* 70: 223–9.

(2006) *Counting the People. Population Registers from Ptolemaic Egypt.* 2 vols. Cambridge.

Clarysse, W. and K. Vandorpe (1997) 'Viticulture and wine consumption in the Arsinoite nome (P.Köln V 221)', *AncSoc* 28: 67–73.

(1998) 'The Ptolemaic apomoira' in *Le culte du souverain dans L'Égypte ptolémaïque au IIIe siècle avant notre ère.* Stud.Hell. 34: 5–42.

Coase, R. (1937) 'The nature of the firm', *Economica* 4: 386–405.

Cohen, B. (1998) *The Geography of Money.* Ithaca.

(2004) *The Future of Money.* Princeton.

Cohen, D. (1995) *Law, Violence and Community in Classical Athens.* Cambridge.

Cohen, E. E. (1992) *Athenian Economy and Society. A Banking Perspective.* Princeton.

(2003) 'Progressive taxation and the fostering of maritime trade in classical Athens' in Lo Cascio (2003): 17–32.

(2008) 'The elasticity of the money-supply at Athens' in Harris (2008): 66–83.

Collis, J. R. (1984) *Oppida. Earliest Towns North of the Alps.* Sheffield.

Corbier, M. (1985) 'Dévaluation et évaluation des prix (Ier-IIIe siècle)', *RN* 27: 69–106.

Cornell, T. J. (1995) *The Beginnings of Rome. Rome and Italy from the Bronze Age to the Hannibalic Wars (c. 1000 to c. 264 BC).* London.

Coronil, F. (1997) *The Magical State. Nature, Money and Modernity in Venezuela.* Chicago.

Costabile, F. (1992) 'Editio altera et traduzione delle tabelle Locresi' in (ed.) *Polis ed Olympieion a Locri Epizefiri.* Soveria Manelli: 229–307.

Crawford, M. (1969) *Roman Republican Coin Hoards.* London.

(1970) 'Money and exchange in the Roman world', *JRS* 60: 40–8.

(1974) *Roman Republican Coinage.* 2 vols. London.

(1985) *Coinage and Money under the Roman Republic*. London.

(1986) *La moneta a Grecia et a Roma*. Bari.

Creighton, J. (2000) *Coins and Power in Late Iron Age Britain*. Cambridge.

Crosby, M. and M. Lang (1964) *Weights, Measures and Tokens* (Athenian Agora 10). Princeton.

Cunliffe B. (ed.) (1981) *Coinage and Society in Britain and Gaul. Some Current Problems*. London.

Cuvigny, H. (2003) 'Les avatars du chrysous dans l'Égypte ptolémaïque et romaine', *BIFAO* 103: 111–30.

Davies, G. (1994) *A History of Money*. Cardiff.

Davies, J. K. (1998) 'Ancient economies: models and muddles' in H. Parkins and C. Smith (eds.) *Trade, Traders and the Ancient City*. London 1998: 225–56.

(2001) 'Temples, credit and the circulation of money' in A. Meadows and K. Shipton (2001): 117–28.

(2006) 'Hellenistic economies' in G. R. Bugh (ed.) *The Cambridge Companion to the Hellenistic World*. Cambridge: 73–92.

Debord, P. (1982) *Aspects sociaux et économiques de la vie religieuse dans l'Anatolie Gréco-Romain*. Leiden.

De Callataÿ, F. (1989) 'Les trésors achéménides et les monnayages d'Alexandre: espèces immobilisées et espèces circulantes', *REA* 91.1–2: 259–76.

(2005) 'A quantitative survey of Hellenistic coinages: recent achievements' in Z. Archibald, J. K. Davies, and V. Gabrielsen (eds.) *Making, Moving and Managing. The New World of Ancient Economies*. Oxford: 73–92.

(2005a) 'L'instauration par Ptolémée I Soter d'une économie monétaire fermée' in F. Duyrat and O. Picard (eds.), *L'exception égyptienne? Production et échanges monétaires en Égypte hellénistique et romaine*. Actes du colloque d'Alexandrie, 13–15 avril 2002 (Etudes Alexandrine 10). Cairo: 117–33.

(2005b) 'The Graeco-Roman economy in the super-long run: lead, copper, and shipwrecks', *JRA* 18: 361–72.

De Callataÿ, F., G. Depeyrot, and L. Villaronga (eds.) (1993) *L'argent monnayé d'Alexandre à Auguste*. Leiden.

De Jersey, P. (ed.) (2006a) *Celtic Coinage: New Discoveries, New Discussions*. BAR International Series 1532. Oxford.

(2006b) 'Introduction' in de Jersey (2006a): 1–16.

De Ligt, L. (1990) 'Demand, supply, distribution: the Roman peasantry between town and countryside. Rural modernisation and peasant demand', *MBAH* 9: 24–56.

De Ligt, L. and P. W. De Neeve (1988) 'Ancient periodic markets, festivals and fairs', *Athenaeum* 66: 391–416.

De Neeve, P. W. (1990) 'A Roman landowner and his estates: Pliny the Younger', *Athenaeum* 68: 363–402.

Depeyrot, G. (1991) *Crises et inflation entre antiquité et moyen âge*. Paris.

De Vries, J. (1994) 'The Industrial Revolution and the Industrious Revolution', *Journal of Economic History* 54: 249–70.

Dignas, B. (2002) *Economy of the Sacred in Hellenistic and Roman Asia Minor*. Oxford.

Donlan, W. (1981) 'Scale, value and function in the Homeric economy', *AJAH* 6: 101–17.

(1981–2) 'Reciprocities in Homer', *Classical World* 75: 137–75.

(1989) 'The pre-state community in Homer', *SO* 64: 5–29.

Drexhage, H.-J. (1991) *Preise, Mieten, Pachten, Kosten und Löhne im römischen Ägypten bis zum Regierungsantritt Diokletians*. St. Katharinen.

Duncan-Jones, R. (1976) 'The price of wheat in Roman Egypt under the principate', *Chiron* 6: 241–62.

(1982) *The Economy of the Roman Empire. Quantitative Studies*. Cambridge.

(1990) *Structure and Scale in the Roman Economy*. Cambridge.

(1994) *Money and Government in the Roman Empire*. Cambridge.

(1997) 'Numerical distortion in Roman writers' in Andreau *et al.* (1997): 147–59.

(2003) 'Roman coin circulation and the cities of Vesuvius' in Lo Cascio (2003): 161–80.

Duyrat, F. (2005) 'Le trésor de Demanhur (IGCH 1664) et l'évolution de la circulation monétaire en Égypte hellénistique' in Duyrat and Picard (2005): 17–52.

Duyrat, F. and O. Picard (eds.) (2005) *L'exception égyptienne? Production et échanges monétaires en Égypte hellénistique et romaine*. Actes du colloque d'Alexandrie, 13–15 avril 2002. Etudes Alexandrine 10. Cairo.

Eddy, S. K. (1973) 'Some irregular amounts of Athenian tribute' *AJP* 94: 47–70.

Edwards, C. H. (1991) *The Politics of Immorality*. Cambridge.

Eggertson, T. (1990) *Economic Behaviour and Institutions*. Cambridge.

Einzig, P. (1966) *Primitive Money*, 2nd edn. Oxford.

Engelmann, H. and D. Knibbe (eds.) (1989) *Das Zollgesetz der Provinz Asia: Eine neue Inschrift aus Ephesos*. Epigraphica Anatolica 14. Bonn.

Erdkamp, P. (2005) *The Grain Market in the Roman Empire*. Cambridge.

Fales, F. M. (1995) 'Assyro-Aramaica. The Assyrian lion-weights' in van K. Lerberghe and A. Schoors (eds.) *Immigration and Emigration in the Near East. Festschrift E. Lipinski*. Orientalia Lovaniensia Analecta 65. Leuven: 33–56.

Figueira, T. (1981) *Aigina: Society and Economy*. New York.

(1998) *The Power of Money. Coinage and Politics in the Athenian Empire*. Philadelphia.

Finley, M. I. (1951) 'Some problems of Greek law: a consideration of Pringsheim on sale', *Seminar* 9: 72–91.

(1952) *Studies in Land and Credit in Ancient Athens, 500–200 BC*. New Brunswick [repr. and quoted from New Brunswick 1985 with an introductory essay by Paul Millett].

(1981) *Economy and Society in Ancient Greece* (ed. B. Shaw and R. Saller). London.

(1981a) 'Debt-bondage and the problem of slavery' in Finley (1981): 150–66.

(1981b) 'Land, debt and the men of property in classical Athens' in Finley (1981): 62–76.

(1981c) 'The ancient city: from Fustel de Coulanges to Max Weber' in Finley (1981): 3–23.

(1985) *The Ancient Economy*. 2nd edn. London.

(1986) 'The alienability of land in ancient Greece' in (ed.) *The Uses and Abuses of History*. 2nd edn. London: 153–60.

Foxhall, L. and H. A. Forbes (1982) 'Sitometreia: the role of grain as a staple food in classical antiquity', *Chiron* 12: 41–90.

Frier, B. W. and D. Kehoe (2007) Law and economic institutions' in I. Morris, W. Scheidel and R. Saller (2007): 113–43.

Gabrielsen, V. (2003) 'Banking and credit operations in Hellenistic times' in Z. Archibald, J. K. Davies and V. Gabrielsen (eds.) *Making, Moving and Managing: The New World of Ancient Economics*. Oxford: 136–64.

Galinsky, K. (1996) *Augustan Culture. An Interpretive Introduction*. Princeton.

Gallant, T. W. (1991) *Risk and Survival in Ancient Greece*. Stanford.

Gara, A. (1976) *Prosdiagraphomena e circolazione monetaria. Aspetti dell'organisazione fiscale in rapporto alla politica monetaria dell'Egitto Romano*. Milan.

(1984) 'Limiti strutturali dell'economia monetaria nell'Egitto tardo-tolemaico' in B. Virgilio (ed.) *Studi Hellenistici* I (Bibliotheca di studi antichi 48). Pisa: 107–34.

Garland, R. (1987) *The Piraeus*. London.

(1992) *Introducing New Gods*. London.

Garnsey, P. (1988) *Famine and Food Supply in the Greco-Roman World*. Cambridge.

Garnsey, P. and R. Saller (1987) *The Roman Empire. Economy, Society, Culture*. London and Berkeley.

Gatz, B. (1962) *Weltalter, goldene Zeit und verwandte Vorstellungen*. Hildesheim.

Geginat, V. (1964) *Prodoma in den Papyri aus dem ptolemäischen und römischen Ägypten*. Cologne.

Gernet. L. (1981) 'La notion mythique de la valeur en Grèce', *Journal de psychologie* 41 (1948): 415–62. [Engl. trans. (and quoted from) 'Value in Greek myth' in R. Gordon (ed.), *Myth, Religion and Society: Structuralist Essays by M. Detienne, L. Gernet, J.-P. Vernant and P. Vidal-Naquet*. Cambridge: 111–46.].

Giacomin, A. and M. C. Marcuzzo (2007) (eds.) *Money and Markets*. London.

Graf, F. (1999) 'Mythical production: Aspects of myth and technology in antiquity' in R. Buxton (ed.) *From Myth to Reason? Studies in the Development of Greek Thought*. Oxford: 317–28.

Gruel, K. (1989) *La Monnaie chez les Gaulois*. Paris.

Harl, K. W. (1987) *Civic Coins and Civic Politics in the Roman East.* AD *180–275*. London.

(1996) *Coinage in the Roman Economy. 300* BC *to* AD *700*. Baltimore and London.

Harris, D. (1995) *The Treasures of the Parthenon and Erechtheion*. Oxford.

Harris, W. (1993) 'Between archaic and modern: some current problems in the history of the Roman economy' in (ed.) *The Inscribed Economy*.

Production and Distribution in the Roman Empire in the Light of Instrumentum Domesticum. Ann Arbor: 11–29.

(2006) 'A revisionist view of Roman money', *JRS* 96: 1–24 (repr. as 'The nature of Roman money' in Harris (2008): 174–207).

(2007) 'The Late Republic' in Morris, Scheidel and Saller (2007): 511–39.

(ed.) (2008) *The Monetary Systems of the Greeks and Romans.* Oxford.

Harrison, A. R. W. (1968) *The Law of Athens.* Vol. 1. Oxford.

Hart, K. (1986) 'Heads or tails. The two sides of the coin', *Man* 21: 637–56.

Haselgrove, C. (1987a) 'Culture process on the periphery: Belgic Gaul and Rome during the late Republic and early Empire' in M. Rowlandson, R. A. G. Carson, and K. Kristiansen (eds.) *Centre and Periphery in the Ancient World.* Cambridge: 104–24.

(1987b) *Iron Age Coinage in South-East England: The Archaeological Context.* (BAR 174). Oxford.

(2006a) 'Early potin coinage in Britain: an update' in de Jersey (2006a): 17–29.

(2006b) 'The impact of the Roman conquest on indigenous coinages in Belgic Gaul and southern Britain' in de Jersey (2006a): 97–116.

Hazzard, R. A. (1984) 'The silver standard of Ptolemaic coinage', *RN*: 231–39.

(1990) 'The composition of Ptolemaic silver', *Journal of the Society for the Study of Egyptian Antiquities* 20: 89–107.

Healey, R. F. (1990) *Eleusinian Sacrifices in the Athenian Law Code.* New York.

Hedlund, R. (2008) *". . . Achieved Nothing Worthy of Memory". Coinage and Authority in the Roman Empire c.* AD *260–295.* Studia Numismatica Upsaliensia 5. Uppsala.

Heichelheim, F. (1930) *Wirtschaftliche Schwankungen der Zeit von Alexander bis Augustus.* Jena.

(1954/5) 'On ancient price trends from the early first millennium BC. to Heraclius I', *Finanzarchiv* 15: 498–511.

(1970) *An Ancient Economic History.* Vol. III. Leiden (German orig. Leiden 1938).

Hendy, M. F. (1985) *Studies in the Byzantine Monetary Economy. c. 300–1450.* Cambridge.

(1993) 'From antiquity to the Middle Ages: economic and monetary aspects of the transition' in *De la antigüedad al medievo: siglos IV–VII.* III Congreso de Estudios Medievales. Fundacion Sanchez-Albornoz: 325–60.

Herman, G. (1987) *Ritualised Friendship and the Greek City.* Cambridge.

Herrmann, J. (1958) *Studien zur Bodenpacht im Recht der gräko-römischen Papyri.* Münchner Beiträge zur Papyrusforschung und Rechtsgeschichte 41. Munich.

Hitchner, B. (2005) 'The advantage of wealth and luxury: the case for economic growth in the Roman Empire' in Manning and Morris (2005): 207–22.

Hollander, D. (1999) 'The management of the mint in the Late Republic', *Ancient History Bulletin* 13.1: 14–27.

(2005) 'Veterans, agriculture, and monetization in the late Roman republic' in Z. Varhelji and J.-J. Aubert (eds.) *A Tall Order: Writing the Social History of the Ancient World. Essays in Honour of William V. Harris.* Munich and Leipzig: 229–39.

(2007) *Money in the Late Republic.* Leiden.

(2008) 'The demand for money in the Late Roman Republic' in Harris (2008): 112–36.

Hopkins, K. (1978) 'Economic growth and towns in classical antiquity' in P. Abrams and E. A. Wrigley (eds.) *Towns in Society. Essays in Economic History and Historical Sociology.* Cambridge: 35–77.

(1980) 'Taxes and trade in the Roman empire', *JRS* 70: 101–25.

(1995/6) 'Rome, taxes, rents and trade', *Kodai* 6/7: 41–75 [repr. in Scheidel and von Reden (2002): 190–230].

Horden, P. and N. Purcell (2000) *The Corrupting Sea. A Study of Mediterranean History.* London.

Hörisch, J. (1996) *Kopf oder Zahl. Die Poesie des Geldes.* Frankfurt.

Horster, M. (2004) *Landbesitz griechischer Heiligtümer in archaischer und klassischer Zeit.* Leiden.

Howgego, C. (1990) 'Why did ancient states strike coins?', *NC* 150: 1–25.

(1992) 'The supply and use of money in the Roman world: 200 BC to AD 300', *JRS* 82: 1–31.

(1994) 'Coin circulation and the integration of the Roman economy', *JRA* 7: 5–21.

(1995) *Ancient History from Coins.* London.

Howgego, C., V. Heuchert, and A. Burnett (eds.) (2005) *Coinage and Identity in the Roman Provinces.* Oxford.

Hultsch, F. (1862). *Griechische und römische Metrologie.* Berlin (repr. 1971).

Humphrey, C. and S. Hugh-Jones (eds.) (1992) *Barter, Exchange and Value: An Anthropological Approach.* Cambridge.

Huss, W. (1994) *Der makedonische König und die ägyptischen Priester. Studien zur Geschichte des ptolemäischen Ägypten.* Historia Einzelschriften 85. Stuttgart.

Huston, S. M. and C. Lorber (2001) 'A hoard of Ptolemaic bronze coins in commerce, October 1992 (CH 8, 413)', *NC* 161: 11–40.

Jones, D. (2006) *The Bankers of Puteoli. Finance, Trade and Industry in the Roman World.* Stroud.

Jongman, W. (2003) 'A golden age: death, money supply and social succession in the Roman Empire' in Lo Cascio (2003): 181–96.

(2007) 'The early Roman empire: Consumption' in Morris, Scheidel and Saller (2007): 592–619.

Kallet-Marx, L. (1993) *Money, Expense and Naval Power in Thucydides' History 1–5.24.* Oxford.

(1994) 'Money talks: rhetor, demos and the resources of the Athenian Empire' in R. Osborne and S. Hornblower (eds.) *Ritual, Finance, Politics. Athenian Democratic Accounts Presented to D. M. Lewis.* Oxford: 217–51.

(2001) *Money and the Corrosion of Power in Thucydides: The Sicilian Expedition and its Aftermath.* Berkeley.

Kaminski, G. (1991) 'Thesauros. Untersuchungen zum antiken Opferstock', *JDI* 106: 63–181.

Katsari, K. (2005) 'The monetization of Roman Asia Minor in the third century AD' in S. Mitchell and K. Katsari (eds.) *Patterns in the Economy of Asia Minor*. Swansea: 261–88.

(2008) 'The monetization of the Roman frontier provinces' in Harris (2008): 242–66.

Kehoe, D. (1988) 'Allocation of risk and investment on the estates of Pliny the Younger', *Chiron* 18: 15–42.

(1997) *Investment, Profit and Tenancy: The Jurists and the Roman Agrarian Economy*. Ann Arbor.

Kessler, D. and P. Temin (2008) 'Money and prices in the Early Roman Empire' in Harris (2008): 137–59.

Kim, H. (2001a) 'Small change and the moneyed economy' in Cartledge, Cohen and Foxhall (2001): 44–51.

(2001b) 'Archaic coinage as evidence for the use of money' in Meadows and Shipton (2001): 7–22.

Koenen, L. (1994) 'The Ptolemaic king as a religious figure' in A. Bulloch (ed.) *Image and Ideologies. Self-Definition in the Hellenistic World*. Berkeley and London: 25–115.

Körner, R. (1993) *Inschriftliche Gesetzestexte der frühen griechischen Polis*. Cologne.

Kraay, C. (1964) 'Hoards, small change and the origins of coinage', *JHS* 84: 76–91.

(1976) *Archaic and Classical Greek Coins*. London.

Kraus, C. (1999) 'Jugurthine disorder' in (ed.) *The Limits of Historiography*. Leiden: 217–46.

Kroll, J. (1976) 'Aristophanes' *ponera chalkia*: A reply', *GRBS* 17: 329–41.

(1979) 'A chronology of early Athenian bronze coinage, ca. 350–250 BC' in O. Mørkholm and N. M. Waggoner (eds.) *Greek Numismatics and Archaeology: essays in Honor of Margaret Thompson*. Wetteren: 139–154.

(1998) 'Silver in Solon's laws' in R. Ashton and S. Hurter (eds.) *Studies in Greek Numismatics in Memory of Martin Jessop Price*. London: 225–32.

(2001) 'Observations on monetary instruments in pre-coinage Greece' in M. Balmuth (ed.) *Hacksilber to Coinage: New Insights into the Monetary History of the Near East and Greece*. New York: 77–92.

(2008) 'The monetary uses of weighed bullion in archaic Greece' in Harris (2008): 12–37.

Kurke, L. (1991) *The Traffic in Praise. Pindar and the Poetics of Social Economy*. Ithaca and London.

(1995) 'Herodotus and the language of metals', *Helios* 22: 36–64.

(1999) *Coins, Bodies, Games and Gold*. Princeton.

(2002) 'Money and mythic history: The contestation of transactional orders in the fifth century BC' in Scheidel and von Reden (2002): 87–113.

Lambert, W. G. (1993) 'Donations of food and drink to the gods in Ancient Mesopotamia' in J. Quaegebeur (ed.) *Ritual and Sacrifice in the Ancient Near East*. Leuven: 191–201.

Laum, B. (1914) *Stiftungen in der griechischen und römischen Antike*. Leipzig.

(1924) *Heiliges Geld*. Tübingen (repr. Berlin 2006).

Le Goff, J. (1986) *La bourse et la vie. Économie et religion au Moyen Âge*. Paris.

Le Rider, G. (1986) 'Les alexandres d'argent en Asie Mineure et dans l'Orient séleucide au IIIe siècle av. J.-C. (c. 275–225). Remarques sur le système monétaire des Seleucides et des Ptolémées', *JdS*: 3–51.

(1989) 'La politique monétaire du royaume de Pergame après 188', *JdS*: 163–90.

(2001) *La naissance de la monnaie: Pratiques monétaire de l'Orient ancien*. Paris.

(2003) *Alexandre le Grande. Monnaie, finances et politique*. Paris.

Lewis, D. M. (1968) 'Dedications of *phialai* at Athens', *Hesperia* 37: 368–80.

Linders T. (1972) *Studies in the Treasuries of Artemis Brauronia*. Stockholm 1972.

(1987) 'Gods, Gifts, Society' in T. Linders and G. Nordquist (eds.) *Gifts to the Gods*. Uppsala: 115–222.

(1992) 'Sacred finances: some observations' in Linders and Alroth (1992): 2–9.

Linders, T. and B. Alroth (eds.) (1992) *The Economics of Cult*. Uppsala.

Lippert, G. (1967) *Über die Rechtsformen altgriechischer Stiftungen*. PhD Erlangen.

Lo Cascio, E. (1981) 'State and coinage in the Late Republic and Early Empire', *JRS* 71: 76–86.

(1996) 'How did the Romans view their coinage and its function?' in C. E. King and D. G. Wigg (eds.) *Coin Finds and Coin Use in the Roman World*. 13th Symposium on Coinage and Monetary History (SFMA 10). Frankfurt: 215–45.

(ed.) (2003) *Credito et Moneta nel Mondo Romano*. Bari.

(2008) 'The function of gold coinage in the monetary economy of the Roman Empire' in Harris (2008): 160–73.

Loomis, W. T. (1998) *Wages, Welfare Costs and Inflation in Classical Athens*. Ann Arbor.

Lüddeckens, E. (1960) *Ägyptische Eheverträge*. Ägyptische Abhandlungen 1. Wiesbaden.

Manning, J. (2001) 'Demotic papyri (664–30 BC)' in R. Westbrook (ed.) *Security for Debt in the Ancient Near East*. Leiden: 307–26.

(2003) *Land and Power in Ptolemaic Egypt*. Cambridge.

(2005) 'The relationship of evidence and models in the Ptolemaic economy' in Manning and Morris (2005): 187–206.

(2007) 'Hellenistic Egypt' in Morris, Scheidel and Saller (2007): 434–59.

(2008) 'Coinage as code in Ptolemaic Egypt' in Harris (2008): 84–111.

Manning, J. and I. Morris (2005) (eds.) *The Ancient Economy. Evidence and Models*. Stanford.

Maresch, K. (1996) *Bronze und Silber. Papyrologische Beiträge zur Geschichte der Währung im ptolemäischen und römischen Ägypten bis zum 2. Jh. n. Chr.* Cologne.

Martin, T. R. (1985) *Sovereignty and Coinage in Classical Greece*. Princeton.

Meadows, A. (2001) 'Money, freedom, and empire in the Hellenistic world' in Meadows and Shipton (2001): 53–64.

(unpublished) *Coins and standards; rhetoric and practicality* [2005].

Meadows, A. and K. Shipton (2001) (eds.) *Money and its Uses in the Ancient Greek World*. Oxford.

Meikle, S. (1995) *Aristotle's Economic Thought*. Oxford.

Meissner, B. (2000) 'Über den Zweck und Anlaß von Diokletians Preisedikt', *Historia* 49: 79–100.

Melitz, J. (1970) 'The Polanyi school of anthropology on money: An economist's view', *American Anthropologist*: 72: 1,020–40.

Menu, B. (1982) 'Le prêt en droit égyptien ancien (Nouvel Empire et Basse Epoque)' in B. Menu, *Recherches sur l'histoire juridique, économique et social de l'Ancienne Égypte*. I. Versaille: 217–300.

(1998) 'Modalités et réglementation du prêt en Égypte à l'époque de la première domination Perse', in B. Menu, *Recherches sur l'histoire juridique, économique et social de l'Ancienne Égypte* II. Cairo: 385–99.

Migeotte, L. (1984) *L'Emprunte Publique Dans Les Cités Grecques*. Quebec.

(1997) 'Le contrôle des prix dans les cités grecques' in Andreau *et al.* (1997): 33–52.

(2002) *L'économie des cités grecques*. Paris. (Engl. transl. *The Economy of the Greek Cities*. Berkeley and London 2009.)

Millett, P. (1982) 'The Attic horoi reconsidered in the light of recent discoveries', *Opus* 1: 219–49 (repr. in the second edition of Finley (1952).

(1984) 'Hesiod and his world', *PCPS* 30: 84–115.

(1990) 'Sale, credit and exchange in Athenian law and society' in P. Cartledge, P. Millett and S. Todd (eds.) *Nomos. Studies in Athenian Law and Society*. Cambridge: 167–94.

(1991) *Lending and Borrowing in Ancient Athens*. Cambridge.

Mitchell, T. C. (1990) 'The bronze lion weights from Nimrud' in C. Jullien and F. Jullien (eds.), *Prix, salaires, poids, et measures*. Res Orientales 2. Bures-sur-Yvette: 129–38.

Momigliano, A. (1975) *Alien Wisdom. The Limits of Hellenization*. Cambridge.

Mørkholm, O. (1991) *Early Hellenistic Coinage. From the Accession of Alexander to the Peace of Apamea (336–188 BC)*. Cambridge.

Morley, N. (1996) *Metropolis and Hinterland*. Cambridge.

(2007) *Trade in Classical Antiquity*. Cambridge.

Morris, I. (1987) *Burial and Ancient Society: The Rise of the Greek City State*. Cambridge.

(1994) 'The ancient economy twenty years after *The Ancient Economy*', *CPh* 89: 351–66.

(1996) 'The strong principle of equality and the archaic origins of Greek democracy' in J. Ober and C. Hedrick (eds.) *Demokratia. A Conversation on Democracies, Ancient and Modern*. Princeton: 19–48.

(2001) 'Hard surfaces' in Cartledge, Cohen and Foxhall (2001): 8–43.

(2005) 'Archaeology, standards of living and Greek economic history' in Manning and Morris (2005): 91–126.

Morris, I. and J. G. Manning (2005) 'Introduction' in Manning and Morris (2005): 1–46.

Morris, I., W. Scheidel, and R. Saller (eds.) (2007) *The Cambridge Economic History of the Greco-Roman World.* Cambridge.

Mrozek, S. (1975) *Prix et rémuneration dans l'occident romain* (31 av.n.è. – 250 de n.è). Gdansk.

Muhs, B. C. (2006) *Tax Receipts, Taxpayers and Taxes in Early Ptolemaic Thebes.* Chicago.

Murphy, T. (2004) *Pliny the Elder's Natural History. The Empire in the Encyclopedia.* Oxford.

Murray, O. (1990) 'Cities of Reason' in O. Murray and S. Price (eds.) *The Greek City from Homer to Alexander.* Oxford: 1–29.

Nafissi, M. (2005) *Ancient Athens and Modern Ideology. Value, Theory and Evidence in Historical Sciences. Max Weber, Karl Polanyi and Moses Finley.* London.

Nash, D. (1978) 'Plu ça change . . . : currency in central Gaul from Julius Caesar to Nero' in R. A. G. Carson and C. Kraay (eds.) *Scripta Nummaria Romana. Essays Presented to C. H. V. Sutherland.* London: 12–31.

   (1981) 'Coinage and state development in central Gaul' in Cunliffe (1981): 10–17.

   (1987) *Coinage in the Celtic World.* London.

Nelson, L. W. and U. Manthe (1999) *Gaii Institutiones III 88–181.* Berlin.

Nicolet, C. (1971) 'Les variations des prix et la "théorie quantitative de la monnaie" à Rome, de Cicéron à Pline l'Ancien', *Annales E.S.C.* 26: 1,208–227.

Niehans, J. (1987). 'Transaction costs' in *The New Palgrave: A Dictionary of Economics*, v. 4: 677–80.

Noeske, H.-C. (2000) 'Zum numismatischen Nachweis hellenistischer Stiftungen am Beispiel ptolemäischer Geldgeschenke' in Bringmann (2000), vol. ii: 221–48.

North, D. (1990) *Institutions, Institutional Change, and Economic Performance.* Cambridge.

North, D. and B. R. Weingast (1989) 'Constitutions and commitment: the evolution of institutions governing public choice in seventeenth-century England', *Journal of Economic History* 49: 803–32.

Ober, J. (2008) *Democracy and Knowledge. Innovation and Learning in Classical Athens.* Princeton.

Ober, J. and C. Manville (2003) *A Company of Citizens.* Boston.

O'Gorman, E. (1993). 'No place like Rome: identity and difference in the *Germania* of Tacitus', *Ramus* 22: 35–54.

Osborne, R. (1985) *Demos. The Discovery of Classical Attica.* Cambridge.

   (1991) 'Pride and prejudice, sense and subsistence: exchange and society in the Greek city' in J. Rich and A. Wallace-Hadrill (eds.) *City and Country in the Ancient World.* London: 119–45. [repr. in Scheidel and von Reden (2002): 114–32].

   (1996) *Greece in the Making. 1200–479 BC.* London.

Parise, N. (1997) 'Metallic currency and weight units in the Mediterranean before coinage' in C. Morrison *et al.* (eds.) *A Survey of Numismatic Research 1990–1995*. Berlin: 5–9.

Parker, R. (1996) *Athenian Religion: A History*. Oxford.

Parry, J. and M. Bloch (eds.) (1989) *Money and the Morality of Exchange.* Cambridge.

Pestman, P. (1961) *Marriage and Matrimonial Property in Ancient Egypt. A Contribution to Establishing the Legal Position of Women*. Pap. Lugd. Bat. 9. Leiden.

Phillipson, D. E. (1968) 'Development of the Roman law of security', *Stanford Law Review* 20: 1,230–48.

Polanyi, K. (1957) 'The economy as instituted process' in K. Polanyi, C. Ahrensberg, and H. W. Pearson (eds.) *Trade and Markets in the Early Empires*. Glencoe: 243–70.

(1977) *The Livelihood of Man*. New York.

Preisigke, F. (1910) *Girowesen im griechischen Ägypten enthaltend Korngiro, Geldgiro, Girobanknotariat mit Einschluss des Archivwesens. Ein Beitrag zur Geschichte des Verwaltungswesens im Altertum*. Strassburg.

Price, M. J. (1991) *The Coinage in the Name of Alexander the Great and Philip Arrhidaeus*. Zurich and London.

Pringsheim, F. (1950) *The Greek Law of Sale*. Weimar.

Rathbone, D. W. (1983) 'The weight and measurement of Egyptian grains', *ZPE* 53: 265–75.

(1989) 'The ancient economy and Graeco-Roman Egypt' in L. Criscuolo and G. Geraci *Egitto e storia antica dall'ellenismo all'età araba*. Bologna: 159–76 [repr. in Scheidel and von Reden (2002): 155–72].

(1991) *Economic Rationalism and Rural Society in Third-Century* AD *Egypt*. Cambridge.

(1996a) 'The imperial finances' in *The Cambridge Ancient History*, 2nd edn, Vol. 10: 309–23.

(1996b) 'Monetization not price inflation' in C. E. King and D. G. Wigg (eds.) *Coin Finds and Coin Use in the Roman World*. 13th Oxford Symposium on Coinage and Monetary History (SFMA 10). Frankfurt: 321–39.

(1997) 'Prices and price formation in Roman Egypt' in Andreau *et al.* (1997): 183–244.

(2003) 'The financing of maritime commerce in the Roman empire' in Lo Cascio (2003): 197–229.

(2009) 'Earnings and costs: living standards and the economy of the Roman empire' in Bowman and Wilson (2009): 299–326.

Rathbone, D. and P. Temin (2008) 'Financial intermediation in first-century AD Rome and eighteenth-century England' in Verboven *et al.* (2008): 371–420.

Reckford, K.-J. (1958) 'Some appearances of the Golden Age', *CJ* 54: 79–87.

Reekmans, T. (1948) 'Monetary history and the dating of Ptolemaic papyri', *StudHell* 5: 15–43.

(1949) 'Economic and social repercussions of the Ptolemaic copper inflation', *Chronique de'Égypte* 24: 324–42.

(1951) 'The Ptolemaic copper inflation', *StudHell* 7: 61–119.

Reger, G. (1994) *Regionalism and Change in the Economy of Independent Delos.* Berkeley.

(1997) 'The price histories of some imported goods on independent Delos' in: J. Andreau, P. Briant, and R. Descat (eds.) *Économie antique. Prix et formation des prix dans les économies antiques*, Saint-Bertrand-de-Comminges: 53–71.

(2006) 'The economy' in A. Erskine (ed.) *A Companion to the Hellenistic World.* Oxford: 331–53.

(2007) 'Hellenistic Greece and Western Asia Minor' in Morris, Scheidel and Saller (2007): 460–86.

Rhodes, P. and R. Osborne (2003) *Greek Historical Inscriptions, 404 – 323* BC. Oxford.

Rhodes, P. J. (1988) *Thucydides. History II.* Warminster.

Rickman, G. (1980) *The Corn Supply of Ancient Rome.* Oxford.

Robinson, E. S. G. (1947) 'The Tell El-Maskhuta hoard of Athenian tetradrachms', *NC* 7: 1–6.

Rogers, G. M. (2001) *The Sacred Identity of Ephesos. Foundation Myths of a Roman City.* London and New York.

Rosivach, V. (1994) *The System of Sacrifice in Fourth-Century Athens.* Atlanta.

(1998) 'Some economic aspects of the fourth-century Athenian market in grain', *Chiron* 30: 31–64.

Rostovtzeff, M. (1935/36) 'The Hellenistic world and its economic development', *AHR* 41: 231–52.

Rowlandson, J. (1996) *Landowners and Tenants in Roman Egypt.* Oxford.

(ed.) (1998) *Women and Society in Greek and Roman Egypt.* Cambridge.

Rupprecht, H. A. (1967) *Untersuchungen zum Darlehn im Recht der Graeco-Ägyptischen Papyri der Ptolemäerzeit.* Munich.

(1994) *Kleine Einführung in die Papyruskunde.* Darmstadt.

Rutter, K. (1981) 'Early coinage and the influence of the Athenian state' in B. Cunliffe (ed.) *Coinage and Society in Britain and Gaul.* London: 1–9.

Saller, R. (2005) 'Framing the debate over growth in the ancient economy' in Scheidel and von Reden (2002): 251–69 [also in Manning and Morris (2005): 223–38].

Sandy, D. B. (1989) *The Production and Use of Vegetable Oils in Ptolemaic Egypt* (BASP Suppl. 6). Atlanta.

Schaps, D. (2004) *The Invention of Coinage and the Monetization of Ancient Greece.* Ann Arbor.

(2007) 'The invention of coinage in Lydia, in India and in China', *Bulletin du Cercle d'Études Numismatiques* 44: 281–300; 313–22.

(2008) 'What was money in ancient Greece?' in Harris (2008): 38–48.

Scheidel, W. (1996) 'Finances, figures and fiction', *CQ* 46: 222–38.

(2007) 'Demography' in Morris, Scheidel and Saller (2007): 38–86.

(2008) 'The divergent evolution of coinage in eastern and western Eurasia' in Harris (2008): 267–86.

Scheidel, W. and S. von Reden (eds.) (2002) *The Ancient Economy. New Approaches*. Edinburgh.

Schmitz, W. (1986) 'Händler, Bürger und Soldaten. Die Bedeutung von Münzgewichtsveränderungen in der griechischen Poliswelt im 5. und 4. Jahrhundert v. Chr.', *MBAH* 5: 59–87.

Schönert-Geiss, E. (1987) 'Bemerkungen zu den prämonetären Geldformen und zu den Anfängen der Münzprägung', *Klio* 79: 406–42.

Seaford, R. (1994) *Reciprocity and Ritual: Homer and Tragedy in the Developing City State*. Oxford.

(1998) 'Tragic money', *JHS* 118: 119–39.

(2004) *Money and the Early Greek Mind*. Cambridge.

Seidl, E. (1962) *Ptolemäische Rechtsgeschichte*. Ägyptologische Forschungen 22. Glückstadt.

Shaw, B. (1981) 'Rural markets in North Africa and the political economy of the Roman Empire', *Ant. af.* 17: 37–83.

Shell, M. (1982) *Money, Language and Thought*. Baltimore and London.

Shelton, J. S (1977) 'Artabas and Choinikes', *ZPE* 24: 55–67.

Sills, J. (2003) *Gaulish and Early British Gold Coinage*. London.

Snell, D. C. (1995) 'Methods of exchange and coinage in western Asia Minor', in: J. M. Sasson (ed.) *Civilisations of the Ancient Near East*. New York: 1487–97.

Sokolowski, F. (1954) 'Fees and taxes in the Greek cults', *HThR* 47: 153–64.

Spawford, P. (1988) *Money and its Use in Medieval Europe*. Cambridge.

Strøm, I. (1992): 'Obeloi of pre- or proto-monetary value in Greek sanctuaries' in T. Linders and B. Alroth (eds.) *Economics of Cult in the Ancient World*. Uppsala: 41–51.

Szaivert, W. and R. Wolters (2005) *Löhne, Preise, Werte. Quellen zur römischen Geldwirtschaft*. Darmstadt.

Tenger, B. (1993) *Die Verschuldung im römischen Ägypten (1. und 2. Jh n. Chr)*. St Katharinen.

Thomas, R. (1992) *Literacy and Orality in Ancient Greece*. Cambridge.

Thompson, D. J. (1999) 'New and old in the Ptolemaic Fayyum' in A. Bowman and E. Rogan (eds.) *Agriculture in Egypt From Pharaonic to Modern Times*. Oxford: 123–38.

Thompson, W. E. (1970) 'The golden Nike and the gold coinage of Athens', *NC* 10: 1–6.

(1979) 'A view of Athenian Banking', *MH* 36: 324–42.

Turner, E. G. (1984) 'Ptolemaic Egypt' in *The Cambridge Ancient History*, 2nd edn, Vol. VII. Cambridge: 118–74.

Van Alfen, P. (2002) 'The owls from the 1989 Syria hoard with a revision of pre-Macedonian coinage in Egypt', *AJN* 14: 1–52.

Van de Mierop, M. (1992) *Society and Enterprise in Old Babylonian Ur*. Berlin.

Vandorpe, K. (2000) 'The Ptolemaic epigraphe or harvest tax (shemu)', *APF* 46: 169–232.

Verboven, K. (1997) 'Caritas Nummorum. Deflation in the Late Republic?', *MBAH* 16: 40–78.

(2002) *The Economy of Friends. Economic Aspects of Amicitia and Patronage in the Late Republic*. Brussels.

Verboven, K., K. Vandorpe, and V. Chankowski (eds.) (2008) *Pistoi Dia ten Technen. Bankers, Loans and Archives in the Ancient World. Studies in Honour of Raymond Bogaert*. Studia Hellenistica 44. Leuven.

Verhoogt, A. (2005) *Regaling Officials in Ptolemaic Egypt*. Pap. Lugd. Bat. 32. Leiden.

Villard, P. (1994) 'Aristophane et l'argent' in M.-C. Amouretti and P. Villard (eds.) *Eukratia. Mélanges offerts à Claude Vatin*. Provence: 87–92.

von Freyberg, H.-U. (1989) *Kapitalverkehr im römischen Kaiserreich*. Freiburg.

von Reden, S. (1995) *Exchange in Ancient Greece*. London.

(1997) 'Money, law and exchange: coinage in the Greek polis', *JHS* 117: 154–76.

(1999) 'Re-evaluating Gernet: Value and Greek Myth' in R. Buxton (ed.) *From Myth to Reason? Studies in the Development of Greek Thought*. Oxford: 51–70.

(2001) 'Demos' *phiale* and the rhetoric of money in fourth-century BC Athens' in Cartledge, Cohen and Foxhall (2001): 52–66.

(2002) 'Money in the ancient economy: a survey of recent research', *Klio* 84: 141–74.

(2007a) *Money in Ptolemaic Egypt*. Cambridge.

(2007b) 'Wirtschaftliches Wachstum und institutioneller Wandel' in G. Weber (ed.) *Der Hellenismus. Eine Kulturgeschichte*. Stuttgart: 177–201.

(forthcoming) 'Power, Consumption and "New Demand" in Hellenistic Egypt' in Z. Archibald, J. K. Davies and V. Gabrielsen (eds.) *Proceedings of the Third Symposium on Hellenistic Economies (24–26 September 2006)*. Oxford UP.

Wagner-Hasel, B. (2000) *Der Stoff der Gaben. Kultur und Politik des Schenkens und Tauschens im Archaischen Griechenland*. Frankfurt.

Wallace, M. B. (1984) 'Texts, amphoras, coins, standards and trade', *AncW* 10: 11–14.

Wallace, S. L. (1938) 'Census and poll-tax in Ptolemaic Egypt', *AJP* 59: 422–6.

Wartenberg, U. (1995) *After Marathon. War, Society and Money in Fifth-Century Athens*. London.

Weber, F. (1932) *Untersuchungen zum gräko-römischen Obligationenrecht*. Munich.

Weikart, S. (1986) *Griechische Bauopferrituale*. Berlin.

Weiser, W. (1995) *Katalog Ptolemäischer Bronzemünzen der Sammlung des Instituts für Altertumskunde der Universität Köln*. Papyrologica Coloniensia 23. Cologne.

Wells, H. B. (1978) 'The arrow-money of Thrace and southern Russia', *SAN* 9: 6–9 and 24–6.

Whitehead, D. (1986a) 'Festival liturgies at Thorikos', *ZPE* 62: 213–20.

(1986b) *The Demes of Attica 508/7 – ca 250 BC. A Politcal and Social Study*. Princeton.

Wierschowski, L. (1984) *Heer und Wirtschaft. Das römische Heer der Prinzipatszeit als Wirtschaftsfaktor*. Bonn.

Will, E. (1954) 'De l'aspect éthique des origines grecques de la monnaie', *RH* 212: 209–31.

(1955) 'Réflexions et hypothèses sur les origines du monnayage', RN 17: 5–23.

Willetts, R. F. (1955) *Aristocratic Society in Ancient Crete*. London.

Williams, J. (ed.) (1997) *Money. A History*. London.

Williamson, O. E. (1975) *Markets and Hierarchies. Analysis and Antitrust Implications*. New York.

Wilson, A. (2002) 'Machines, power and the ancient economy', *JRS* 92: 1–32.

(2007) 'The metal supply of the Roman Empire' in E. Papi (ed.) *Supplying Rome and the Roman Empire* (JRA Supplement 69): 109–25.

Wörrle, M. (1988) *Stadt und Fest im kaiserzeitlichen Kleinasien. Studien zu einer agonistischen Stiftung aus Oinoanda*. Munich.

Wolters, R. (1999) *Nummi Signati. Untersuchungen zur römischen Münzprägung und Geldwirtschaft*. Munich.

Woolf, G. (1992) 'Imperialism, empire and the integration of the Roman economy', *World Archaeology* 23: 283–93.

(1993a) 'The social significance of trade in Late Iron Age Europe.' in C. Scarre and F. Healey (eds.) *Trade and Exchange in Pre-Historic Europe*. Oxford: 211–18.

(1993b) 'Rethinking the *oppida*', *OJA* 19: 223–34.

(1998) *Becoming Roman. The Origins of Provincial Civilisation in Gaul*. Cambridge.

Zaccagnini, C. (2000) 'A note on Old Assyrian weight stones and weight systems' in S. Graziani (ed.) *Studi sul Vicino Oriente Antico dedicati alla memoria di Luigi Cagni*. Naples: 1,203–13.

Zanker, P. (1988) *The Power of Images in the Age of Augustus*. Ann Arbor.

Index